*We did it our way*

# FOREST GREEN ROVERS

## TRIUMPH AT WEMBLEY

### CHRIS GARDNER

To Jilly Cooper and her 'right-hand lady' Amanda Butler, who encouraged my first book and told me I had to write a second. I owe them both more than words can say. Ultimately it is their fault that my prose has been inflicted on the public (again)!

Also to Rich Joyce, Phil Butterworth, Peter Whitbread, David Kerry, Crispin Thomas, 'Chef Em' and FGR's student ambassadors, too numerous to mention. Without you, this book would have been duller and much thinner.

All the author's profits from this book will go to
Gloucestershire Deaf Association (GDA)
Charity No. 1015937, Company Registered by Guarantee No. 2692718
www.glosdeaf.org.uk

Published in 2017 by:

C. J. F. Gardner
2 Archway Cottages
Main Road
Whiteshill
Stroud
Gloucestershire GL6 6AU
England

Typeset by Aura Technology and Software Services, India
Cover design by iinde.com
Printed in the UK by CPI Anthony Rowe Ltd.

ISBN: 978-0-9956043-5-3

British Library Cataloguing-in-Publication Data
A catalogue record for this book is available from the British Library

# CONTENTS

Living confidently with
deafness and hearing loss

# Gloucestershire Deaf Association (GDA)
*by Jenny Hopkins (CEO)*

GDA is an award-winning, Gloucestershire-based charity whose vision is of a society that actively supports ways to break down communication barriers for people who are deaf or hard of hearing.

Deafness is invisible but it marginalizes and its effect on relationships can be crippling. When a profoundly deaf child is born into a hearing family with little or no experience of how to overcome the communication challenges that deafness brings, social isolation can start at home. When an older person gradually loses their hearing, an early sign is their withdrawal from conversation.

We live in a hearing world which at best appears to lack understanding or empathy with deafness, and at worst stigmatizes it. You only have to consider how many organizations today can only be reached by telephone. As a result, deaf people are left feeling unable to access the everyday services hearing people take for granted.

GDA provides a range of services and social activities which bring deaf people back into the conversation, to enjoy greater independence and ultimately better physical and mental wellbeing.

The people whom GDA supports include adults and children who have been born deaf and whose preferred method of communication is sign language, and also those with an acquired hearing loss, who have speech but can no longer hear. Our services include deaf-awareness training, communications support (BSL interpreters), employment support, listening-aid equipment, hearing-aid clinics, lip-reading classes, and deaf children's and deaf youth clubs.

As well as being a besotted fan of Forest Green Rovers, this book's author, Chris Gardner, is himself severely deaf and is closely connected with GDA, initially as a beneficiary and now as Chair of Trustees of the charity.

The first link between the two organizations came about in 2015 when FGR directors and supporters donated and bought lots at a GDA Promises Auction. In 2016 the Club hosted representatives of GDA's Deaf Football Team at a home match.

As with this new book, the profits of Chris' first book: *The Rise of Forest Green Rovers – The Road to Wembley,* were passed to GDA, the launch being held at The New Lawn Stadium on 22nd October 2016. It raised in excess of £4,500 for the charity from sales and sponsorship of nearly 500 copies. In dedicating his profits from the new book to our cause, Chris's commitment to helping deaf and hard-of-hearing people in Gloucestershire continues. By buying a copy, you help too. We thank you.

# Foreword
## by Dale Vince, Chair Ecotricity & Forest Green Rovers FC

Dale Vince Chair Ecotricity & FGR

Chris's books are coming round as fast as the seasons themselves, and why not – there's plenty to write about.

A year ago I wrote about waking up on a Sunday morning, eyes still closed, feeling a smile and realising why – the game the day before. It's something plenty of football fans will be familiar with. That feeling the next day, and maybe the one after, when your team does something special.

And FGR did that at Wembley, 'with knobs on'. Months later, I'm still getting those same feelings, that inner smile, that feeling of invincible joy.

FGR is in the Football League.

And there are reminders everywhere: when the fixtures came out, when the draw for the League Cup was made, the preparations we're making to play new teams in a new league. It's a fantastic feeling – an amazing achievement for our club.

Chris is an excellent chronicler, and here he charts the journey we made last year, and the 'fairy tale' ending on that incredible day at Wembley.

Enjoy his story – it's the latest chapter of what could be a long running series … :)

# Foreword
## *by Mark Cooper, Manager Forest Green Rovers FC*

Mark Cooper Manager FGR

I was delighted to be offered the opportunity to write this Foreword for Chris Gardner's new book.

As a past player and captain of Forest Green Rovers, I had a better idea than most of our hamlet club's astonishing ambitions to reach the promised land of the Football League. When Dale Vince offered me the opportunity to take over the reins, only one outcome was on the agenda – promotion. The season had the usual ups and downs associated with any competitive sport, but we prevailed in fine style with that magnificent win at Wembley. Yet achieving promotion to the EFL is simply the first step on the ladder as the challenge to scale further heights now begins. Quite an ambition for the smallest club of 92.

As Manager, my main concern is coaching the best from my players. That is pressure enough over what amounts to a 10 month season, including the pre-season friendlies. Chris' book tells the story of the 2016/17 season as supporters experienced it, game by game. Supporters and coaches do not always see eye to eye, but they go through the same torture and euphoria. For all, the win at Wembley was an explosion of joy and huge relief!

The influence of Forest Green Rovers reaches far beyond Nailsworth, as evidenced by the interest in the club from national and international media. Importantly though, the community has played a huge role in the club's unrelenting growth and it has reached out to many charities along its journey. The charity Chris chairs, GDA is one such. Deafness is not an obvious disability but it can be desperately isolating for sufferers. Supporting of, and involvement with a football club like Forest Green helps to break down barriers and allow deaf people to enjoy a level playing field with their hearing friends and families.

In hope Chris's book sells in great numbers and raises substantial funds for GDA.

Best wishes, Mark.

# Introduction
## *The making of a Forest Green Rovers addict – how I succumbed*

In one respect, Supporting FGR is no different to supporting numerous other football clubs the world over. Sooner or later, your nearest and dearest or latest acquaintances will ask "why do you put yourself through this agony". It is a good question and has no simple answer. The roots run deep, at least in my case.

I am cursed an optimist. For me, optimism is the justification for leaving my bed in the morning. Yet as a football supporter, optimism causes death by a thousand cuts. I view pessimism as an attempt to provide armour against the hurt of disappointment. It is also a self-fulfilling prophecy and marks a refusal to rationalise the supporter's malady. Ultimately, pessimism makes you feel worse and can drive your friends and family to distraction.

Optimism is a harder task master. It offers something other than pain as reward, but just as you are convinced of success, the vagaries of sport will cut an optimist to the quick. However, given the rare event of success, an optimist can experience the high of all highs. At 17.00 on May 14th 2017 we optimists supporting FGR were in nirvana. It was unforgettable and worth decades of unrealised dreams and living on our nerves. A wonder drug and then some!

My route to *supporterdom* came through participation in sport. As advancing age reduced my ability to partake actively in the sports I have loved, my status as a supporter grew from casual to engrossing interest. In the best Hollywood tradition, I am obliged to time travel back to my childhood to trace my encounters with my favourite sports, and how they led to the first symptoms of the supporter disease. Cue wobbly screen and sepia images.

I was born in Bristol in 1953, the youngest of 4 brothers. The eldest being Peter, 9 years my senior then Richard, a gap of 7 years. Anthony was born in February 1952 so naturally we stuck around together far more than with our older brothers. Nonetheless, we all grew up in the post war world that embraced sport enthusiastically, a reaction to the horrors of conflict experienced by the country for the second time in four decades.

My father, David, had fought with the Gloucestershire Regiment in Burma, so say the forgotten theatre of war that continued beyond the European theatre. He was invalided home before the Atomic Bombs ended the world conflict.

Dad was a tee total Methodist, a faith inherited from his parents. Yet neither he nor they were strict and did not visit their beliefs on their friends or offspring. Less promisingly for the direction my life was to take, he was a 'Rugger Man' but that did not blind him to the value of a variety of sports for his gang of sons – in fact he supported us in anything for which we showed keenness or aptitude, even that other code of football played by hooligans.

My mother found herself in an unrelenting masculine world, even by the standards of the time. A WREN during the war, she reverted to the accepted role of housewife afterwards and for the remainder of her life. So far as sport was concerned, her task was usually to drive her sons to where ever the sporting fixture list dictated, often in and around Bristol and what we now call South Gloucestershire. Only at weekends, as his work permitted, did Dad take over the ferrying and importantly, watching and supporting role.

It is fair to say that I grew apart from my mother as I became a teenager and adult though I always respected my father and valued his advice and company. As my family and offspring have frequently commented, I am my father's son. As the years pass, I identify many of the things he encouraged in my behaviour and pursuits, and sadly many more that he did not.

Like most of his peers, Dad did not talk about his war time service. He kept in close touch with those with whom he served, and many of his regimental friends stayed with us over the years. He also became Chair of the local branch of the Royal British Legion, helping veterans and their families. In a small way, I have helped to encourage Forest Green Rovers' support for RBL around Remembrance Day. RBL is a marvellous organisation which supports service men and women and their families throughout their lives, the majority of whom are now in old age.

The most passionate Dad became on the subject of the war itself was during Britain's attempts to secure membership of the (then) Common Market in the 1970s. As I put childish, deliberately contrary arguments to him, he snapped "imperfect as it is, if the Common Market prevents the annihilation of another generation of young men and women, I'm all for it". I've never forgotten the depth of emotion conveyed in that short sentence and was bereft on his, as well as my behalf, when the xenophobic Brexit campaign took hold in 2016.

Dad had played various sports himself before the war, along with his 2 sisters Mary & Peggy and younger brother Charles (the only current survivor). And though post-war he would happily play and coach his four boys in rugby, football, cricket and so on, he abstained from playing other than in 'father's matches'.

Instead, straightaway after his demob, he applied to become a rugby referee and did that for 25 years. At that time, the game was amateur and he received a letter of invitation for every fixture. His 'home base' was the Memorial Ground, then fortress of Bristol RFC, the big power in the region. He died in 2002, before Bristol Rovers became the owner of the stadium through the financial crisis into which Bristol Rugby plunged. How he would have felt about Bristol Rugby moving to Ashton Gate I cannot be sure, but he would no doubt have been sorrowful at the loss of significance of the founding of the Memorial Ground.

In 1958, with me aged 5, we moved from our tall terraced house in the Clifton area of Bristol, not far from the Suspension Bridge, to a rambling 1930s house, 'Green Acres', 7 miles out in the village of Almondsbury. As his work permitted, Dad set about repairing and decorating the interior, barely stopping in the 20 or so years during which it was the happy family home.

Aside from meeting the spatial needs of his boisterous brood, Green Acres gave dad everything he wanted – a vegetable garden in which he spent his daylight hours after work, and thickly turfed, striped lawns to indulge his sport mad children. For four boys it was Wembley and Lords rolled into one.

The lawns were famous amongst friends and family for their lush turf. No one else's came close. Even now, in our far smaller homes, my brothers and I try to replicate dad's luxurious, striped lawns but fail miserably. The work entailed in keeping the lawns and gardens expertly tended, which he did on his own is mind boggling to me now.

Such was his unselfishness that the front lawn became the focus of our sporting needs. Regardless that we'd create muddy goal mouths, excavate divots galore and generally lay waste to the hedges. That all seemed to fit with his grand plan.

So it was that the front lawn reflected the school sporting curricular. When we played football or hockey in the autumn, winter and spring, there was a goal at the top of the lawn. All sorts of rules and penalties were invoked if the balls flew out of the garden into neighbours' properties or onto the road. But Dad also let the hedges grow tall, planted conifers to protect the neighbours and used fruit nets as back up!

I remember Anthony and I retreating to the garden to take turns in goal or attack, as the tension of watching the 1966 World Cup Final on the family black and white TV became unbearable. West Germany had just equalised at 2-2 and extra time was about to start. We did not return to the lounge until our older brothers had assured us England had won!

Oddly, rugby rarely got a look in on the lawn. Probably as rugby in those days seemed to be about kicking for touch or position. That would not have pleased the traffic or long suffering neighbours.

In summer, a diagonal set allowed for a proper sized, narrow cricket pitch. Ever game, Dad helped us to mow and roll the batting strip and got creative with fruit netting and scaffold poles. The result, a perfect, fully enclosed net at the bottom of the lawn. The hedge at the top of the lawn was reinforced with pig wire netting and strict penalties eliminated the risk posed by lofted straight hits.

Thus I was coached from an early age to hit the ball along the ground and avoid the airborne route. As my batting style developed as I got older – a hard hitting batsman in the top 5 – my team mates might have noticed a rebellion against the 'on the deck' upbringing!

I think I must always have had a short attention span, so wanted to bowl as much as bat and unsurprisingly became an all-rounder. Fred Truman was the most feted English fast bowler of my pre-teenage years, so naturally I fancied myself as his successor. But there was a problem. The chief limitation of the cricket net at Green Acres was the length of the bowler's run up, as even the crossways orientation of the 'square' meant just a couple of yards of grass beyond the bowler's crease. As ever, necessity is the mother of invention. I paced out a curling run up which started on the concrete plinth of the garage, crossed the drive, and circumvented a gnarled old oak tree before straightening towards the stumps. In all, 12 to 15 paces. Thus it was that in a 40 year club cricket stint, I always used a short run up and developed most speed from a windmill arm action.

Primary school sports were taken more seriously than now, or so my memory would have it. At any rate, during term time throughout the year I played school matches on Saturdays and often midweek too, principally Football, Hockey and Cricket. That continued in to secondary education too, though at Wycliffe College (then a Rugby orientated school that shunned the beautiful game), I courted trouble by arranging informal games of football with the willing youth of Stonehouse.

The point of all these rose tinted recollections is to demonstrate that I always wanted to play sport, first and foremost, with spectating being a bonus.

My father made it possible to do both. Not just for me, but my elder brothers too. In my pre-teens, Saturdays were always dominated by sport.

The 6 of us sat round a circular table next to the kitchen counter. The weekend treat would be Corona 'pop' plus sausages and chips or similar fare. Not much talking occurred as we were too busy listening to the Clitheroe Kid or Round the Horne on the trusty, veneer clad valve radio.

Food scoffed, it was off to whatever match Anthony and I were playing, whilst Richard and Peter went to play their more adult games. Depending on the season, that meant rugby or cricket for the Clifton Club, then based at Eastfield Road in Clifton. A big club at the time, the ground was sold for housing in the Seventies and the cricket and rugby sections parted company. Rugby moved to Cribbs Causeway, still its home. Cricket amalgamated with Flax Bourton CC but eventually disappeared.

Even outside term time, I was not necessarily supporter material. Cricket was my first love, and I'd go with Richard and Peter to watch them play, or more honestly, to hope that one of the team (Clifton 3rd XI) failed to turn up. That was not unusual, so at the tender age of 9 or 10 I started to get a taste of Club Cricket with adults.

In the cold months, if Richard and Peter did not have rugby matches, they switched codes to watch Bristol's football teams. In those years, both City and Rovers spent most of their time as middle of the table clubs in the old Third Division.

Being a Rugby man, my father regarded neither team with much enthusiasm, besides, he had his Rugby Refereeing schedule to occupy his thoughts. As for his sons, the older 3 kept a foot in both camps, rugby and football, but rugby did not interest me at all.

Peter was, and still is, dyed in the wool Bristol Rovers. Anthony similarly Bristol City, for whom he and his son Dave are presently Scouts. Richard, always the most even tempered and considerate of the foursome, played his cards closer to his chest. So much so, that I always thought him to be for City and said as much in my 2016 book, *The Rise of Forest Green Rovers – The Road to Wembley*. Only afterwards was I corrected. He was a closet Pirate – the Rovers!

My loyalty was never in doubt. Bristol Rovers, they of Alfie Biggs, Geoff Bradford and Harold Jarman. To my mind, City's star player of the time – big John Atyeo – did not signify.

Until I was 9 or 10, it did not matter which team I supported. Support for Anthony and me meant only hearing what our older brothers told us of the games, changing the positions of the teams in our cardboard wall charts after every round of matches and reading the Bristol Pink'un or Green'un (the *Bristol Evening Post*'s Saturday evening sports editions). Otherwise, even if we did not have school matches, we were deemed too young to watch. Except that is for Rugby at the Bristol Memorial Ground.

From as young as five or six years, Anthony and I were taken off to Dad's home refereeing appointments, overwhelmingly 'The Mem', but occasionally Clifton's Eastfield Road ground at Westbury on Trym. Once there, we were placed 'in the care' of responsible adults in the draughty old wooden floored grandstands at either venue.

My overriding memory was being cold. In the 60s and early 70s, there appeared to be a law in force that a child was not allowed to wear long trousers until he became a teenager. Presumably character building stuff for which I blame Baden Powell! Inevitably, come rain, hail, sleet, snow and gales, there we would be in calf slapping wellington boots, worsted shorts, itchy woollen jumpers and duffel coats.

Even as we stood there, teeth chattering, our ordeal was far from over. As dad, clad in his Clifton Rugby garb (it was the habit then for rugby referees to wear their 'ancestral' club kit) went about his work, those around us in the stand kept up a torrent of foul abuse aimed at him. And they say Rugby is a game played by gentlemen! For me at least it was an education in language I'd not heard elsewhere and disbelief how my dearly loved father could be so misunderstood.

My first proper football match was in the early 60s, an uninspiring 0-0 draw at Ashton Gate between City and Walsall to which I had been taken by Peter and Richard. Not the start I wanted. But as I got older, I'd make increasingly regular visits to Eastville Stadium, usually watching a mid-table 'long ball' Gas slogging it out in old Division 3 (and choking on the fumes emitted by the gasometers beyond the Tote End). In those days, you could sit on the enormous open terrace (later clipped by the M32) with few around you to interrupt the panoramic pitch view.

So, I was engaged but not besotted. The highs included winning the Watney Cup by defeating Burnley and promotion to Division 2 under Don Megson's management. Relegation soon followed. After the exile to Twerton Park, Bath, Gerry Francis steered the best Rovers team I ever watched back into Division 2, thumping Bristol City 3-0 in the penultimate home game to claim the championship. Once he left, again, relegation was not far behind. Apart from some fun under the inimitable Ian Holloway, Rovers fell away to Division 4 (3 by then) back to 2 then sliding away remorselessly, eventually joining FGR in the National League, before the Phoenix like rise back to Division 1 for 2016/17.

By the mid-1970s, I had moved from Bristol as my career took me north to Sheffield before marriage and family meant a settled life back in

Bristol, then Stroud since 1985. Bristol Rovers were not forgotten but did not really tug at the heart strings. Even so, some of their notable players from the sixties, seventies and eighties still resonate with me and several moved on to greater careers in the top flight. They include Geoff Bradford the first Rovers player to win an England cap, Alfie Biggs, Harold Jarman, Bobby Jones, Bryn Jones, Phil Roberts, Gary Mabbutt (later Spurs and England), Ray Graydon (Aston Villa), Robin Stubbs (Torquay highest goal scorer) Stuart Taylor, Larry Lloyd (Liverpool, Notts Forest & England) Smash & Grab (Warboys & Bannister), 'Duke' Ellington (West Brom), Jason Roberts (also West Brom) & Jamie Cureton (multi-teams, still playing).

It is difficult to say when I first came across Forest Green Rovers. Before moving to Stroud, I'd returned from Sheffield for a spell in Bristol during the mid-seventies and early eighties. The Bristol Evening Post used to pick up reports about FGR and got excited about the FA Vase win in 1982. But in all honesty, I hadn't a clue where Forest Green was.

I had my first direct contact with FGR in around 1980. Then Manager Steve Millard would take his squad to train at Easton Sports Centre off the M32 close in on Bristol's East side. With a group of work friends, I played 5-a-side football there regularly on Thursday evenings from 8.00-9.00. FGR was the next squad on, having warmed up with a run around the locality. They seemed like decent guys. After the reports of their FA Vase win, my curiosity was whetted.

In 1984, I took a job in Gloucester and I moved to Stroud a year later with my wife Jenni. But I was not yet cured of the playing bug, and turned out for Whiteshill United in the Gloucestershire Senior League Division 2, carving out a niche as a non-scoring centre forward. But they trained too hard for my liking, so I swapped back to my other autumn/winter sport, Hockey with Stroud HC. I am one of few still alive and kicking who played for all 5 of its Saturday teams, Veterans & mixed X1s.

And my passion for Alpine skiing had kicked in too. Our children Suzi & Phil could ski when they were 2 and to my delight, soon took to the competitive national slalom skiing circuit, our base being the dry slope at Matson, Gloucester. They encouraged me to join them and that required no second invitation. Training twice a week, a May-November race calendar in England, training and racing on European mountains – it was truly a consuming passion. Suzi and Phil ceased racing in their late teens but obtained coaching licences. I stopped barely 8 years ago, but still trek to the mountains with Jenni whenever I can, which usually explains my absences from FGR matches during winter.

Inconveniently, the modern football calendar encroaches on the cricket season too. In 1986, I switched over to Stroud CC, parent club of ardent FGR fan and sometime goalkeeping coach, Jack Russell MBE, and continued to play for them until aches and pains called time in the 'noughties'. Jack was already established with the County but in those days was allowed to turn out for his club when the County had no game. I played alongside him just a few times.

Two tragedies stood out from those years. First being the waste of David Russell's life, Jack's younger brother and seen as a batting prodigy. As a teenager, he scored a maiden century at Cardiff, returning home to celebrate with his team mates at the Alpine Lodge opposite the old Farmhill ground. Somehow, he fell from the balcony and died the next day from a brain haemorrhage. So sad and a dreadful waste.

Second was the death at just 14 of Tom Moore. Tom was the son of Whiteshill FC team mate Brian. Brian is known to many at The New Lawn Stadium as, fair weather or foul, he is on 'gate duty' for FGR home matches. During the summer, he and I watch cricket at Frocester CC together. Tom was a very popular, smiling lad with bags of talent who starred for the junior teams at Stroud CC. Without warning, he contracted Leukemia then complications that resulted from the disease. He did not recover. Shivering in a local Church at his funeral on a scorching hot day is engraved on my memory. There are few things so awful as a young life taken, when so much is promised. Much as sport can help us negotiate the challenges of daily life, tragedies such as this put our partisan disappointments into their true perspective.

Playing or supporting, winning and losing mean everything at the time. Yet those two 'imposters' have little to do with to the rigours of life in general, the long game. I try not to let all consuming supporter views dominate my life, hard though that is. Back in the 70s, if I ranted about Bristol Rovers being outplayed, like as not a brother or adult friend would retort that "there are two sides playing out there". It did not help much but is correct. The only thing that separates partisan support and conflict is sportsmanship.

Other sport aside, living in Stroud meant exposure to the weekly Stroud News & Journal. Then as now, it was always full of the exploits of 'The Little Club on the Hill'. Curious, and recalling my Bristol encounters, I took in occasional midweek and Saturday matches at The (Old) Lawn. The bug was beginning to infect me and my attendance became increasingly regular. By the time promotion had been gained to the Conference in 1998, I was properly hooked, more so than Bristol Rovers had ever managed.

Nerve jangling does not begin to cover the FGR experience in the noughties. Yet the great relegation escapes at the end of most seasons simply drove my habit to greater depths. As BBC Radio Gloucestershire began to take closer interest in FGR in the comparative success of the Jim Harvey era (2007-09), I joined the inimitable Bob Hunt in the live commentary box. After 2 years, worsening deafness began to make this an impossible task, so I bowed out, fun though it had been to work with such a true professional (and hopeless FGR fan) as Bob. My final contribution was a staggering game at Altrincham when Rovers turned a 2-0 first half deficit into a 5-2 triumph. It would have come over brilliantly on Radio had Bob and I not left the commentary equipment in the BBC Radio Gloucestershire car park. Ever resourceful, Bob did what he could using his mobile phone until the battery expired.

Some occasions in sport, maybe life in general, are life-changing. With FGR, my epiphany was at a small Essex Club called Grays in April 2010, the last game of the season. Dale Vince's involvement was just around the corner. Rovers needed just a point at already relegated Grays and 100s turned out from the 5 Valleys to see the job done on a sunny day in deepest Essex. Sure enough, we took the lead, then one of our legends, Jonathan Smith (since with Luton) missed a sitter. As tension mounted, Grays scored twice in the final ten minutes as elsewhere our rivals had similarly late revivals of fortunes. Rovers were relegated.

All supporters were inconsolable. I felt bereft and could not face the lonely drive back to Stroud, so stayed in London at my daughter's flat. She was then a student at Central St Martins. Even so, what should have been an easy journey on a Saturday evening was a nightmare as London was being set up for the following day's Marathon. I have never felt so bad after watching a game.

Anyhow, on such cruel moments you either walk away or commit for life. I did the latter. Only weeks later, during the summer, did Rovers earn a reprieve. Salisbury City's financial problems sent them down in our place. In the interim there had been speculation to add to the agony, spreading the angst over weeks. When Rovers very nearly repeated the dose the following year – losing a final day 6 pointer at Tamworth, only to find that our rivals had also surrendered late on in their games – I endured the pain with practised calm!

In 2010, worsening severe and profound deafness forced early retirement from my Development Surveying career. At the invitation of long-time friend and FGR Vice-Chair, David Drew (now MP again so recently resigned as V/C), I gladly joined the Club's new Advisory Board which initiates and coordinates Rovers' community activities. When asked, I chip in with media interviews and other appointments for the Club, write for the Match Day magazine as Rambling Man and do whatever I can to help out and/or promote the Club.

The Rambling Man accounts of Rovers away trips are a deliberate ploy to stem the pain of bad results and to help me and my fellow travellers to be more rounded souls. In short, not to sulk or have tantrums when things do not go well on the turf. Most of my companions, Foggy, Compo, Clegg, Deep-throat, Sir Tomcat, Woody and others are National Trust Members. Some (me being the worst) are also very poor coach travellers. We meet early on match days with an itinerary of notable castles, mansions and gardens, taking turns to drive our cars. Occasionally, we stay overnight. Thus the journey tempers poor Rovers performances but makes good ones even more memorable. In summary, my alter ego, Rambling Man, gives me control of my addiction.

At The New Lawn, I was a season ticket holder at the South & West Terrace for many years. There I chewed the fat with friends at the 'wet' terrace. It's the closest thing we can find to our favoured spot at the 'Old' Lawn. However, last term, the launch of *The Rise of Forest Green Rovers – The Road to Wembley* and regular voluntary duties for the club meant much time spent warming the seats of the East Stand and switching my season ticket there. I still feel like a fish out of water!

To end this section, a few words about deafness. As with *The Rise of Forest Green Rovers* the purpose of writing this tome is to raise money for the charity I have the honour to chair, GDA (formerly known as Gloucestershire Deaf Association). Whether deafness occurs from birth or through early or later illness such as meningitis, it can result in social isolation. You avoid being in noisy places or where you do not feel comfortable around people.

A wonderful gift from sport, playing or spectating, is that it can transcend disability. Whether in the East Stand or the Wet Terrace or at all the other stadiums I visit, I can yell my head off in the sure knowledge that everyone else is doing the same, and few of us can hear conversational exchange. The playing field is level.

At home, though I have an 'induction loop' to help me hear the TV, I still use the subtitling service most of the time. Unnoticed by my hearing family or friends, subtitles get things hilariously wrong on many occasions.

Subtitles for pre-recorded programmes or films are easier for the broadcasters as they can be analysed more carefully, or tailored from the scripts. I am not sure how subtitles are done on live programmes like news or sport, but I think they are electronic software like predictive text. I prefer to think of a Flintstone-like guy wrapped in animal skin, listening hard then chipping onto a stone tablet.

Recent football matches give two examples how small mistakes can make a big difference. On 14th April 2017 I was watching Norwich City v Brighton in the Championship. Brighton had just secured promotion and the commentators were eulogising about their leading goalscorer, Anthony Knockaert. As the compliments gushed out, the subtitles acknowledged the value to the team of "The girls he has scored". Puts a new slant on taking one for the team!

On Sunday 21st April, I tuned into BT Sport for the FA Trophy Final at Wembley between Macclesfield Town and York City. I was delighted to see ex FGR favourite John Parkin rise like a killer whale to score for York City, only for Town's Antigua-born Rhys Browne to equalise. I am pretty sure that the commentary went something like "That's just what Macclesfield had needed, someone pacy out wide". But what came out in subtitles on the screen was " ... someone pastie white ... " The machine or person involved needs further training to address his/her/its deep seated xenophobia!

Welcome to my *subtitular* world! I hope you enjoy the book

## REWIND TO SUNDAY 15TH MAY 2016

Were we supporters devastated by the 3-1 Wembley defeat to Grimsby Town, some 9 points behind us in the league standings? Oddly, I do not think we were, as least I wasn't. And my equanimity had nothing to do with the multi-legged delayed trip to Montenegro, starting directly after the final whistle had blown.

No, truth be told, I don't think I believed deep down that we'd do it. Before I invite opprobrium from aghast readers from the Five Valleys, there was a more pragmatic reason for my lack of faith. With dreadful ill fortune, the team's engine room had broken down in the previous fortnight. At home to Halifax on 23rd April, Sam Wedgbury collapsed with a serious leg injury that would deprive him of first team football for 9 months. In the first leg of the Play Offs at Dover, Marcus Kelly limped off with a season ending strain. And at Wembley we learned that hard tackling play maker Rob Sinclair failed his fitness test. The three joined left back James Jennings as spectators.

That left David Pipe and Darren Carter to shoulder the burden. Both fine experienced players but with legs whose age aggregated, fulfilled the requirements for a pension and bus pass. That was never going to cut it on Wembley's lush expanse of green. Rovers competed well, might have taken an early lead, and scored the best goal of the game through Keanu Marsh-Brown. Yet by the end, Grimsby were worthy winners. Perennial bridesmaids as their likeable Paul Hurst Manager pointed out, they had surely completed their apprenticeship for a return to the English Football League?

And beyond defeat, there was hope. The preceding seasons had recorded 10th then 5th (despite a harsh 3 point penalty for a disputed administrative error in Luke Oliver's registration) and now 2nd place & play-off final for our hamlet club. In so many ways, Rovers were on the way up.

To cap the feel good factor, days before the 2016 Play-Off Final, Mark Cooper had been appointed as manager, though ever popular Academy Manager Scott Bartlett would manage on the day.

Ady Pennock's appointment years before had taken everyone by surprise – Ady who? Mark Cooper's though had been well trailed despite his position on a short term contract at Notts County.

Mark had been a popular player at FGR back in the day, towards the end of his career. Club captain, biting midfielder and top scorer. What's more he was a known devotee of the beautiful game. Keep it on the deck, keep possession with a rat-a-tat of passing and play it out from the back. No greater contrast to his predecessor would have been possible. And Mark often made visits to The New Lawn and was known to hold the club in high esteem

And stood behind him, our singular Chair Dale Vince still had his eyes focussed on long term progression. So, fair to say that The New lawn was a buoyant place, not one filled with gloomy types licking their wounds. Without that prevalent mood, I don't think I'd have written *The Rise of Forest Green Rovers: The Road to Wembley,* cathartic though the task was!

One thing saddened me though and it still does – negative coverage in some areas of the media of what Dale Vince is trying to accomplish at FGR. The world of football is not renowned for original thinkers nor Chair or Directors who question the old ways or invest in the long term. More often, it's about clichés, the blame game, constant calls for more money, and sackings by the boat load. Just occasionally, someone breaks the mould. Dale Vince. Yet, whether he craves thanks or recognition or not, he's had precious little except scorn from some of football's organs and saddest of all, Gloucestershire's daily paper, The Citizen/Echo.

I have got to know Dale and his family but he is not a friend as such. However I assure anyone reading my words that he is the real deal – 100% genuine. Dale is a Stroudie, living in a prominent mansion that most know. His company, Ecotricity has become as synonymous with Stroud as Norwich Union (now Aviva) at Norwich. As the 2008 recession loomed and Coventry Building Society upped anchors, Ecotricity's rise was a blessing. Thanks to Ecotricity and substantial employers like Renishaw, Stroud enjoys high quality employment statistics. Many such companies sponsor FGR.

At the close of the nineties and into the noughties, Rovers had enjoyed (or rather, endured) 11 seasons in Non League's top flight before Dale invested. Chairs like Trevor Horsley and Colin Gardner (no relation) and many predecessors had overseen the progression of the hamlet club. Legendary manager Frank Gregan and others like Colin Addison, Jim Harvey and yes, Dave Hockaday coached a quality of football that cemented Rovers' place as modern Davids in a Conference that increasingly featured Goliaths. Because of their efforts, the Club was surviving, albeit with increasing financial difficulty, in a modern stadium in the Conference Premier, soon to become National League.

Of course, Rovers were more popular with its opponents then too. Its small support was library-quiet, averaging barely 1,000. Endearingly quaint. And on the field play Rovers were generous to a fault, often meaning easy pickings for more fancied outfits. That said, the basis was in place for someone with fresh ideas and deeper pockets.

In the unlikely event of a huge cash injection, a risk might have been that FGR could simply become a tiny version of their counterparts in the Premiership. Franchise teams with little else to distinguish them one from another. How then could little Forest Green Rovers retain any semblance of identity if such investment occurred? Oh boy, were we all in for a shock when Dale revealed his game plan!

Dale was not, and has never been about being an old fashioned 'money bags' Chair. He saw a Club which he could help, albeit not initially on the scale that he later invested. The payback from his viewpoint was the ability to realise his ambitions for an eco-friendly, vegan-fuelled, ethical sporting business. Eventually, to become sustainable through its own momentum.

Certainly he was in a hurry. Red meat was consigned in favour of free range fowl, swiftly followed by meatless vegan menus. Photo-voltaic panels appeared on the south stand roof, chemical fertilisers were banned from the pitch, rainwater was harvested for re-use on the now organic pitch which was patrolled by solar powered Mowbot, and the strip and badge were changed. Outlying land was laid to wild flowers. Ticketing became paperless. The club also threw its support behind sporting and ecological charities and many others – like RBL and GDA – who will always be grateful for its help.

The Green in Forest Green Rovers swiftly took on another meaning. Far from losing identity, the Club was seizing it in chunks. Shock and amusement of locals and supporters was balanced by admiring reports by national press and media. Why shouldn't a football club lead in ethical and ecological affairs and why hadn't its *athletes* adopted sounder dietary habits? Years on, much of Dale's initial revolution is becoming more mainstream. Ecotricity and FGR were proving to be a good match.

Behind the scenes, the Club was restructured on a more professional basis. Administrators, marketing & commercial staff all left their mark. Catering was becoming famed for the quality of the vegan menu, and the supporters voted with their feet and stomachs as the restaurant and hospitality suites filled. Again unusually for a football club, customer was king not turnstile fodder.

On the playing side, coaches and medical back up were recruited with greater depth of expertise central to fitness training of players, and their recovery from injury. The academy and development set up was similarly strengthened. And volunteer efforts were redoubled with purpose.

The Ambassador scheme led by Phil Butterworth was embraced with enthusiasm by Dale's team and blossomed. At the last count, there are a remarkable 53 schools and colleges in Gloucestershire and South Gloucestershire at Primary, Secondary and Tertiary level boasting 73 individual ambassadors. They draw in fellow students, their school friends and different generations of their families. I have come across nothing like it at any other club. Despite the modest population of Forest Green and Nailsworth (less than 5,800 souls) Rovers average home league gate nears 1,800. This has put FGR's support ahead of most National League clubs and on a par with much larger outfits such as Torquay United, unthinkable a few short seasons ago.

This has not been to everyone's liking. Some traditionalists take a principled view about clubs accepting investment from a new owner and effecting change. Nothing personal, just that they see the future of their football club differently.

Elsewhere, green eyed jealousy has taken hold in surprising places. It was to be expected that opponents, particularly languishing former league clubs, would not enjoy the reversal of fortunes. Less predictable though was the offence taken by the Gloucester Citizen/Echo who saw their favoured team – Cheltenham Town – being upstaged by the upstart country bumpkins. Long serving FGR reporter Pete Orchard was given the elbow and replaced by a series of Robins' cast offs or students, all who preferred to carp about, rather than enthuse over FGR's rise.

Fortunately, Stroud News & Journal's excellent coverage more than filled the void. And the daily updating of its website offsets the lack of meaningful coverage of the Citizen. Also, such is the strength of the FGR's media presence these days that the Citizen's carping has been shrugged off and is more a cause for mirth by FGR supporters than concern.

The reaction in the Non-League Paper has also been disappointing. Their writers have had little good to say of FGR in recent years. Sad hacks who cannot see a good story when it slaps them in the face, nor the ethically minded work that backs up FGR's rise. They prefer to trot out the same tired 'moneybags club' epithets rather than objective reporting. Their loss.

Back to the impending start of the 2016/17 season. Once Mark Cooper's selection, player off-loads and recruitment had got under way in earnest, the scar of Wembley 2016 was muted though not forgotten. Attention focussed on the new season and the promised swash buckling passing game. It evoked happy memories of Jim's Harvey's best days.

As the July friendlies played out in the sunshine, Mark's team began to show off its new faces and 'play it from the back' style. Sam Russell was back at the team he loves. Ethan Pinnock began to show why he such a highly rated young prospect. Geordie Liam Noble assumed manager's role on the pitch and Christian Doidge appeared to win every high ball tossed up to him. That cruel taskmaster optimism was in the air again.

Compo, Foggy and I saw each other regularly during the close season and friendlies. To us, everything in the garden was adopting a rosier hue, and the ridiculous mid-summer restart of the National League was eagerly awaited. The National Trust's yearbook promised much.

Regrettably, 2016/17 would be the first any of us could recall without a hint of a local derby. Long gone were Yeovil Town, Bath City, Hereford United, Bristol Rovers, Cheltenham Town and even Kidderminster Harriers. Closest clubs geographically were Aldershot Town, Eastleigh and newbies Solihull Moors. Add the ever increasing diet of northern clubs and we were left wondering how our league gates would hold up and whether our cars would survive the journeys. We should not have worried.

Once again, what follows is the season's calendar of fixtures told mainly through the supporters' first hand experiences. Rich Joyce plays straight man with his summary match reports. In my alter ego, Rambling Man, I concentrate on the journey more that the pig's bladder. Jokerman tells the supporters' and match tales in detail (between downing quarts of real ale and boxes of cakes) The Ambassadors report matches observed by their sharp young eyes – always simple and devoid of cynicism. The Farmcotian & Football Poets and several others translate the season's emotions into telling verses. A few tasty tit-bits are added, like the recipe for FGR's famed Q-Pie. And many illustrations.

Hopefully, what shines through is our love of the beautiful game and irrational support for our proud hamlet team, ever the little club on the hill, Forest Green Rovers. Read on. For this was the season of our lives.

It was clear from the pre-season friendlies that Coops' Rovers were a work in progress. When the new 'pass it from the back' style worked, the team purred but when opponents pushed up on our midfield, hasty clearances or players caught in possession might embarrass. The Manager and the supporters expected the team to score more but concede more too.

So, after a stumbling defeat at Boreham Wood and unconvincing home performances against Sutton United and Gateshead, Coops would have been pleased to see out August in second place with 5 increasingly dominant wins and a single defeat. On the plastic of Maidstone and at home to Southport, Rovers purred and delighted.

*Now so long, National league, it's time that we began*
*to laugh and cry and cry and laugh about it all again*

(ChrisGump11 muses pre-season – some prophesy)

### Saturday 06.08.16
### Boreham Wood 1 FGR 0
### FRUSTRATING START ON FIRST DAY FOR ROVERS
*Richard Joyce*

Ricky Shakes' first half goal ensured Forest Green Rovers began the National League campaign with defeat at Boreham Wood.

The Guyana international smashed home from inside the area to cement what was an impressive opening day performance from the home side, who restricted Mark Cooper's charges in his first game in charge.

Dale Bennett was handed the captains armband in the middle of the Rovers back three as eight players were given their FGR debuts.

From the start, the danger carried by the hosts' front line was clear, and both Bruno Andrade and Angelo Balanta offered a threat in shooting positions.

Openings were rare for FGR, but Christian Doidge was presented with a great chance on 27 minutes, only to be scuppered by Grant Smith's brilliant decision to rush out of his goal and block his shot.

And the game's only goal came just a couple of minutes later just before the half hour mark when Shakes struck.

Bennett had initially done well to prevent Balanta's shot from finding a way through, however from the rebound Shakes was on hand to place the ball in the back of the net.

Mohamed Chemlal was a real bright light for Rovers throughout the afternoon, and the French wide man was involved in two chances towards the end of the first half as Cooper's troops tried to draw level before the break.

His deep cross towards Elliott Frear was volleyed wide by his fellow wing back, and his shot after tucking inside was well struck but not on target.

A step up in quality was needed in the second half, and the early chances for Forest Green did little to threaten from Doidge's low hit and Darren Carter's deflected strike.

The introduction of Matt Tubbs saw the former Portsmouth man almost head home after a good team move, however Boreham Wood came very close to doubling the lead on 65 minutes when Kenny Davis' turn and smash hammered against the crossbar.

And again they came close, only to be denied by Sam Russell on 71 minutes, when Adriano Moke had burst through from midfield.

Time was running out for Rovers, but it was the home side who were edging nearer to scoring the next goal, with Morgan Ferrier and Andrade both forcing efforts on goal in the closing stages.

As the clock ticked into stoppage time there would be just one final opportunity for Rovers.

It fell to the feet of Chemlal. However from a difficult position the star man's dug out attempt flew well over to frustrate FGR on the opening day, and to leave a determination to put things right when newly promoted Sutton United visit The New Lawn on Tuesday.

## DESTINATION BOREHAM WOOD

*Rambling Man*

The hottest day of August 2016 to date. Opening day of the Olympics at Rio. Definitively mid-summer. Am I getting old, or is our national game simply encroaching too far beyond its early autumn tradition? Whatever, Boreham Wood beckoned for Rovers first fixture of the National League season.

Last term had taken its toll of the 10 year old Passat. Emergency surgery was needed, notably new springs and anti-roll bars. But the operation was successful and it gambolled like a dirty grey lamb to the Glider, to pick up Foggy and Compo. Deep-throat had sent his last minute apologies having elected to travel by iron horse with the press pack.

Unseasonality aside, optimism was rife on the journey. Fine new manager, players to drool over, expansive football in prospect. Isn't life just dandy?

For Rovers, Boreham Wood is virtually a local derby for the 2016/17 season. Fact is, for the first time ever, we do not have one. The diminutive

Hertfordshire club is however 20 miles less distant than the Boxing Day/ New Year's Day double of Torquay United.

After the scant break, our appetite for culture had been refreshed. A year ago, Waddesdon Manor's gates had been closed to Compo and me but we would not be denied a second time.

Waddesdon Manor is eye candy and then some. Not yet 150 years old, it was commissioned by Baron Ferdinand de Rothschild (who was not short of a bob or two) from French Architect Gabrielle-Hypolyte Destailleur. Good name that. The brief was to deliver Renaissance Chateau style to a sleepy home county hamlet. The result is stunning and challenges the senses. The whole was bequeathed to the National Trust in 1957.

Honeyed Cotswold stone supports soaring fairytale turrets and towers. It is far more elaborate than your average Loire chateau, more Wedding Cake meets Disney. And the endless floral gardens and vistas would not look out of place at Versailles.

Of our distinguished threesome, Compo is far in a way the most erudite. He's had more education than Foggy and I have had hot dinners. Innit? Yet I was honoured to teach him some new vocabulary at Waddesdon – 'finials' and 'carpet bedding'. There are none so fine as at this palace.

90 minutes did not go far for our visit – a quick circuit with refreshments – but we'll be back *en famille*.

Boreham Wood FC is as friendly a little club as you might wish to visit, set in a smart, modern stadium that also hosts Arsenal Ladies. Tiny crowds mean that they live off relative scraps. The Club did well to survive its first foray into the National League, last season.

Even with 100+ from the Five Valleys, the total crowd was not much more than 500. But generosity was not in evidence on the pitch, as the hard working hosts dismantled a confused and confusing Rovers team. The 1-0 reverse could have been worse.

Highlight for me was the ice cream cart doing the circuit of the stadium at half time, and a roaring trade too. Unlikely to be present come the winter, I think.

So, steaming hot summer had been interrupted by the giant ice bucket of reality. The National League does not suffer half-hearted performances.

## THE TEAM THAT FELL TO EARTH

*Jokerman*

A new dawn, a new manager, new players and forty six games to realise great expectations. Dickens of a job but hey this team is wired to succeed. Most agree Mark Cooper is a strong choice to lift the club into the

Football League and Chairman Dale Vince has backed him to do just that. The better players remain and further quality has been added by the bucket full.

Forest Green Rovers supporters will be hoping the players can engage to create a strong bond and with a Welsh leprechaun striker surely all things are possible. The journey begins today with an away trip to Boreham Wood, the first step on the ladder. Kendo is on station again this season. The scenic route is chosen through Bibury, twinned with Yokohama, to Oxford and beyond. Red Kites circle languidly under a blue sky and blazing sun above the M40.

Arriving in good time several fans head for The Hart & Spool on main street, Doom Bar on draught two forty nine a pint. Wetherspoon, a friend to the poor. Back at Meadow Park, the home of Boreham Wood, Cooper has named his first team. Russell has the gloves and Doidge and Murphy lead the attack. Bennett is skipper with Racine on the bench.

Ten minutes before kick off a crowd of well over a hundred Rovers fans gather at the away end but one could have fired a gatling gun around the ground and not hit anyone. Atmosphere zero. From the kick off Boreham Wood took the game to Rovers and immediately the visitors looked unprepared. Balanta put Andrade in on the left and the skilful winger forced a good block from Russell at his near post.

Fifteen minutes in and no reply from Rovers. On twenty minutes Chemlal was fouled on half way and needed treatment. In the warm conditions the players used the interruption for a drinks break having not sweated as much since they sat their last spelling test. Twenty five minutes and Rovers created their first real chance when Frear cut the ball inside the area to Doidge in space but Boreham custodian Smith was quickly off his line to block the shot, which rebounded to Carter, whose effort was narrowly too high. Boreham Wood took the lead on thirty minutes taking advantage of a hesitant defence with an attack down the right. Balanta was allowed to run into the area, Bennett blocked his shot but the ball dropped to Shakes who turned and lashed a shot across Russell high inside the left hand post. It was a sickner for Rovers fans but couldn't come as any shock and it just went from bad to worse. Far from stinging the visitors into life it boosted the home side. Andrade was taking Rovers apart and on thirty six minutes he picked out Shakes at the back post who beat Carter knocked the ball inside and forced Pinnock to make a goal saving block. Forty minutes in and Chemlal created a rare chance for Rovers launching a terrific cross field ball from the right to the unmarked Frear, who hit a first time volley over the bar from ten yards. The only

**A U G U S T**

thing Rovers won in the first half was the first corner of the match in added time. Temperatures were in the high twenties as FGR fans queued at the ice cream cart and wondered if there was a scientific explanation of why their team was 'frozen stiff'. Cooper would need a 'blow torch' to sort this out. Unfortunately the second half almost turned to farce after five minutes when Russell twice made suicidal short clearances. Boreham Wood failed to punish him. Cooper had seen enough and soon brought on Tubbs and Robert for Murphy and Carter. Matters improved slightly when rare link-up play saw Chemlal cross the ball for Tubbs whose header cleared the cross bar. Boreham Wood came very close to doubling their lead on sixty six minutes when Andrade again picked out Shakes who knocked the ball inside to Davis, who under pressure, crashed a shot against the angle of post and bar from close range. A minute later Forest Green had their one real chance to square the match. Clough from just inside the Boreham half on the right crossed to the edge of the box where Doidge rose to meet the ball. For reasons known only to himself Smith rushed out to punch and missed by a country mile. Agonisingly for Rovers fans behind the goal the looping header dropped inches wide of the right hand post. Racine replaced Traore on seventy minutes but the home side continued to boss the game and create better chances with Moke bringing a good save from Russell after exchanging passes with Balanta. Frustration set in with ten minutes remaining and Bennett and Ferrier were booked after an altercation.

Rovers were desperate and tried in vain to press forward but could not bypass the two giant defenders Paine and Stevens. They shall not pass was the motto for Boreham Wood whose players picked up several yellow cards as the game ended, but Forest Green can have no complaints they were clearly second best on the day. Cooper will have to contact Coles Electrical to re-wire his squad in time for Tuesday night's game against Sutton where anything short of a victory will cause the forum to explode.

**Tuesday 09.08.16**
**FGR 1 Sutton United 1**
**ROVERS GET THEIR FIRST POINT ON THE BOARD**
*Richard Joyce*
Newly promoted Sutton United denied Forest Green Rovers a winning start in Mark Cooper's first competitive home game in charge thanks to Nicky Bailey's second half penalty.

Last season's National League South winners picked up a point on their first ever visit to The New Lawn as they cancelled out Matt Tubbs' first FGR goal.

It was Rovers first recorded point of the season after losing on the opening day at Boreham Wood, and Cooper's men will now be licking their lips at the prospect of another home encounter on Saturday when Gateshead visit Gloucestershire.

Used as a substitute on Saturday, Tubbs was one of five changes to the FGR starting XI, and he made an instant contribution when after only seven minutes he nodded his side into the lead.

Mohamed Chemlal's fantastic free kick found the summer signing at the back post, and he guided home past Ross Worner with an excellent header.

Tubbs' goal was reflective of Forest Green's dominant start to the match, however Sutton came into the game past the quarter of an hour mark, and after Roarie Deacon had tested Sam Russell, former FGR trialist Ryan Burge chipped onto the crossbar with a fantastically produced effort.

Chances continued to fall to Rovers though. A stunning team move ended with another Tubbs attempt being saved by Worner after Dale Bennett had fired a low cross into the box.

Meanwhile Sutton's former Charlton Athletic keeper produced an easy save from a curling Chemlal hit, and he even had to make an acrobatic save off his own defender, Jamie Collins, when the former FGR man had deflected the ball towards his own goal.

Deacon's early second half strike for the visitors served as an early warning for Rovers, who after seeing Tubbs scuppered by Worner after a marvellous Chemlal through ball, saw their opponents draw level.

Drissa Traore brought down Bedsente Gomis in the box, and that allowed the experienced Bailey the opportunity to slam home from the penalty spot.

There were plenty of opportunities for Rovers to hit back with much of the half left. Although a number of half chances made it difficult for a winner to present itself.

Keanu Marsh-Brown's drive from distance went over, and a spin and volley from just outside the area by Tubbs ended with the strikers effort flying wide.

Substitute Christian Doidge tried to make an impact, but he only saw one difficult chance fall his way late on from a narrow Bennett long ball, which the Welsh forward could only nod off target.

## SUTTON SOW EARLY SEEDS OF DOUBT AT THE NEW LAWN
*Jokerman*

Following on from Forest Green's disappointing performance in their opening fixture of the new season at Boreham Wood, fans will be hoping for a positive response from Coopers much lauded players. Talk in the bar is guarded, however Jilly Cooper eulogises how beautiful the players are. A real plus there then.

Mark Cooper has made some changes to the starting line-up with Racine partnering Clough in defence and Tubbs and Moore leading the attack. A slight cooling breeze flutters the black flag possibly designed by a Hells Angel from the Devil's Kitchen as the teams parade to warm applause. Thirteen hundred are in attendance and the Rovers fans are in effing good voice behind the goal. The low sun is blinding the East Stand supporters but it doesn't stop Forest Green make a promising start to the game. Five minutes in and Rovers win a free kick on the right and Worner the Sutton keeper dives to punch Chemlal's cross away. Two minutes later Rovers are in front. Stearn fouls Robert on the right touchline and his deep cross to the back post finds Tubbs who deftly headed the ball past Worner.

FGR were playing more football in the first quarter of an hour than fans saw in ninety minutes on Saturday. Sadly it didn't last. A few words from the Sutton bench and Sutton came into the game. Gomes put Deacon in on the right following a good counter move. The striker cut into the box and forced Russell into a save low down that he had to scramble to collect at the second attempt. On twenty minutes Sutton were unfortunate not to be level when hesitation on the edge of the box gave the ball away and allowed Burge to hit a sublime shot over Russell only to see the ball strike the crossbar. Only when Rovers upped the pace did they again threaten the Sutton defence. Moore was booked for a foul on Worner which incensed the Sutton fans behind the goal who thought he should have received an early bath. On thirty five minutes Chemlal and Robert combined well and the cross from the right was met by Tubbs at the near post, but he was denied by a good save from Worner. Chemlal then sent Bennett on the overlap and his cross was nearly turned in to his own net by Stearn but for an acrobatic save from his keeper.

The earth had revolved away from the sun to ease the eyes of the east standers but was replaced by the broken scoreboard that flashed like a strobe for the remainder. Sutton were still very much in the game and from a Stearn corner on the left Clough was beaten to the ball by Beckwith, whose glancing header went wide from close range.

On half time Clough gave away a free kick on the edge of the area. The kick deflected off the wall to Deacon six yards out, but his contact was poor and Russell was relieved to smother the effort. Plenty to discuss at half time. Rovers were playing well in patches but Sutton were bullying them and crossing the ball too easily from the flanks.

The game was fairly even and remained so at the start of the second half, both sides launching attacks. Around the fifty minute mark Deacon should have levelled for the visitors when he created loads of space in the area with a quick side-step and hit a ferocious shot narrowly wide of the right hand post with Russell beaten.

Rovers replied when Robert threaded a superb ball through to Tubbs inside the box but Worner was quickly out to smother his effort. On fifty five minutes Bennetts block on the left side by-line failed to stop the ball being knocked back to Deacon who was fouled by Traore and the referee pointed to the spot. Bailey stepped up and leathered the ball past Russell's left hand despite going the right way.

A few minutes later things got worse for Rovers when Clough went to ground with what looked like a dislocated shoulder. Doidge replaced him. Frear replaced Robert on the hour but Rovers were running out of ideas and one had the feeling the game was there for the taking from the Sutton point of view.

Tubbs and Keanu had shots over the bar from distance and Rovers resorted to balls lofted over the top. Wishart up from the back for Sutton ran right through the Rovers defence to hit a shot wide. It was a bit uncomfortable for the Rovers fans. Sinclair came on for Traore with fifteen minutes remaining but the game just petered out and ended in anti-climax for the home supporters. There were some positives and with Noble and Kelly on the horizon there is plenty of time to put things right. Ten games in will give a clearer indication. However this was not the plan and another home game against Gateshead on Saturday will see the pressure intensify. Three points there will make the world of difference.

## FGR AMBASSADOR REPORT
*Elsie Heslop, Sir William Romney Secondary School, Tetbury*
Elsie's FGR Experience. Hi I'm Elsie, a 13 year old student from Sir William Romney's school. This year I am again lucky to have been asked to be an Ambassador for FGR. Being an Ambassador last year was great, as it gave me an opportunity to spend time with my family, sharing something that we love: football. Promoting the club has been fun too! To hear people at my school talking about the club makes me feel proud to know that I am helping the club by influencing people to come and support their local team. Personally, I do reports to develop the support of the Rovers and they get published in my village magazine. Last season we went to Wembley for the first time and it was easily the best experience I've had, despite the end result. But hey, that's why I love football: the atmosphere,

**A U G U S T**

the emotions and the community spirit it brings. Hopefully this season we can get back up to the top and get promoted to league 2.

At the start of this game FGR needed to boost their confidence after losing to Boreham Wood, and after just 7mins Matt Tubbs scored an excellent goal making it 1-0. However, Sutton came up the field and nearly scored, but it hit the crossbar. The game was exciting and getting tense as FGR had more opportunities to score. You could tell that the crowd were on the edge of their seats as it went a little silent, until someone shouted a funny comment at Sutton's goalkeeper, which made everybody laugh!

Then 10 Minutes in to the second half the ref, for no reason, gave a penalty to Sutton, making it 1-1. After this FGR did all they could to get another goal but the ref kept making strange decisions and Forest Green just couldn't get ahead. The game ended with man of the match deservedly going to Mohamed Chemlal.

**Saturday 13.08.16**
**FGR 1 Gateshead 0**
**ROVERS LEAVE IT LATE TO BAG FIRST VICTORY**
*Richard Joyce*

Dale Bennett's stoppage time winner earned Forest Green Rovers a first win of the season against Gateshead at The New Lawn.

The right back, whose last goal for Rovers was an identical strike in an April 2015 clash with Macclesfield, struck at the death to secure Forest Green a first three point haul of the season.

Both sides had chances in an entertaining end-to-end encounter, with Mohamed Chemlal hitting the woodwork for FGR and Antony Sweeney doing the same for the visitors.

However it was Mark Cooper's side who came out on top as he registered his first win as Forest Green boss.

The lively Chemlal was a threat to the away side early on, and he produced a number of chances in the opening quarter of an hour, with Drissa Traore and Keanu Marsh-Brown also seeing opportunities go close.

Neil Aspin's Gateshead came into the tie, and Paddy McLaughlin should have done better when he drilled a left footed strike wide on 20 minutes.

The ex-York City man again should have put his side in front ten minutes before the break, only to be foiled by a crucial save by Sam Russell, who kept out the midfielder's effort when he had broken through in the box.

At the beginning of the second half the action continued in a similar vein. Marsh-Brown tried his luck with two long range efforts that weren't far away.

Matt Tubbs was looking to add to his goal from midweek, but the former Bournemouth man was foiled by Sam Johnson in the Heed Army's goal when he turned and shot from inside the area.

Cooper's men continued to work openings, and on the midpoint of the second half they came close to finding the net, but Chemlal was denied by the crossbar after Johnson had been beaten.

Gateshead changes introduced new impetus to their attack with the introduction of Ryan Bowman and Danny Johnson. And on 72 minutes they themselves hit the bar when Sweeney nodded onto the woodwork.

It was a vital moment for a Forest Green side who grabbed the game by the scruff of the neck in the final ten minutes.

Tubbs forced Johnson into a spectacular tip over the bar, before Bennett crowned the performance with the winning goal at the start of stoppage time.

Forward down the right hand side, his speared ball into the danger zone from the corner flag area was inch perfect, and it dropped in over Johnson via the post to send The New Lawn crowd into raptures.

Rovers had left it late, but it was the first of what will hopefully be many victories in the pursuit for promotion this season.

There was still time for one last piece of drama near the finish as the visitors ended the game with nine men in stoppage time. Former FC Halifax man Williams kicked out at Guthrie in an incident near the corner flag, and after expressing his views to the officials a little too forcefully, he managed to earn himself a head-start on his teammates when it came to the walk down the tunnel.

## BENNETT OPENS THE GATES

*Jokerman*

Forest Green have no time to dwell on their slow start to the season, having nearly two games a week in the first month. One point from six was some way below expectations but signs of improvement against Sutton on Tuesday, a penalty denying a win, gave grounds for optimism.

Today's visitors Gateshead have two wins from two games and will no doubt be up for the challenge against the stuttering favourites for the title. It is a warm afternoon and thirsty fans are in The Green Man maxing out their credit cards as Hull City stuff Leicester City in the early kick-off. It's a funny old game.

**A**
**U**
**G**
**U**
**S**
**T**

FGR manager Mark Cooper has an enforced change with Clough injured and brings in Jefford while partnering Doidge with Tubbs in attack. Frear does not feature today. Forest Green start the match dominating possession and Gateshead are content to sit back rather than chase and harry.

Despite being in control it is nearly fifteen minutes before the game sparks into life with both Robert and Traore hitting shots wide of the mark. Keanu then made the first of several eye-catching runs. Skipping through the middle before pushing the ball to Tubbs whose shot just cleared the bar.

As on Tuesday there was then a lull in proceedings that allowed Gateshead to reply. York on the right wing beat Pinnock for pace and crossed to McLaughlin who fired wide from the edge of the area.

After some head tennis in the Rovers defence following a corner, Brundle hit the ball wide. On thirty three minutes McLaughlin struck the first shot of the game on target from the edge of the 'D' that Russell caught comfortably. A minute later they came closest catching Rovers out with a quick throw-in on the right, allowing York to cut inside and square the ball to McLaughlin at the near post. The striker was denied only by a fine save by Russell diving low to his left.

Despite these efforts Forest Green still looked the better side in possession and by far the more adventurous side going forward, as the half time whistle sounded. Rovers had played good football but just lacked that final flourish to cap their build up play. Temperatures were a bit too high for football and the heat was getting to Shaun and his mates in the field opposite who were doing a lot of frolicking.

The second half started in the same vein with Rovers on the offensive. Keanu hit a shot from distance that Gateshead keeper Johnson gathered easily. Jefford was having a solid game at the back for Rovers while Racine hardly put a foot wrong all afternoon. On fifty five minutes after good movement, Keanu curved a shot goalwards but not enough to trouble Johnson. Around the hour Cooper made a change replacing Robert with Murphy. He was soon in action with a deft pass to Tubbs on the right who struck a good shot from a narrow angle that Johnson blocked away. Gateshead had also made a change and it was substitute Dan Johnson who latched on to a clearance down the centre. Only a superbly timed tackle from Pinnock denied him a one-on-one with Russell. Rovers reply was instant and a mesmerising turn by Keanu in mid-field saw him slip the ball through to Chemlal in the left corner of the area. He hit his shot over Johnson only to see the ball strike the crossbar.

Fans began to wonder if Rovers were ever going to score for all their superiority. Then as often happens Gateshead forged the chance their tactics were geared to. A quick counter from defence put Dan Johnson in acres of space on the right. He reached the by-line and crossed perfectly for fellow sub Sweeney unmarked to head powerfully past Russell. As Rovers fans jaws dropped to knee level the ball smashed against the bar and was cleared.

Carter replaced Chemlal on seventy two minutes and Sinclair for Traore around the eighty minute mark as FGR desperately searched for the goal their play merited. Tubbs forced Johnson to tip a stinging shot over the bar and Racine driving forward put the ball through to Keanu inside the area on the right. Johnson raced out to meet it and Keanu went down and was booked for simulation. It was frustrating for all in the Rovers camp as time was ticking away. The board went up three minutes added. As the game began to die some fans thought it was all over and left their seats, heading home. Most Forest Green fans good naturedly know that Dale Bennett only has one leg, his right, to play football with. His left allows him to do so. On ninety one minutes Bennett took a pass from Carter wide near the right hand corner. It's long been his trademark to hit this ball on the run aiming for the back post. Just a few minutes earlier too much adrenalin made him over hit the ball. This time the high looper dropped out of the sun like a meteor blinding Johnson, evading his desperate stretch, striking the inside of the back post and bounced nicely into the back of the net in front of several delirious Rovers fans. Flat on the ground Bennett was mobbed by his team mates. The feeling was tangible. Not just relief, the team got what their commitment and efforts deserved, but gave a lift to the whole football club. Forest Green Rovers will look to capitalise on this performance at Woking on Tuesday night.

### Tuesday 16.08.16
### Woking 0 FGR 1
### MARSH-BROWN STRIKE DOWNS WOKING
*Richard Joyce*

For the first time in eight years, Forest Green Rovers recorded an away victory at Woking thanks to Keanu Marsh-Brown's first half goal.

The Rovers hoodoo when on their travels to Kingfield was brought to an end following a commanding performance – the best yet of Mark Cooper's short tenure in charge.

Controlling much of the play, FGR needed just the one strike from Marsh-Brown to settle the tie, but could and should have added more to their tally.

**A**
**U**
**G**
**U**
**S**
**T**

In what was the two teams' 33rd league meeting in the fifth tier, an encouraging opening 15 minutes saw Marsh-Brown try his luck with two long distance attempts.

With debutant Liam Noble bringing quality in midfield, a fine FGR team move on 17 minutes saw Rhys Murphy almost fire home, only to be denied by Michael Poke after he had latched onto strike partner Christian Doidge's lay off.

Noble played his part in the game's only goal two minutes later when he showed terrific vision to tee up Marsh-Brown with an outstanding assist.

His lifted ball found Marsh-Brown in room just inside the area, and he swept home first time with a hooked right footed effort to give Rovers the lead.

The hosts were struggling to see much of the ball, although in response to going behind they did see Dennon Lewis fire just wide, and then Zak Ansah forced Sam Russell into a good stop.

After Darren Carter had hit a powerful shot just over the bar, Rovers had the ball in the back of the net again on the stroke of half time.

This time however the linesman had his flag up to deny Noble a goal on his debut after he had met a header inside the box.

A quiet opening to the second half saw little but half chances for either side. It wasn't really until the final quarter of an hour did the action catch the eye again.

Noble's magnificent free kick looked set for the top corner before Poke got across to produce an excellent save, while the former Torquay United keeper also denied Marsh-Brown's strong attempt after he had burst through.

The hosts had lacked a goal threat all evening, but yet in the final stages they began to make life difficult by putting pressure on the FGR goal.

Focussed defending though kept Garry Hill's men at bay, and if anything it was Forest Green who should have added a second goal, only for Poke to again pull off another excellent stop.

This time substitute Matt Tubbs found a way round the back of the Cards defence in the final moments of stoppage time, but his right footed shot was well blocked by Poke to keep FGR's victory down to just the one goal.

### DESTINATION WOKING
*Rambling Man*

"Phew, wotta scorcher! Hotter than Tossa Del Mar (at midnight)!" The Sun and Daily Getsworse headline writers live for weather like this.

Admittedly it was a trifle warm as we met at The Glider, mid-afternoon. We being Cleggy, Deep-throat and me, with the former piloting Dagenham's finest automotive machinery. This was the first of our season's jousts with pre rush hour M4, a guessing game at the best of times but smooth as silk today.

Our intermediate target was The National Trust's Runnymede riverside site. As every primary school child knows (or used to know?), John was a 'bad' king who properly brassed off his barons. As a result, in 1215 they forced him to sign Magna Carta at Runnymede. Why Runnymede? Well, I suppose it was considered convenient for the M25, refuelling their horses at Chobham Services and resuming their homeward journeys after.

As a modest student of history, I always thought Magna Carta was about the bolshy aristos securing their rights and power, faced by an unjust tyrant. But commentators now have it as the underpinning of modern democracy. Buy a copy on Amazon and decide for yourself. One thing I can confirm is that the signing of Magna Carta is not one of Mark Cooper's Gallic additions to the FGR squad nor any relation of our Darren's.

Should you wish to explore Runnymede's attractions, you'll be able to enjoy The Magna Carta and JFK memorials in woodland on the hillside, a lovely riverside park with visitor centre, the RAF Memorial and Ankerwyke wood, home to a 2,500-year-old tree. Great place for picnics and cycles too. Oh and it is only 14 miles from the Kingfield, sorry the Laithwaite Community Stadium, chez Woking FC. It made for a pleasant sun soaked visit.

I've travelled to Kingfield over two millennia, and seen but one FGR win – a Kaid Mohammed blast from distance in the Harvey era. Since then misery, even at the hands of former tenants Hayes & Yeading. The welcome is always as good as anywhere it's just that the on-pitch generosity sucks!

As last year, enormous sausages were served up by the hosts. I didn't ask, but was confident that the delicious Zeppelins were constituted from Quorn & seaweed extract and so on. Anyhow, they didn't touch the sides.

The game? A rare thing indeed in this corner of Surrey. A convincing 1-0 win and a relaxed experience for we nerve-affected FGR supporters. Coop's charges are up to 80% on the performance meter and going ever higher. Possession was slick, the side dominated and frustrated their opponents. Noble's chip over to KMB and his volleyed winner will have sent the Forum's poets racing for their smocks and quills.

**AUGUST**

So, 10 days in to the new season, Rovers inauspicious start has receded and momentum is building. Next away trip is a new date on our calendar – the plastic turf of Maidstone United.

**Saturday 20.08.16**
**FGR 2 York City 1**
## TUBBS HOLDS HIS NERVE TO EARN LATEST WIN
*Richard Joyce*

Matt Tubbs' dramatic late penalty helped Forest Green Rovers to three points against York City to make it three wins on the bounce.

The experienced front man stepped up and kept his cool at the death to deliver Forest Green's third win in the space of seven days having had to come from behind from Richard Brodie's fine first half finish.

Rovers are now up to sixth after five games, although saw York active in front of goal early on at The New Lawn as they looked to respond to their 6-1 hiding at Gateshead in midweek.

Former FGR favourite Yan Klukowski went close after eight minutes with a low shot inside the box that just rolled past the post, and then a couple of minutes later Sheffield United loan youngster Jake Wright nodded wide from the impressive Aidan Connolly's ball into the box.

After Rhys Murphy had headed wide Forest Green's first opportunity on the quarter of an hour mark, York silenced the home crowd when they broke the deadlock.

The much-travelled Brodie despatched a brilliant volley, out of the reach of Sam Russell, to slam the hosts ahead.

And he almost doubled his team's lead only to be thwarted by Russell's wonderful fingertip save.

The search for a Forest Green equaliser came in the final sector of the half, and after Aarran Racine had narrowly headed over Mohamed Chemlal's corner, Murphy bagged his first goal since joining the club.

He slid in from close range as he met Ben Jefford's dangerous low cross into the six-yard box to draw the two teams level.

In additional time at the end of the first half York debutant goalkeeper Luke Simpson was required to make two crucial saves to keep things all square heading into the break.

He denied Tubbs with a smart stop and then produced another key block to leave the sides level.

Simpson again kept Tubbs at bay, who was looking to make FGR the sixth club he has scored against York for, with another save early after the break as Rovers sought the game's next goal.

York though had chances themselves with the impressive Russell saving well from Matty Dixon, but their ambition to win the game was pegged back when on 73 minutes their captain Simon Heslop was given his marching orders after picking up his second yellow card of the afternoon.

The impetus was now with FGR to claim three points, and Tubbs was again in a good position to get a shot off on goal as the match entered the final ten minutes, but he stroked the ball just wide.

Russell though was called upon to make a sensational save in the closing stages of the 90 minutes when he tipped away Racine's goal-bound touch on the ball, pushing it superbly onto the woodwork.

Last week FGR had claimed their first victory of the season in the depths of stoppage time, and it was to be the same again in even more dramatic fashion this time round.

A delivery into the box saw Racine hauled down, and referee Steven Rushton pointed straight to the spot to offer Rovers the chance to claim a maximum haul of points.

Tubbs snapped up the opportunity in courageous style, chipping the ball home off the underside of the crossbar, to make it three wins in a row and to send FGR into the August Bank Holiday double-header with another win under the belt.

## TUBBS DINES OUT ON A YORKIE BAR CHIP

*Jokerman*

The wheels of progress are beginning to turn at Forest Green Rovers with a second success away at Woking on Tuesday night. Having outclassed their rival's manager Mark Cooper was decidedly unhappy with the margin of victory (0-1) and has demanded improvement from his strike force. Today the Yorkists are travelling south having been trashed at Gateshead 6-1 in mid-week. Following such a beating Cooper will not be underestimating the reaction York boss McNamara will be expecting from his players this afternoon.

Sinclair is on the injury list so Chemlal starts while the strikers continue to rotate with Murphy and Tubbs given the office up front. Under storm clouds with high winds blowing heavy showers down the pitch from the south, Rovers choose to play against the conditions in the first half.

On seven minutes York win the first corner that gives ex-FGR man Klukowski a sight of goal but his shot is wide. From a Rovers corner at the other end York defender Whittle breaks clear and runs the length of the pitch, flicks a pass to Connolly who crosses for Wright to glance a header wide.

**A U G U S T**

York are looking far more dangerous in attack and on 20mins take the lead. The industrious Connolly on the left hits the ball into Brodie twelve yards out who shrugs off a challenge from Pinnock, turns and smashes a left foot shot high inside the left hand post. The hundred and fifty travelling supporters behind the goal are in raptures. Brodie may have had more clubs than one would find in a Neanderthals armoury but he can still do a job at this level. Four minutes later he has Russell at full stretch to fist away his shot from the edge of the area. To complete his range of abilities, all in six minutes, he hacks Keanu down from behind to receive a yellow card.

Forest Green's first real chance comes on thirty four minutes from a Chemlal corner that Racine meets head on, but the ball bounces down and over the bar. Rovers begin to dominate in the ten minutes before half time and draw level on 40mins. Noble, who was having a sterling game, hit a superb lofted pass inside the full back for the overlapping Jefford to seize onto and square along the six yard box, for Murphy, under pressure to slide past keeper Simpson. With slick build up play Rovers laid siege to the York goal. Keanu and Tubbs fired shots over the bar and in time added on Simpson made crucial saves from both Tubbs and Murphy to keep the scores level going into the break. FGR were in a game and York's performance had belied their Gateshead debacle.

The second half began with both sides going for a win. A brilliant Keanu 'dummy' wrong-footed the York defence and sent Bennett down the right flank. He crossed from the by-line to the near post for Tubbs, who was thwarted by Simpson, who dived courageously at his feet. York replied on sixty minutes when Brodie looked to have beaten Russell with a header, but Pinnock was on hand to hook the ball clear. Hit straight back in, Wright went down but his penalty appeal was waved away. Dixon then hit a shot from distance that had Russell conceding a corner at full stretch.

Both sides made subs on sixty three minutes, Doidge replaced Murphy in attack for Rovers. Keanu and Chemlal's trickery on the ball was frustrating for the substantially heavier York rearguard and their discipline began to waver in the final twenty minutes of the match. The main protagonist was Heslop who in the space of four minutes hacked Chemlal from behind and then literally rugby tackled him over the touchline to give referee Rushton yellow fever and finally a deserved red card. York immediately made tactical changes bringing on Kamdjo to put up the shutters.

As the game entered the closing stages with Rovers all out for the winning goal there usually comes a chance of a break out and so it transpired. Dixon took a pass near the right corner flag and crossed dangerously over the six yard line. Racine facing his own goal and under pressure from Brodie headed powerfully downwards and looked to have put through his own goal until Russell, with lightening reflexes, dived to his left and scooped the ball up against the crossbar and away for a corner. Banks would have approved.

After such an escape Rovers fans emotions were in turmoil as the game went deep into stoppage time. The skies had been the colour of gunpowder all afternoon over TNL and as the seconds ticked away the game exploded in the faces of the York fans behind the goal. An innocuous free kick thirty five yards out saw Noble hit a cracking ball into the box. Racine diving full length to connect was held back and the referee pointed to the spot and served up another yellow card. Tubbs stepped up and audaciously jinked the ball over Simpson and into the net via the underside of the crossbar. Wheeling away to the corner flag he ripped off his shirt to reveal his wired bra and be mobbed by his team mates. The referee brandished the mandatory yellow card but the players, staff and supporters of Forest Green Rovers didn't give two monkeys or a Maggie Thatcher, they had three points in the bag. Nothing's routine at Forest Green.

## FGR AMBASSADOR REPORT
*Seth Tiley, Uley Primary School*
Hi, my name is Seth Tiley. I am 8 years old and I go to Uley Primary School where I will be going into year 4 in September. I am very excited to be an ambassador for FGR and the opportunities this will present.

Me and my family are huge FGR fans. The Tiley family have been supporting FGR for many years, starting with my Grandad, Trevor Tiley when he was a Director here many years ago. As a result, my Dad has been a fan since he was a teenager as well, so now my whole family regularly attend any game we can go to. We were lucky enough last season to go to Wembley stadium to watch FGR in the Playoff final which was an amazing experience for me.

Here is my match report for the game against York City. FGR came into the game on good form with 2 great wins against Gateshead and Woking. York City however came to the New Lawn off the back of a 6-1 defeat against Gateshead, so were looking to put that right against FGR. Looking to continue their good run, FGR only made a few changes from mid-week's team and started the game strongly. However 20 minutes into the game York City's Striker Richard Brodie found space in the

**A**
**U**
**G**
**U**
**S**
**T**

18 yard box to turn with the ball and volley it into the back of the net. York City were 1 up! Shortly after Brodie almost struck again but Sam Russell pulled off a fantastic save to keep the score 0-1. FGR came back strong with many great chances coming forward, the best of which was converted into FGR first goal when a brilliant cross came in from the left by Ben Jefford who found Rhys Murphy sliding into the 6 yard box to convert for FGR equalizer. 1-1 the score at half time.

Both teams came out and started the second half strong with opportunities both ends. Sam Russell again, pulled off a fantastic save when Aaron Racine's defensive header found its way goal bound forcing Russell into an athletic dive guiding the ball onto the cross bar. With Christian Doidge now on as a sub upfront with Matt Tubbs, the pair had some good chances saved as the game was going on. Finally the breakthrough came in stoppage time as Aaron Racine was brought down in the penalty area, penalty to FGR! Up steps Matt Tubbs to try and Secure another 3 points for FGR, he calmly placed the ball in the top right of the goal just coming off the underside of the bar, 2-1 to FGR.

A good 3 points for FGR, hopefully they can continue this run now throughout the season.

**Saturday 27.08.16**
**Maidstone United 1 FGR 4**
**FOUR ON THE BOUNCE FOR FLYING ROVERS**
*Richard Joyce*

A formidable attacking performance saw Forest Green Rovers clinch all three points in magnificent style on the club's first ever visit to Maidstone United's Gallagher Stadium.

Rovers' debut on a 3G playing surface saw a double from Rhys Murphy, plus further strikes from Darren Carter and Christian Doidge, inflict a sizeable win over last year's National League South play-off winners with what was a stylish display.

At one point the hosts had been level thanks to Jack Evans' well taken free kick, but Rovers raced away with it after clinching an important half time lead on the stroke of the interval.

Having trained all week on a 3G surface to get used to the conditions, FGR made the ideal start, when after only five minutes Carter ran onto Keanu Marsh-Brown's perfectly weighted pass and slotted brilliantly.

Maidstone, backed by an impressive home crowd, drew level a short while later though as Evans found a way past Sam Russell on his 150th league appearance for the club with a pin-point set piece effort.

On a run of three straight wins heading into the tie, FGR set about searching for the game's next goal. They did have the ball in the back of the net on 25 minutes, although the linesman had his flag up after Doidge had turned the ball home.

A series of chances before the break saw Liam Noble's terrific free kick well saved by Lee Worgan, while Murphy fired wide and then forced Worgan into a good stop.

It would be a cross into the box from Ben Jefford though that would see Forest Green restore their lead on the stroke of half time.

His fizzing ball into the danger zone found Doidge who guided home for his first goal since joining in the summer from Dagenham & Redbridge.

After the break FGR showed no signs of settling on their one goal lead. Carter was denied early on by a great Tom Mills block, and Marsh-Brown also watched a strongly hit strike zip past the post.

Maidstone enjoyed a five minute attacking spell that almost saw them level as they looked to get back into the contest.

Substitute Tom Murphy almost made an instant impact when he curled off target, while Drissa Traore's block from a Ben Greenhalgh hit was brilliantly executed. The latter then glanced a header just wide when he met a cross from former Dover man Murphy.

FGR put the game beyond their hosts with two goals in quick succession from Murphy towards the finish.

The ex-Oldham attacker notched his first with a sizzling strike from distance that left Worgan with no chance.

And then it was four for Rovers, and two for Murphy, when fine work by substitute Kieffer Moore allowed Murphy to slam home from inside the area.

The stuffing had been knocked out of Maidstone, although to their credit they pushed late on for another goal, only to be denied by the woodwork after Alex Flisher had worked a good opportunity down the left hand side.

Elliott Frear, returning from injury as a substitute, almost made it five late on. But his bursting run and low hit slipped just wide, as Rovers settled for four goals and four wins in a row in Kent.

## DESTINATION MAIDSTONE

*Rambling Man*

The day's fixture in Kent promised something completely different. Temperate, drizzly Cotswolds swapped for the sweatbox of the South East, organic turf for evergreen plastic 3G wrapped in a new stadium.

**A
U
G
U
S
T**

With Compo detained beyond the Iron Curtain searching for Ferenc Puskas, Deep-throat, Foggy and I met at the Glider at 8.45 am. Bright and early, heeding the warnings about Bank Holiday Weekend chaos. Foggy's little black Corsa would surely squeeze its way through any jams?

As it happened, the outward leg was a breeze, despite a couple of unwarranted detours as my navigating failed the Garmin test. Intended intermediate cultural visit was Leeds Castle so called "most beautiful castle in the world" and the third in our Kent castle trilogy for 2016. Not sure that the boast would stand up to some of France's finest chateaus or fairytale Rhineland forts but who am I to argue?

A stronghold as long ago as 857 the present castle has Norman origins and was built in 1119. Whereas Hever Castle was the seat of Anne Boleyn, in the sixteenth century Henry VIII decked out Leeds for his first wife Catherine of Aragon, his late brother's widow and destined to be dumped for the ill-fated Anne.

Sadly, all that inspiring history was to be lost on us. Underestimating the journey time, our arrival left barely one hour for a peak around. And at £24 per adult, beauty gave way to pragmatism. Deep-throat bought the ices as we rescheduled. The Park Gate Pub adjacent was a bit castle-ish and much better value. Another time maybe for Leeds?

Oblivious to collapsing bridges on the M20, we negotiated the A20 towards the Gallagher Stadium. First contact was a cheerful, quick witted steward, the first of many truly welcoming people we met that day. "Head down to the gate and look out for Gillian, she's Australian". Gillian was full of the joys too and escorted us in.

Next to welcome us was joint owner, the towering Oliver Ash, Chartered Surveyor thus a decent chap(!) He commutes from France daily, stayed at Coops' hotel overnight but failed to convince him of the merits of 3G! He gave Foggy and me the full tour and story of the stadium – a sustainable community based project where the surface allows full 7 day use. The Gallagher is as shiny as a new pin, has a further new stand planned and feels refreshingly different. Averaging 2,100 for National League South games last term, the friendly Kent folk have taken the Stadium to their hearts and I for one salute their enterprise and values.

The match was played in sweltering humidity in the high twenties. Though our manager does not like 3G, his players took to it like plastic ducks. The 4-1 beating was high on quality and bore the Cooper stamp. It is a long time since I left an opponent's ground where generous home supporters were complimenting a team that humbled them. It was a memorable performance.

We were not anxious to leave. In part because the amicable atmosphere continued with Coops and Scott Lindsey in the bar afterwards but also because we were figuring out how to bypass the closed-off M20.

I'm glad we stayed awhile. Who would have missed the sight of both sets of players chilling in the thoughtfully providing inflatable plunge pool? Hilariously, 2 wheelie-bins were also water filled with Liam Noble and Rhys Murphy for tenants! And Gillian speaking in broken Australian accented French to Simon Lefebvre and Fabien Robert, offering them refreshments before the Team Coach left.

All in all, a perfect day at an impressive club.

## PITCH PERFECT – ROVERS ON SONG

*Jokerman*

The final Bank Holiday weekend of the summer and commitments elsewhere are reflected in the half full Forest Green Flyer. Perhaps they knew the M25 would again become the road to nowhere on time. With Maidstone a long way off the coach diverted south past Gatwick and travelled through East Grinstead and on to Tunbridge Wells with time beginning to tell.

Team news came via RJ, also trapped on board this Motor Psycho Nightmare. Cooper continues to rotate his squad with Monday's game in mind. Carter replaces Chemlal and Doidge partners Murphy in attack. To save on laundry bills Maidstone have installed an artificial playing surface. FGR have been training on similar in Bristol in preparation, so no excuses. Around East Barming Carter scores for Forest Green. As the coach enters the suburbs Evans equalises for Maidstone. On twenty minutes Rovers fans passed through the turnstiles for a fiver per head, a generous and welcome concession from Maidstone after a frustrating journey.

Soon after Murphy risks his no claims bonus with a prolonged exchange of 'pleasantries' with the giant Maidstone defender Acheampong. The Rovers striker is receiving plenty of attention from his markers and wins a free kick on the 'D' after thirty five minutes. Noble strikes the ball around the 'wall' but Maidstone keeper Worgon makes a good save diving low to his right to gather. A minute later Noble plays Murphy in but he curls his effort inches wide of the post. Forest Green are moving the ball quickly and accurately while Maidstone are mainly chasing shadows. Another impressive exchange of passes into the area ends with Murphy blasting

**A U G U S T**

a shot from six yards to be denied by a miracle block from Worgon. The home side cannot retain any possession and Rovers are relentless. In time added on Rovers take a deserved lead when Jefford, overlapping on the left, takes the ball in his stride and hits a killer ball low along the six yard line where Doidge, running in at the back post, strikes it high into the net past the stranded Worgon. The stadium is very compact and looks full with the two thousand three hundred fans inside. A shame so few FGR supporters to witness a fine display, the nylon surface proving no hindrance to their side.

The sun breaks through the haze as the second half gets under way and pushes the temperature into the high twenties. Rovers' rampage continued for a good ten minutes as they turned the Maidstone goal into a cocoa nut shy. Keanu shooting on sight and Carter denied a second goal only by a point blank block by Mills on the line.

Maidstone sub Tom Murphy did give the home side some momentum on the hour and a spell of possession unsettled the Rovers' rearguard. A free kick on the left by Greenlalgh found its way to Flisher who seemed sure to score until a timely intervention by Traore. Cooper doesn't hesitate and replaces Traore with Frear.

On seventy minutes Maidstone again threaten when a cross from the left is almost converted at the back post by Greenlalgh. Cooper again reacts and replaces Doidge with Moore on seventy five minutes. Immediate impact as the tall striker, under pressure, slips the ball inside to Murphy who in turn nicks it under the foot of Loko the last defender and races clear. From the edge of the area he hits a vicious right foot shot inside the left hand post past a despairing Worgon and Rovers have daylight. This all but kills off any Maidstone chance of revival and four minutes later, the 79th, Carter puts Moore through. He races into the box and unselfishly squares the ball to the unmarked Murphy to score his second goal of the game.

Although outplayed Maidstone kept on and in a show of defiance Flisher ran through on the left and crashed a shot against the near post that Russell will probably claim he had covered. Murphy limped off very near the end with a foot injury, too late for Maidstone. The game ended with a thirty yard run by Frear who in two minds whether to shoot or cross put the ball wide. The faithful few cheered the victors to the echo on the final whistle and were applauded by the players. It was a fine all round display by Forest Green who are beginning to show more than a glimpse of their potential. On a surface alien to grasshoppers Forest Green Rovers just took a giant leap upwards.

**Monday 29.08.16**
**FGR 5 Southport 1**
**ROVERS SHINE AND MAKE IT FIVE IN A ROW**
*Richard Joyce*

The goals continued to rain in as Forest Green Rovers made it an August Bank Holiday weekend to remember with another high scoring victory against Southport.

Mark Cooper's side followed up Saturday's 4-1 success at Maidstone with another emphatic victory with lowly Southport this time the victims, as Rovers made their mark in the sun at The New Lawn.

Kieffer Moore found the back of the net twice, while Mohamed Chemlal and Charlie Clough also bagged their first goals of the season.

Rhys Murphy then followed up his brace at Maidstone by coming off the bench and sealing the win with FGR's fifth.

The visitors made a bright start when within the first minute Sam Russell was forced into action to deny Louis Almond's shot from distance.

Southport though, who had conceded 15 times in six matches heading into the tie, were behind after only six minutes when Moore headed home Liam Noble's superb ball into the box.

It was two four minutes later. Chemlal was the beneficiary this time as he latched onto Moore's through ball and finished past Swindon Town loanee stopper Tyrell Belford.

Rovers were looking irresistible going forward, and on 15 minutes Moore almost extended the lead after he slammed onto the post following Drissa Traore's delicious diagonal ball.

A good Belford save just before the interval from Elliott Frear ensured Southport were only two goals down at the break, but they hit back early on at the start of the second half.

The Sandgrounders player/boss Andy Bishop showed all of his attacking experience to stoop and head home cleverly at the front post.

Suddenly Forest Green looked rattled as Southport for the first time in the afternoon dominated the contest.

Russell was called upon to make two tremendous saves. He firstly denied James Caton by tipping his shot over, and then clawed away Bishop's reactive effort from off his line when fully outstretched.

Rovers had their goalkeeper to thank for keeping them in front. But having survived a short scare they were on the front foot for the rest of the half.

Former Celtic defender Josh Thompson was required to make a crucial last second clearance from a dangerous Noble delivery, and shortly after another Noble ball into the box, this time a corner, was headed home off the underside of the crossbar by Clough.

FGR's fourth saw Moore confirm his brace with a finely executed header when under pressure in the box.

Southport's desire to shoot from distance again kept Russell on his toes five minutes from the end. He produced another tip over the bar to deny the visitors.

It had been Murphy who had found the net twice on Saturday in the Bank Holiday weekend's first game, and he would round off proceedings with a calm finish shortly before full time.

Forest Green broke with speed and it was Noble who was again the supplier as he laid the ball on for Murphy to stroke home.

## GREEN TSUNAMI SWAMPS 'PORT

*Jokerman*

Forest Green Rovers, following a sparkling performance at Maidstone, will be warm favourites to overcome Southport this afternoon. Today's opponents showed resilience on Saturday to halt the winning run of league leaders Tranmere Rovers, having strengthened the defence after a poor start to the season.

Mark Cooper will ensure his players give them due respect as they work to continue to their improvement. There is a good Bank Holiday crowd of sixteen hundred present on a very warm afternoon as the teams take the field. There can certainly be no complacency within the squad that Cooper continues to keep fresh. Racine and Clough link up at the back while Moore is alongside Tubbs up front. Chemlal starts as Carter drops to the bench and Jefford has the day off.

It is Southport who are quickest off the mark when Almond has Russell tipping his thirty yard effort over the bar in the first minute. Rovers reply by winning a corner on the left that Noble hits wide out to Traore, who volleys the ball into the ground goal wards, and Clough heads into the net but is adjudged offside. Rovers are looking confident in possession and on 6mins take the lead. A free kick on the right is hit with precision by Noble to the back post where Moore rises majestically to head firmly past keeper Belford, into the right hand side of the net.

Rovers are rampant and Frear forces a save from Belford at his near post on eight minutes and two minutes later they double their lead. Moore rises and heads the ball towards Chemlal on the edge of the area and, as Belford comes off his line to block the French star, lifts the ball over him into the net.

Traore then picks out Moore in the area. He chests the ball down, turns and shoots but his effort is wide. Rovers are dominant even Bennett on the overlap hits a shot just wide with only sixteen minutes gone. The only reply from Southport is a shot from distance by Stanley that Russell gathers comfortably.

There is a drinks party on twenty three minutes while Almond receives treatment, allowing the players to re-hydrate. Southport use it to make a change and Stanley is replaced by Caton. This change has a positive affect for the visitors and as half time approaches they come close to scoring.

From a free kick they force a corner on the right which Almond delivers brilliantly. The ball drops in the six yard box inches out of reach of his strikers with Rovers defence nowhere. It is a warning as the teams go in for the break.

Southport kick off the second half a different proposition altogether and have obviously had an ear full. They press Rovers back moving the ball much quicker and after a couple of promising moves are rewarded with a goal on 50mins. Raiding down the right, full back White on the overlap hits a great cross into Jones running to the near post and he deftly thumps a header past Russell inside the right hand post. On fifty three minutes sub Caton cuts in from the right and forces Russell to tip his shot over the crossbar. It's all Southport and Russell has to claw away a shot from Almond before Rovers get some respite.

Southport defender Howe is booked for clattering Moore near the left touchline. Noble crosses superbly but the ball drops behind the rushing attackers who are unaware the ball is loose near the goal line and the chance is gone. Cooper has seen enough and Robert replaces Tubbs on sixty minutes - genius. On 61mins Rovers win a corner on the left. Noble hits it to the near post with pace where Robert stoops makes contact and the ball deflects across goal to Clough steaming in, anticipating a higher cross. His head makes perfect contact, the ball almost explodes into the net via the underside of the cross bar and Rovers, as on Saturday, take the initiative away from their opponents at a crucial stage.

FGR are once again on the rampage and threaten to overwhelm the visitors. Chemlal has played well and is none too pleased to be subbed on seventy minutes replaced by Murphy. 78mins and Rovers go further ahead. Robert has a good shot blocked away for a corner on the left. Noble takes a return from Frear and crosses for Murphy, who can get no direction on his header and the ball loops to Moore standing ten yards out who directs a firm precise header out of Belford's reach, low inside

**AUGUST**

the left hand post. Southport reply with a fierce shot from distance by Caton that takes a deflection which Russell palms over the bar.

86mins sees a fine run by Noble down the centre he slips the ball left to Murphy who runs on and puts the ball under Belford. There is no pace on the effort but the ball has crossed the line before Moore can claim his hat trick. It's game over. Another fine display by Forest Green who just keep on improving with thirty nine league games remaining.

## FGR AMBASSADOR REPORT

*Daisy-May Griffiths, Nailsworth Primary School*

My name is Daisy-May and I am the ambassador for Nailsworth Primary School. This is my first year as an ambassador and it is nice to write a report on my team.

It was a lovely day here at the 'New lawn' and I was hoping FGR can do as well as they did against Maidestone, winning 4-1...only time would tell.

The players entered the stadium all pumped up and ready to win! As the players took their positions the crowd and I went wild. Southport started and nearly scored in the first 30 seconds but FGR stopped them from doing so. FGR's number 14, Kieffer Moore, scored, I was thrilled! Our previous attempt to score went to the back of the net, but sadly it was offside. Then Southport took a corner kick and it went further towards the net but FGR's goalie, Super Sam Russell stopped them from doing so. It wasn't long before we scored again this goal was scored by Mohammed Chemlal.

During the second half Southport played well scoring in the 50th minute. Soon after that, Charlie Clough scored a great header. The score was then 3-1, we were looking good. After our next corner kick, Kieffer Moore scored again! What a player!! Finally Rhys Murphy scored our 5th with only minutes to go.

1621 attended that match including 66 from Southport. (Well I suppose they would have to drive a long way so that is pretty good.) The man of the match was 14 FGR Kieffer Moore.

Overall it was a breath-taking match with lots of goals! I loved it and will tell all my friends to come and watch the great FGR. Final score 5-1 to FGR :)

A sixth win on the bounce (at Chester) delivered top spot for the first time in the season. But defeat in a freakish 4-3 televised match at Dover applied a bucket of cold water. 2 more wins at the month's end consolidated second place. Dover aside, the defence was looking impregnable with young summer signing Ethan Pinnock attracting admiring reviews as 'the new Alan Hansen'. Rovers attackers were spurning chances but were still capable of going to town on their day. Thus, the goal difference was looking very healthy. Optimism was picking up – never a good thing for FGR!

*The plans of men we can understand, but the mice? What're they planning?*

(Voodoobluesman after Eddie Izzard, of Mice & Men)

**Saturday 03.09.16**
**Chester 1 FGR 2**
**DOMINANT ROVERS SEAL VICTORY AT CHESTER**
*Richard Joyce*

Goals from midfield duo Liam Noble and Darren Carter made it six consecutive wins for Forest Green Rovers at Chester.

Rovers' moved to the top of the National League table as a goal in either half proved to be enough for what was also FGR's seventh win on the bounce against the Lookers Vauxhall Stadium side.

Noble scored his first for the club, while Carter added to his goal a week before at Maidstone United, however Chester did threaten a comeback that was confidently extinguished after Elliott Durrell had slammed home late on.

Mark Cooper's side dominated the occasion from the early exchanges. Kieffer Moore, starting up front after his brace on Monday against Southport, had a good chance early on with a header from a Noble free kick but he couldn't keep his effort down.

The former Viking striker glanced another headed effort wide on 20 minutes shortly before Rovers took the lead through Noble's first in an FGR shirt.

His fierce free kick from a wide position was too hot to handle, and found itself settled in the back of the net.

Forest Green's possession of the ball continued, and ten minutes from half time another good opportunity fell to Moore but he was unable to hook home acrobatically after Ben Jefford's brave header had flown across the six yard box.

**S
E
P
T
E
M
B
E
R**

Chester had a fantastic opportunity to draw level just before half time. Durrell's low free kick was gloved away superbly by Sam Russell who was at his best to keep the shot out.

Rovers would bag a second not long into the second half, but Kane Richards firstly had a shot on goal for the hosts that was drilled wide, before Carter doubled the advantage.

A composed build-up of passes saw FGR expertly work the ball to the former Birmingham City midfielder whose finish from outside the area was superbly placed out of reach of the home side's keeper Jon Worsnop.

Former Alfreton stopper Worsnop was then called upon to make a key double save on 71 minutes. He saved well from recently introduced substitute Matt Tubbs, and then blocked Keanu Marsh-Brown's follow up effort.

The control Cooper's men had enjoyed throughout the day was for the first time dented ten minutes before the finish when Chester got one back. Durrell was the man who got it after he turned excellently in the box following Jordan Chappell's good work.

For the first time FGR were under pressure to hang onto their lead, and after Noble had seen a free kick from 30 yards go narrowly over, the composed Ethan Pinnock was called upon to make a much needed headed clearance off the line as Chester pushed to draw parity.

From that point onwards Rovers successfully saw the game out, deservedly holding onto three points for the sixth time in a row as the second month of the season got off to an impressive start.

## DESTINATION CHESTER
*Rambling Man*

September bowls in with a cool, wet Autumnal day. And with it, the season's first outing in Compo's silver beamer, starting with a rendezvous at Stonehouse Court Hotel to pick up Foggy, Deep-Throat and me.

Chester beckons, the chosen intermediate stop-off being National Trust's Tatton Park near Knutsford in Cheshire. Faced with a choice between Tatton and nearby Knutsford M6 services, the former gets our vote. We are men of culture.

Tatton Park is a huge estate around a modest and rather austere, classically styled eighteenth century Mansion. There is a fifteenth century Tudor Hall too too if you persist with your expedition. In fact, the park is big enough to have its own climate – monsoon rains today – and the 2 lakes are like inland seas. It is vast.

Unsociably from our point of view, the mansion does not open until 1pm in the 'summer', by which time we needed to be at the Lookers Stadium (as we have to call the Diva these days). So, we had coffee in 'The Stables' went for a tramp around the walled orchard & veg gardens, arboretum and Japanese garden, getting more soaked by the minute.

Frustratingly, the intriguing Japanese Garden was bamboo fenced-off from visitors, simply visible from a sort of viewing path around it. Disappointing that. At home, you can view my cabbage patch from the warm shelter of the lounge and I won't charge you £6 for the privilege! Still, the walkabout did us good and freshened us for the hour's journey to the Lookers.

In all honesty, this is not one of my favourite stadia. New but short on creature comforts, accessible through the interminable spine road of an industrial/retail park and habitually providing a tepid welcome. 5 times I've been here, and 5 times Rovers have won, so in fairness the locals probably wish that we would stay away. But this fixture was different.

I had the pleasure of meeting Chester's FD, Lawrence Kirby. Local businessman and lifelong Chester fan and best friend of Jim Harvey. He was good company and told me much about Manager John McCarthy's approach to bringing along a young squad and how the club is run on a good house-keeping basis. I had the clear impression that a previously troubled club is beginning to rediscover its heart. Anyhow, I wish them well, if not at Rovers' expense.

Certainly, as the game got underway, the 1,800 crowd seemed to be patient with its young charges. It needed to be. Rovers refused to give them the ball and created many clear chances to score. Liam Noble's first half free kick was too good for a hesitant defence, and the classy second by Carter followed a mesmerising period of keep ball. But for some millionaire finishing by Rovers, and generous interpretation of what constitutes handball in the penalty area by a poor official, the margin could have been 5 or 6 goals.

Yet the home side did not lose heart, and scored a fine individual goal themselves (as Rovers went to sleep whilst bringing on the third sub, Fabien Robert) setting up a tense finish.

Thus, 6 out of 6 and top of the League for the first time in 2016/17. No prizes yet, but another good season of jousting for honours is in prospect. I am away for a week now and miss the next fixture at Dover and at home against improving Eastleigh. 2 tough ones – please look after my team when I'm gone!

S
E
P
T
E
M
B
E
R

### FLYING ROVERS REACH FOR THE SKY
*Jokerman*

All roads lead north for Forest Green fans today, M5 Chester bound. Thirty eight souls on board the Kendo Flyer. Beyond Worcester the forecast residue of the Atlantic hurricane washes in and the rain is constant. Excellent progress through the M6 link and time for a stop at Stafford services.

It was on leaving the aforementioned that a sickening rumble beneath the floor preceded a cessation of forward momentum of the conveyance. The rain just fell heavier leaving passengers on the verge of regurgitating recently purchased vittles. Kendo's driver grabbed the Bat Phone and summoned Dave from the cave who arrived with Staffordshire Coaches and swept the stranded through the storm to the Deva Stadium. This hero not only saved the mission, but with an hour to spare.

Arriving at the bar the appropriately named Spitting Feathers soothed away all qualms. Even the weather relented as the teams took the field. Cooper has given Chemlal and Traore the day off and reinstated Jefford and Keanu. Murphy and Moore start in attack.

Forest Green start confidently and five minutes in Noble delivers a free kick onto the head of Moore who heads over the bar from six yards. Soon in to their possession controlled football Rovers make it pay on 24mins. Keanu races down the left to the bye-line where his cross is cleared only to Jefford who is fouled near the left corner of the area. Noble hits a powerful shot in on goal. Worsnop, the Chester keeper, throws his body inaccurately to block the ball which strikes him and bounces under him into the net. Rovers' fans are jubilant.

Chester reply through Durrell who crosses low from the right where the tall centre back Hudson, up in support, completely miscues his effort from ten yards. On thirty minutes a Noble corner from the right is helped on by Murphy at the near post to Jefford, who heads goalwards where Moore hooks the ball over both Worsnop and the cross bar from six yards. Rovers' style of possession will inevitably catch them out occasionally and Chester striker Mahon found himself with a sight of goal only to take too many touches and the chance was gone. On forty one minutes Chester came closer to levelling the scores when Jefford was harshly booked conceding a foul on the edge of the 'D'. Durrell, Chester's best player, stepped up and whipped a terrific shot around the 'wall' only to see Russell produce a fantastic save, diving full length low to his left to keep his side in front going in to the half time break. Although Forest

Green have been the dominant force Chester have had their chances and the game is far from over.

The home side are quickly on the attack from the restart and Rich hits a shot over the bar after cutting in from the right. However Rovers are soon back into their now familiar style and on 52mins add to their advantage with a goal of the highest quality. The build-up not only consisted in the region of fifteen to twenty passes but takes place in the oppositions half of the field. The final pass to Carter, central on the edge of the area with his back to goal, sees him swivel to his right and hit the sweetest of shots, left footed, sending the ball inside the left hand post past the flailing Worsnop. Spellbinding. It was that good.

Chester hit back and Bennett was caught in possession forcing Racine to block a shot from Shaw as Bennett's protestations for a foul were waved away. Frear and Tubbs replaced Jefford and Murphy as Rovers continued to boss the game. Bennett chipped the ball into Tubbs inside the box whose shot was blocked by Worsnop at the near post, and instantly did the same to a follow up effort from Keanu, who was annoyed at not doing better.

On 77mins Chester brought on Chapell on the right flank, now bereft of Jefford, and caused an immediate impact. Gaining possession on the right he charged diagonally into the heart of Rovers defence evading challenges before slipping a reverse pass in to Durrell, clear on goal, who smashed an unstoppable shot that nearly broke the roof of the net. Russell was booked for something he said.

There was no panic from Forest Green despite the inevitable late flurry from Chester in search of an unexpected equaliser. Racine, Clough, Pinnock and co took care of business to see out the final minutes. Four bookings was disappointing and harsh on Rovers whose record has improved. After all one cannot commit so many fouls when in possession for so much of the game. Mark Cooper's style of football is paying big dividends, albeit prone to the odd loss of concentration. But six straight victories have fired Forest Green Rovers to the top of The National league and the smart money would not bet against them any time soon.

**Saturday 10.09.16**
**Dover Athletic 4 FGR 3**
**WINNING RUN ENDED IN HIGH SCORING CONTEST**
*Richard Joyce*
A magnificent Ricky Miller hat-trick ended Forest Green's six match-winning run in emphatic style in front of the BT Sport cameras at Dover.

**S
E
P
T
E
M
B
E
R**

Dover's leading marksman struck with a brilliant individual effort on 88 minutes, just two minutes after FGR had drawn deservedly level, to steal all three points in one of Rovers' most entertaining National League matches for some time.

Liam Noble had put Mark Cooper's men in front early on, only for Dover to equalise when Miller got his first.

And after the former Luton man had struck a penalty after half time, Rhys Murphy levelled the affair.

Another former Luton forward, in the shape of Ross Lafayette, restored Dover's lead, which was then cancelled out by Christian Doidge – only for Miller to strike right at the end.

Having scored his first goal for the club last weekend, Noble gave Rovers the lead in the lunchtime kick off with another free kick, which clipped the Dover wall on its way into the back of the net.

A frenetic start was added to when Fabien Robert forced former FGR keeper Steve Arnold into a fine stop, and Dover then drew parity on 13 minutes.

Miller swept home from inside a busy penalty area after Aswad Thomas had done well to get forward down the left hand side.

Both sides look threatening when in attacking positions. Arnold was kept busy having to keep out efforts from Noble, Darren Carter and Matt Tubbs, while a superb save by Sam Russell down the other end on 38 minutes prevented Lafayette from scoring from a free kick.

The tie was finely poised at the break, and a crazy five minutes followed after the interval with the hosts turning it around to take the lead.

Miller stepped up from the penalty spot to send Russell the wrong way after the referee had tightly judged Noble to have tripped the advancing Thomas in the area.

But within a minute FGR were level. Carter's hanging cross was headed home terrifically by Murphy whose aerial effort had just enough power to take the ball over the line.

Then came a mass of Rovers pressure that the Kent side managed to survive. Tubbs was denied by a good block, while Robert saw Jack Parkinson deny him a clear shot on goal.

On 58 minutes, for the first time in a three minute spell, Rovers hit the woodwork when Noble's cleverly crafted effort pinged off the post, and shortly after Carter's strike smashed onto the underside of the crossbar.

Just past the hour mark Arnold was alert to make a fine block from Tubbs, who had found room on the left hand side in the box from a well worked free kick taken by Noble.

Forest Green looked like they deserved to be in front, but they were dealt a huge blow when completely against the run of play Dover nosed into the lead again.

Lafayette got in on the goal-scoring act this time as his fantastic lob drifted over Russell.

Cooper's charges would again have to come back if they wanted to salvage something, which they more than deserved from the game.

Substitute Doidge looked like he had delivered on 86 minutes when he made it 3-3. He latched onto Noble's superb intricate pass to slide home for what looked set to be the afternoon's final major act.

Miller had other ideas though, and having been invited to run at the FGR defence, he unleashed a wonderful hit that left Russell with no chance, and with Dover all of the points.

## DESTINATION DOVER
*Rambling Man*

Rambling man is AWL today – absent with leave. 9th and 10th games of Rovers improving season and my body calendar is shouting foul.

I found myself destined for the only 'old' European country I have never visited – Portugal. Quite something these days to experience a country and language for the first time. Particularly being the youngest son of an intrepidly adventurous dad who believed that all places were within reach of a Vauxhall Victor towing a Sprite.

My brother and a friend has a place in somewhere called Tavira. For those with a globe, it's nowhere near the 'pink wash' of empire and seems to relate more to Africa than Western Europe. Logical really as it's a darned sight closer to the North African coast than most European capitals, owes a lot to historical Moorish rule and is hotter than hell. Confusingly it is even in the same time zone as UK; how does that work?

Anyhow, generously my bro and sister-in-law invited the Rambling Mans out for a week and Mrs R-M accepted. With the May 15th Wembley v Montenegro debacle still a fresh sore ready to be aggravated, I was in no position to refuse. No consideration for the fact that I wilt when the mercury exceeds 20 degrees whilst in Tavira it tops double that.

My sibling is a Bristol City Season Ticket holder and scout so he's as guilty as me taking furlough in the football season. But when isn't it the football season? From Wembley to the start of the friendlies, FGR's down time was about 7 weeks out of 52. Precious little time to organise your life around if you have a hopeless club addiction.

**S
E
P
T
E
M
B
E
R**

For once, easyJet delivered on its contract, on time to the minute. By 10.15 on a warm night in Faro, we sought the Shuttle Bus to Tavira. Fortune still smiled as it turned out to be a plush Merc taxi. By 11.15 we'd knocked back chicken and chips at the destination apartment and hit the town for a few beers.

If I am to miss some early season games, it was some consolation that BT Sport scheduled to cover the first, Dover, live. Bro said all we have to do is to stroll down to the local sports bar and drink our fill whilst taking in another FGR win. 2 problems with that though:

1 The locals needed to be convinced that they'd rather watch 2 English 5th tier clubs they've never heard of than watching the Manchesters slug it out featuring a pouty Portuguese exile and a locally reviled Spanner.
2 I am the world's worst coward at watching my club when not at the stadium concerned. Stupid as it sounds, I fervently believe that my shouts form a stand will influence the way they play whereas screaming at the TV has no effect at all.

And just for good measure, Deep-Throat wants my player ratings too. Some dedicated Rovers fans take these things seriously and will not be happy with me resorting to 'stick a pin' method.

Predictably, all the plans unravelled. The bar staff laughed at the notion of choosing Dover v FGR over the North West derby, backed up by sweaty hordes in red and sky blue. We tried an Irish pub with multi-screens but they stayed loyal to their Celtic roots with the Glasgow shindig. To cap that, we found our BT accounts would not stream to Portugal so my Mac was no use.

Instead, I was subjected to the death of a thousand cuts as texts and emails tracked the 4-3 reverse at The Crabble. That's put a downer on my break and I now live in fear of the home fixture with Eastleigh on Tuesday.

**Tuesday 13.09.16**
**FGR 1 Eastleigh 1**
**LITTLE CAN SEPARATE ROVERS AND EASTLEIGH**
*Richard Joyce*
Elliott Frear marked his hundredth league appearance for Forest Green Rovers by setting up the equaliser in a hard fought draw with Eastleigh at The New Lawn.

Two of the National League's most fancied sides met under lights for a keenly fought contest, which saw Rhys Murphy's finish from a Frear cross cancel out Mikael Mandron's opener for the Spitfires a few minutes earlier.

Looking to bounce back from Saturday's loss at Dover, Mark Cooper made a number of changes to his starting XI, and one returning player, Ben Jefford, drew a wonderful ball back for Liam Noble to try and finish after just seven minutes in one of the night's early openings.

Sam Russell produced the first of a number of good saves shortly after to deny Mandron, however one of his stand out stops came on 26 minutes, when he reacted brilliantly to deny Luke Coulson's hit that looked destined to find the bottom corner.

After he had saved from Mandron again shortly before the interval, Russell was left with no chance when the former Sunderland youngster slammed the visitors into the lead shortly after half time.

He powered home into the roof of the net after latching onto Coulson's low ball into the danger zone to hand Ronnie Moore's side the lead.

Only a few minutes later Frear was thrown into the battle, and the century appearance maker made an instant impact, setting up the goal that would see Murphy earn FGR a point.

Frear's driving run ended with him drawing the ball back for leading marksman Murphy, who guided home inside the area.

Eastleigh responded by almost stealing the lead back minutes later. Russell came to the rescue though when he pulled off a magnificent stop to prevent James Constable from smashing home when one-on-one after he had broken through.

The tie was finely poised heading into the last quarter of an hour, and Darren Carter's firm drive that flew narrowly over the crossbar almost pushed FGR in front.

There was to be no dramatic finale, and apart from a Noble shot where the midfielder couldn't quite find his range, the match ended in just Forest Green's second draw of the season.

## RUSSELL SAVES A POINT AS ROVERS STUTTER
*Jokerman*

After The Millers Tale was played out at Dover on Saturday, the pallor of Forest Green Rovers connections turned to reflect that of the local cliffs. On Sunday the players were read the lesson that would leave them under no illusions as to what is required of them going forward. This evening's game at TNL against Eastleigh gives the team a quick opportunity to regain the winning thread.

S
E
P
T
E
M
B
E
R

Manager Mark Cooper made it clear through the media that he would again be making changes to his starting eleven. In the event Jefford was reinstated at the back and Doidge linked with Murphy in attack. A crowd of nearly fifteen hundred were present as the teams paraded on a humid evening dampened by earlier thunderstorms.

Rovers were first on the attack and Keanu snapped a shot wide on two minutes and Noble was annoyed at missing the target from a good position soon after. Eastleigh were by no means on the back foot and a good move down the right saw Coulson pick out Mandron who forced Russell to gather his shot low down.

The Eastleigh striker had an even better chance on twelve minutes when the ball came to him in front of goal six yards out but his touch was awful and Rovers escaped. The visitors were looking the more likely side with some promising build up play and on twenty five minutes they brought out the best in Sam Russell.

Again the danger came from the right, the ball into the box found Coulson who hit a venomous shot heading inside the right hand post that had goal printed all over it, until Russell hit the delete key with a reaction save full length to his left. Brilliant. Rovers replied through Carter whose full bloodied drive from fifteen yards was blocked by the giant defender Johnson.

The game was lacking some quality but as the first half ended Forest Green had been second best, certainly in attack. Eastleigh came out with real purpose after the break and over ran the home side in the early minutes and it was no surprise when they took the lead on 50mins.

They were enjoying plenty of success raiding down the right flank and duly punished Rovers, when Coulson beat off a couple of challenges and crossed from the by-line to Mandron at the near post, who promptly lashed the ball into the roof of the net from point blank range. The hundred and fifty plus travelling support behind the goal were suitably impressed, one of whom was carried away by it all to the car park by the stewards after encroaching onto the pitch.

Cooper didn't hesitate and brought on Frear for Traore, a repeat move in recent games. Immediate impact as Frear created danger for the Eastleigh defence making inroads on the left flank. The winger forced a corner which Noble delivered to Keanu on the edge of the area and he hit Rovers first shot on target in the match straight at Flitney, the Eastleigh keeper, who gathered the ball comfortably.

On 57mins Rovers found an equaliser. An excellent build up on the left saw Jefford thread a ball through to Frear, who ran on into the area and hit the perfect cut-back pass to Murphy near the penalty spot, who swept the ball past Flitney sparking wild celebrations from the Rovers faithful. The game then see-sawed but it was the visitors who were more effective in attack and two minutes after the goal, Clough misjudged a bounce that put Constable clean through on Russell, who produced another mighty save to deny the veteran striker. Rovers best moves were all coming through Frear but the Eastleigh defence were sound whereas at the other end the goal had a charmed life. On seventy minutes, the ball criss-crossed the face causing palpitations amongst the home support. On seventy four minutes Carter was annoyed with himself when he hit a cracking shot just too high from the edge of the box which could have captured all three points. The game had it's niggles and no more so than when Drury lashed at a clearance for Eastleigh, only to find Jefford in close proximity consequently hurting himself. A four minute hiatus occurred. After treatment he began haranguing all and sundry as he walked to the touchline and proved to the East Stand supporters he had more gob than a basking shark. Cooper's assistant was ordered to the posh seats probably after explaining to Drury the error of his ways. It added five minutes to the contest but the scoreline remained.

It was not a good performance by Forest Green who remain a work in progress. They can take heart from results elsewhere that all their competitors are in a similar situation.

## FGR AMBASSADOR REPORT
*Jessica Smith, Uplands Primary School, Stroud*
My name is Jessica Smith aged 9, and I am the school ambassador for Uplands Community Primary. So far I have enjoyed being an ambassador for the first time. I have been to most of the home matches and the pre-season games so far.

Match Report – Forest Green Rovers v Eastleigh. My Headmaster Mr Lucas who is an amazing supporter of FGR said that this was going to be a hard game to win and it was!

I think that FGR were good at keeping the ball but when they lost it there was a chance that they would get caught out because Eastleigh were very good on the counter attack. FGR had several shots in the first half but each were wide of finding the back of the net. After 26m Sam Russell made a brilliant save stopping a powerful shot from Luke Coulson who was hoping to find the back of the net. Half time score 0-0

In the second half it didn't take long for the Spitfires to take the lead with Mandron latching on to Coulson's pass to slam home a goal high

**S**
**E**
**P**
**T**
**E**
**M**
**B**
**E**
**R**

in the back of the net. At this moment when the players were celebrating the Eastleigh fans erupted and one of them found his way on to the pitch and started hugging the players but soon after he was hustled off out of the stadium by security.

Traore was then substituted for Frear at 52 minutes who then went on to create a number of chances including a cross to Rhys Murphy in the 56th minute which he put successfully in to the back of the net to equalise and the crowd went wild.

Marcus Kelly made his first appearance this season in place of Marsh-Brown. Both sides had some more chances to take the lead, one of the last being Carter's strike which went just over the crossbar.

Crowd attendance was 1,444 and both teams were quite evenly matched. Overall it was a good performance but sometimes it was left a bit open in defence. Only time will tell how we do in our next game. Come on you Rovers!

**Saturday 17.09.16**
**FGR 1 Bromley 0**
**ROVERS REWARDED AS MARSH-BROWN WINS IT**
*Richard Joyce*

Patient Forest Green had to wait until the final quarter of an hour to claim victory over a resolute Bromley side.

A second goal of the season from Keanu Marsh-Brown helped Rovers bounce back to winning ways and move up to second in the National League table.

The former Fulham man claimed the man-of-the-match award for a lively display, as Bromley's second ever visit to The New Lawn again ended in defeat.

From as early as the seventh minute Marsh-Brown was trying his luck in front of goal, while he was also providing the service, as his whipped-in cross on 13 minutes almost saw Rhys Murphy head home.

The visitors came to life midway through the half. Bradley Goldberg's fierce drive firstly forced Sam Russell into action, and from the following corner Jack Holland should have done better as he made contact with Dave Martin's wicked delivery.

Elliott Frear was starting on the left hand side of FGR's front three, and he shot just wide on 23 minutes, with Martin then fancying his luck down the other end, and forcing Russell into a good stop.

End-to-end action in the final minutes of the first half continued with the experienced Alan Julian saving well from Frear, before one final save from Russell kept Goldberg and the visitors at bay.

Julian is a well-known name at this level, and the 33-year-old made a vital save at the beginning of the second half to keep out Marsh-Brown's attempt after he'd got through.

And Rovers then had the woodwork to thank for keeping the scores level two minutes later. A free kick found its way onto the post before Rob Swaine followed up with a swing at the ball that clattered the upright again.

It was a let off that allowed Forest Green to then take some control of the tie, and to push for a winner.

Liam Noble's free kick, which stayed low, forced Julian into an unorthodox save, and on 65 minutes Marsh-Brown's drive from distance was tipped over.

Eventually Marsh-Brown would find success in front of goal. He hung back in space to allow Frear to find him with a lifted cross from the right, and executed a neat finish to finally break the deadlock.

Rovers had the goal they needed and substitute Drissa Traore almost added to it, only to see his drive inside the area fly wide.

Another top save from Julian denied Ben Jefford who had got forward, but there was drama to come, as the woodwork again proved significant in the final result.

This time Holland's venomous hit that flew towards the FGR goal clipped the bar and slammed behind.

It was Bromley's final say on a battling afternoon at The New Lawn, as Forest Green claimed victory to follow up an already hard earned point against Eastleigh earlier in the week.

## COOL KEANU SINKS BROMLEY

*Jokerman*

After a run of nineteen points from eight games Forest Green Rovers have accumulated just one from six recently. 'Oh my goodness everything is broken I must go and put my head in a vice.' Football Forums eh? Manager Mark Cooper changes tack again today playing Murphy as the lone target man in attack. Both Kelly and Frear, who came off the bench against Eastleigh on Tuesday night, retain their places in the starting line-up.

A crowd of over thirteen hundred saw Rovers make the brighter start with Frear forcing Bromley keeper Julian to concede an early corner, resulting in Keanu shooting wide from the edge of the area. The visitors then gave Noble an opportunity with a free kick from twenty yards the ball hitting the top netting. Keanu failed to get any power on his shot from a Jefford cross and again the ball went wide.

**S
E
P
T
E
M
B
E
R**

Bromley manager Neil Smith then adjusted his side's formation to counter Rovers superiority in mid-field and his players began to enjoy a share of possession. Striker Goldberg stung Russell's palms from thirty five yards as the Rovers keeper pushed the ball over the bar. From the corner the ball fell to Holland in front of goal but he could only stab the ball wide under pressure.

Thirty eight minutes saw Keanu make a good run putting in Frear on the left. The winger struck the ball well but Julian blocked the effort away for a corner. At the other end Goldberg held off two challenges and hit a low shot that brought a solid save from Russell. It had been an unspectacular first half and the 0-0 scoreline was about right.

The first chance of the second half fell to Bromley, after two minutes, when Sho-Silver raced into the area and only a timely block by Clough, close to goal, cleared the danger. Soon after Keanu had Rovers best chance when put through the centre, but he took an extra touch and Julian quickly off his line made a great block.

Another scare for Rovers on fifty two minutes came when a free kick on the left by Swaine eluded defenders and attackers alike, and struck the right hand post with Russell a spectator. This escape seemed to galvanise Rovers and they began to put real pressure on the Bromley defence. Following a series of corners Frear made a run into the box and went to ground, but the referee waved away what would have been a soft penalty. On the hour Noble leathered a free kick that Julian had to punch clear and minutes later crossed to the back post, where a Clough header was just too high. It was all Rovers now and on sixty five minutes Clough went on the charge through the centre and slipped the ball to Keanu who lashed a terrific shot that was deflected over the bar.

Moore replaced the ineffective Murphy on sixty six minutes and was immediately in the action with an ambitious overhead effort that Julian gathered. Traore replaced Kelly on seventy one minutes and soon after Forest Green made the breakthrough.

Frear, having switched flanks with Keanu, cut in on the right and his cut back was blocked back to him. Changing tactics he chipped the ball to Keanu lurking wide of the back post. A good first touch and he calmly passed the ball, with unerring accuracy, low across defenders and goalkeeper to slip the ball less than a foot inside the right hand post. He has his detractors but that was just class.

The confidence flowed and around the eighty minute mark the home crowd were given an illustration of the geometric style of possession football that Mark Cooper is beginning to instil into his playing squad.

With Bromley players merely bystanders a multiple passing move ended with Jefford driving into the box and hitting a vicious shot that brought a terrific save from Julian.

A second goal would have been more comfortable for Rovers who had to withstand late pressure from the visitors. A cross from the left saw Holland hit a searing shot that skimmed the bar and sub Cunnington blasted over from ten yards when he should have done better. Pinnock and Clough stood firm however and Rovers saw the game out, deservedly taking the three points with a much improved second half performance.

Up next for Forest Green Rovers is a visit to Jamie Day's struggling Braintree Town. Anything other than three points and the world will probably end.

## FGR AMBASSADOR REPORT
*Atticus Lynham, King's Stanley Primary School*
My name is Atticus Lynham and I am a Year 3 student at King's Stanley Primary School. I saw my first FGR game in 2014 and loved it (even though we lost!) and so was keen to become an ambassador even though I am so young especially as FGR mix my interests in football and being green, King's Stanley being an eco-school.

FGR's perseverance and determination against an organised Bromley team finally paid off with a Keanu Marsh-Brown winner in the 73rd minute as Rovers kept their unbeaten home record.

The big surprise of the day was that captain Liam Noble had shaved off his green Mohican – he now has the same hairstyle as Charlie Clough!

Rovers dominated possession in the first half but were unable to break down Bromley. Marsh-Brown looked a threat but the visitors held firm and they actually went closest when a long range shot forced a fine save from Sam Russell.

Minutes into the second half, Marsh-Brown broke clear from the defence and was one-on-one with the visiting goalkeeper Alan Julian but Julian managed to make a great save.

Bromley also had a couple of chances and even hit the post but Rovers remained patient and continued playing good football. Cheered on by the home fans, Rovers pressed on again and might have been given a penalty when Elliot Frear went down in the box after contact from Jack Holland but the referee decided there was no foul.

Manager Mark Cooper made a couple of changes with Drissa Traore and Kiefer Moore coming on for Marcus Kelly and Rhys Murphy and soon afterwards, Rovers made the breakthrough they deserved when

**S E P T E M B E R**

Marsh-Brown calmly converted a cross from Frear at the end of a good passing move. Rovers climb to second in the table as their good start continues.

**Saturday 24.09.16**
**Braintree Town 0 FGR 1**
**MARSH-BROWN STRIKES TO EARN BRAINTREE WIN**
*Richard Joyce*

Keanu Marsh-Brown's first half goal, and a Sam Russell penalty save, were enough to help Forest Green Rovers earn another National League victory at Braintree.

A tale of two halves saw Rovers dominate the first, but come under pressure more in the second, as Braintree almost sneaked a point, only for Russell to save the day with a penalty save from Chez Isaac.

Marsh-Brown's terrific first half opener proved to be the difference between the two sides, as Mark Cooper's men followed up last week's narrow win over Bromley with another three points.

Christian Doidge almost put FGR ahead by exploiting space in the Braintree box from as early as the third minute, but a last ditch block denied the Welsh strikers shot.

Braintree's best chance of the half came soon after from a free kick. On loan AFC Bournemouth midfielder Sam Matthews managed to direct his effort over the Rovers wall, but Sam Russell gathered comfortably.

A fairly uneventful opening 45 minutes was brought into life on 38 minutes when Marsh-Brown bagged the opener.

He received the ball 30 yards from goal and produced a sizzling right footed shot that flew past Braintree's debutant keeper Will Puddy and into the bottom corner.

Rovers should have made it two just before half time. Elliott Frear had beaten Puddy to the ball, but saw his left footed effort go wide, although the winger appeared to have been dragged back by the goalkeeper just as he looked to get his strike away.

For the first time the Iron posed a real threat after the break. Matthews hit from outside the area whistled past the post, and Simeon Akinola blazed over after he had eventually gathered Michael Cheek's loose square pass.

After Liam Noble had seen his low drive from distance saved, Braintree were offered a great chance to level, when they were given a penalty.

Russell ensured the hosts couldn't draw parity though as he guessed right to deny Isaac's strike to the right.

The FGR stopper was at it again when he saved Akinola's attempt from inside the box, while the tricky attacker blazed over again for the hosts after Darren Carter had seen his low shot saved down the other end.

Akinola had a late opportunity to rescue a point after Ethan Pinnock had been penalised. However he failed to find the target with his free kick.

Rovers avoided any late scares to register another three points, and to remain second in the National League table.

## DESTINATION BRAINTREE
*Rambling Man*

I love going to Essex. Yes I've said it and I'm proud! Ok, you have to dodge the Ford Capris and puddles of platinum bleach but there is no more welcoming club in the National League than Braintree Town.

Which is possibly why Clegg's gleaming 'Dagenham Dustbin' was full to bursting as Foggy and I met him and Compo at the Glider. Deep-Throat had turned down the option of riding on the roof rails, so travelled separately with the press pack. The day's destination was not the Avanti but the newly re-named Ironmongery Direct Stadium, which has the cachet of an Essex Mullet. Right up there with the World of Smile and the Kit-Kat Stadia.

But that was for later. First port of call was Cressing Barns (sometimes called Cressing Temple) near Witham, just 10 minutes from the Ironmongery Direct. Despite stopping for refreshments at South Mimms, Clegg had parted the traffic so effectively that we rolled up to the Barns by noon. Just as well as there was much to see and admire as well as a crafts fayre.

The venue is usually free to enter, being owned by the County Council. It is a historic estate originally given to the Knights Templar in 1137 though archaeology has revealed Iron Age and Roman remains. It features Grade I listed Barley and Wheat timber structured barns, built in the 13th century, among the oldest and rarest surviving Templar buildings in England. The soaring interiors are like Cathedrals of oak - stout, intricate, twisted and magnificent. Informative displays, tableaux and guidance panels add greatly to the awe inspiring structures.

If that was not enough, amongst Cressing's extensive grounds is the Walled Garden, faithfully reconstructed as a Tudor pleasure garden, with herringbone brick pathways, water features, ornamental hedges and trees groaning with tasty fruits. Compo and I can vouch for the Russet apples! Period crafts, cream teas and much else besides make this a brilliant cheap day out for the family. We left, lugging 3 crates of craft beer.

S
E
P
T
E
M
B
E
R

Our culture buds were not satiated. Clegg drove us around nearby Silver End. "What's that?" I hear you ask. Well, Silver End is Braintree's equivalent of Port Sunlight, conceived as a model village by Henry Crittall who established his world famous window factory there. The Ironmongery Direct Stadium was built on Crittall property. Nice segue R-M.

At last, footy raised its head. The smashing folk at the stadium welcomed us like long lost kin and, as ever, were the fount of countless funny stories. Whatever your mood, a visit to Braintree Town will put a smile on your face – so much more than their nickname "just a pub team from Essex"

Not that Coops was chortling. 'Iron' Manager and FGR old boy Jamie Day had ordered the pitch to remain uncut. Don't think he was after a hay crop rather it was an attempt to thwart Rovers' passing game.

It didn't, at least, not for the first half. Rovers went through the gears, and were as slick as Brylcreem. Keanu delivered one of his specials and it would have been more if Mr Treleaven had worn his prescription glasses. Second half brought a home assault, unfairly timed as most of FGR's finest had decided to take a 45 minute snooze. Yet Sam Russell roused himself to save a penalty so Rovers secured the 3 points with more difficulty than had seemed possible at half way.

Thus we waved a fond farewell to the East, hoping that this latest reverse would not herald Jamie Day's dismissal.

Just a single defeat (a last minute job in the FA Cup at Sutton United), but more to the point none in the League. 4 thumping wins and 2 draws meant Rovers were stretching away at the top and in some style. The New Lawn was packing in regular crowds of 2,200+ and supporters had started to believe this was Rovers' year. Could it be that easy?

*for all of the times that we've been here*
*ahead of the pack in the chase*
*be it fleeting or long we will need to be strong*
*in this joyous precarious place*

(Excerpt from 'Top Today' by Crispin Thomas "Football Poets")

**Saturday 01.10.16**
**FGR 0 Barrow 0**
**PERSISTENT ROVERS EARN BARROW POINT**
*Richard Joyce*
The woodwork twice denied Forest Green Rovers in a competitive clash with play-off chasing Barrow at The New Lawn.

Aarran Racine and Drissa Traore both struck the upright in a tight affair between two of the divisions in form sides, as Rovers kept up their unbeaten home record for a seventh game in a row.

Paul Cox's Barrow proved resolute and at times tricky to break down. They themselves had chances but Sam Russell again impressed to record his third clean sheet on the bounce.

The opening quarter of an hour provided little for a good sized crowd, but on 15 minutes the influential Keanu Marsh-Brown forced Barrow keeper Joel Dixon into a good save with a drive from 20 yards.

Marsh-Brown again did well to cross for Charlie Clough to head narrowly over just before the half hour mark, while Moussa Diarra's hook towards goal for the visitors ended up going over the bar.

Then came a five minute spell where FGR had a glorious opportunity to break the deadlock, only to be denied twice by the woodwork.

Racine's header from a fine Liam Noble free kick saw the recalled central defender head onto the post, and Dixon was again called into service to prevent Christian Doidge from turning and scoring seconds later.

Then, five minutes before the break, Traore this time went close. He did brilliantly to work the ball onto his left foot and saw his speared effort slam against the bar.

Diarra had another good opportunity from a set piece shortly before half time for the visitors that he couldn't convert.

**O**
**C**
**T**
**O**
**B**
**E**
**R**

Rovers attacking play in the final third caught the eye in the second period. Early on Marsh-Brown tested Dixon after being set clear, while Doidge came very close to poking home Dale Bennett's teasing low ball.

Russell recovered well to keep his clean sheet intact. He saved Paul Turnbull's shot but pushed it back into the danger zone, only to then bravely collect the ball from the feet of former Chesterfield man Byron Harrison who came bundling in.

Marsh-Brown was just inches away from breaking the deadlock on 66 minutes as his cross the pitch run from a corner ended with him rifling a shot just past the post.

And the continued Rovers pressure almost saw Noble strike from outside the box, but his right footed shot landed on the roof of Dixon's net.

The game inched towards the finish and it was going to take something heart breaking for at least one of the sides to separate the two. With FGR looking to claim a late win, Barrow were able to utilise the gaps that had opened up at the back.

Jordan Williams found himself in two good positions, only to be denied firstly when Russell saved his low effort, and then again when the experienced keeper made a superb save to push away the attackers attempt four minutes from time, to leave the tie all even in what was Forest Green's first goalless draw of the campaign.

### POINT BLANK

*Jokerman*

Overcoming a lack of application for ninety minutes is required by manager Mark Cooper of his Forest Green team, after all but conceding victory at lowly Braintree Town last week. Certainly today's opponents Barrow, the early season 'springer' in the market and only two points behind Rovers will prove a far sterner test.

With Tubbs on loan at Woking and Kelly and Chemlal given the day off, Cooper has paired Racine and Clough at the back and Doidge in attack supported by Keanu. Heavy showers throughout the morning have ruled out the sprinklers, indeed surface water is evident as the game kicks off in front of a crowd allegedly in excess of two thousand.

Following the early sparring the game springs to life when Jefford releases Keanu down the left. He of the nimble feet races forward and strikes a powerful shot from twenty yards that Barrow keeper Dixon tips over the bar. Barrow are matching Rovers and Racine gets in a timely block to thwart Yates inside the area. Picking on someone half his size Barrow's central defender Diarra chops down Keanu and gets a warning from the referee. Noble's free kick is headed over by Clough.

On thirty minutes a short corner by Barrow gives Turnbull space for a shot but Bennett is on hand to block as the game swings from end to end. The final fifteen minutes of the half belonged to Rovers who were unfortunate not to take the lead. A typical Noble free kick mid-way in the Barrow half on the right was met by Racine at the back post. His powerful header had the crowd on its feet as the ball beat Dixon, but agonisingly for home supporters struck the right hand upright. Bennett chased it down and crossed inside to Doidge on the edge of the area, but his shot brought a good save low down from Dixon. Another fine flowing move ended with a cracking left foot strike by Traore from fifteen yards that bounced high off the crossbar and over.

As the Vegans feasted in the lounge at the interval the rest of us ate cake and very nice it was too. Mercifully the threatening thunder clouds behind the west terrace headed north and the sunshine prevailed during the second half.

Frear replaced Jefford at half time. After an early scare when Traore was caught in possession, Noble slipped a pass to Keanu who forced Dixon to block his snap shot, low down at the near post. Keanu then split the Barrow defence with a pass inside the full back to the overlapping Bennett, who crossed superbly along the six yard line where Doidge was only inches away from reaching it.

There was an immediate reply from Barrow with a passing move, resulting in Turnbull hitting a screamer from the edge of the box that Russell did well to block but could not hold. Ritchie Bennett, the Barrow striker, lashed at the loose ball but Russell still on the floor bravely smothered the ball which was cleared away.

The Forest Green supporters behind the goal were in fine voice during the second period with incessant encouragement to get Rovers over the line. The team responded, Doidge in particular having a fine game. His heading ability is outstanding and on sixty five minutes his knock-down for Pinnock saw his cracking shot blocked away for a corner. Noble played it short to Keanu who jinked inside to create a shot that curled an inch wide of the right hand post. He was understandably miffed to be subbed a minute later along with Traore for Murphy and Robert. A good run by Frear on the left saw his cross nodded down by Doidge for Noble whose well-struck shot hit the top netting.

As the game entered the closing stages it was Barrow who came closest to taking all three points. With Rovers applying pressure they were caught on the break and Williams, from the corner of the area with a clear shot on goal, brought a fine save from Russell that had the Barrow winger holding his head at the missed chance. A minute later Rovers were caught

**O**
**C**
**T**
**O**
**B**
**E**
**R**

in mid-field and it was Williams again through on Russell, and again the Rovers keeper defied him diving low to his left to palm the ball away.

Barrow ran the clock down for the final minutes five of which were added time. It was a frustrating afternoon for the home fans but by no means a disaster. Playing against the form side in the division the defence did well to keep another clean sheet, Russell is in top form. A little more invention in front of goal is needed and will surely come with the ability the squad has. A good chance of three points at Aldershot on Tuesday night will put them well on track.

### FGR AMBASSADOR REPORT
*Nathanael Dover, The British School, Wotton-under-Edge*
Hello my name is Nathanael Dover, I'm 10 years old and I am the FGR ambassador for the British school this season. I enjoy being the school's ambassador I go to all the home matches and went to Wembley to watch the play off final last season. Today FGR are playing against Barrow, FGR are 2nd and Barrow are 4th. Here is my report for the match. Get comfy. FGR apply some good early pressure which ends with a nice shot, but saved. During the game there has been some risky play from goal kicks I wish they wouldn't do that again, it makes me nervous. FGR hit the woodwork twice in the first half. End of the first half, I was hoping for a bit more excitement, time to find grandad to get me a drink. In the 59 minute there was a cracking through ball by Marsh-Brown that ended up going for a corner. The corner is swung in, so close what a great header. FGR had a bit more possession in both half's but couldn't finish their chances off. In the 73 minute Traore had a long shot but hit the crossbar. Barrow had more corners than FGR but could not find the net because of FGR great defence. Finally getting to the end of the match both teams were evenly match but an extremely good performance by FGR. On another day this could have been 3-1 to the green army. Come on you Rovers!

### Tuesday 04.10.16
### Aldershot Town 0 FGR 4
### OUTSTANDING ROVERS STORM TO SHOTS WIN
*Richard Joyce*
Magnificent Forest Green produced a stunning performance to march to victory in a dominant and powerful showing at Aldershot Town's EBB Stadium.

Fabien Robert and Kieffer Moore scored a brace apiece to register four first half goals, as Rovers put a team that boasted the best defensive record in the National League to the sword on their own home turf.

Aldershot themselves were on an eight match unbeaten run heading into the clash, but were blown away by a Forest Green side who extended their own unbeaten run to five games.

Will Evans was shown a red card for the hosts in an astonishing first half. The second 45 minutes was a more conservative affair, as FGR simply wrapped up the win by dominating possession.

The goal scoring frenzy began when Robert swept home with a low drive after the ball had fallen to him on the edge of the area.

And it was two three minutes later. This time Moore got his first as a brilliant break forward saw him slip the ball just inside the post past the on rushing Jake Cole.

The action wasn't just restricted to the Shots box. Sam Russell was called upon to make a good save from Jake Gallagher, while Iffy Allen's right footed strike on 16 minutes clipped the FGR bar.

Another major talking point came a minute later, as former Eastleigh man Evans was sent off for an off the ball incident with Rhys Murphy, as the home sides task became even more difficult.

Cole denied Robert with a brave stop midway through the half, although he let the Frenchman score past him again when an outstanding run saw him slam home his second.

The Shots keeper made a great stop to prevent Murphy's overhead kick from going in on 35 minutes, however for the fourth time in the half he was picking the ball out of his own net again when Moore slid home his second from a superb Robert cross.

It was Moore, seeking his hat-trick, who had the first chance of the second half. Debutant Dan Wishart's good cross from the left was glanced wide though.

Given the eventful nature of the night, it was perhaps unsurprising that a lengthy period that yielded just long periods of Forest Green possession was to follow, with just a Moore effort slammed over the bar providing a notable moment.

Rovers needed to do little but keep the ball against a depleted Shots side who were well and truly beaten, as Mark Cooper's men march on to North Ferriby this coming weekend with a confidence that'll be hard for any side to stop.

## DESTINATION ALDERSHOT

*Rambling Man*

Over 4 straight season's Rovers have played at Aldershot on a Tuesday night. Shame as the Shots are one of few opponents within 100 miles of the Five Valleys and is a superb community based club. A Saturday outing is long overdue.

The Football Club has a proud tradition of honouring the armed forces based in the town, notably the Ghurkas. That chimes with me too, my late father having served in Burma was effusive in his praise of Ghurka soldiers. Earlier in the year, the Club welcomed members of Gurkha Regiment to the EBB Stadium to celebrate the Regiment's award of the Freedom of the Borough of Rushmoor.

Mid-afternoon, Clegg, Compo and I zeroed in on the Glider. Foggy was making his own way to visit his kin. I set the Passat's Satnav; the diesel fired up and we were away. Like the Red Sea, traffic on the nation's motorways parted before us and left us with a hour to play with before rolling up at the EBB.

Clegg had a plan. Suave, urbane he is widely travelled and is acquainted with many of the UK's finest nooks and crannies. He pronounced that one such is Farnham, just a short hop, skip and jump from Aldershot. Surrey borders to the latter's Hampshire. So, that became the interim destination well before sunset robbed the daylight.

To be honest, we did not see the best of Farnham. Nowhere is dazzling in the thick of the evening rush hour. Yet we had a decent stroll around the older parts of the town, admiring the blend of stately red brick elevations blended with stout oak and topped with clay tiled roofs. Then the vista leading up to the castle at the town's high point.

It's a pretty place, reminiscent of Marlborough. Farnham has Roman origins but the modern town began life as a Saxon village on strategic east-west crossroads. It grew into a town under the protection of its castle, built in the mid-12th century by the Bishop of Winchester (or more probably by his work force). A convenient residence for him halfway between the shops and nightlife of Winchester and London. A Bishop has to let his cassock down somewhere. The garrison of the castle formed a market.

The towered church of St Andrews dates from the 7th century the present building from the late 11th. Waverley Abbey was built near Farnham in 1128 but dissolved by Henry VIII in 1536 as Cromwell helped him raid the Church's coffers.

Oh, and in 1854 a new army camp was built at the village of Aldershot. This village quickly grew into a town. Clever link eh? Sure enough,

Farnham is another reason why a Saturday match v the Shots would be just dandy. As expected, a warm welcome from familiar faces at the EBB. But Rovers team were not generous guests.

As unexpected as the Spanish Inquisition, temporarily goal starved FGR tore into the League's meanest defence. 2 each for Fabien and Kieffer meant that at 4-0 was game over by half time – could have been more. Obviously bushed by their efforts, the team played keep ball in a tedious second period.

In front of my seat was a young parent with his 6 or 7 year old son, equipped with hand-drawn banner: "Come On Shots". By the half time break the lad was nearly in tears, making me feel awful. I gifted him my Rovers scarf to cheer him up. Not sure what will happen to it, but I hope it will comprise a better memory of a rotten day for him and a great one for us.

## Saturday 08.10.16
## North Ferriby United 0 FGR 3
## ROVERS CARRY ON TOP FORM WITH AWAY WIN
*Richard Joyce*

Forest Green made it five clean sheets and six games unbeaten to extend their stay at the top of the National League with a good win at North Ferriby United.

Ethan Pinnock scored his first Rovers goal, as further second half efforts from Charlie Clough and Christian Doidge proved enough for FGR to carry on their fine run of form.

Rovers defensive strength proved itself again, as the team's run of shutouts was enough to frustrate an opponent who themselves had only found the net six times all season.

The result means FGR will hold top spot in the division heading into next week's FA Cup fourth qualifying round weekend.

A lively start saw Rhys Murphy produce an effort on goal as early as the first minute, while he reacted quickly to a deflected Kieffer Moore strike by firing another shot just wide minutes later.

Liam Noble then continued a strong FGR start when he blasted off target following an excellent interchange of passes with Fabien Robert, and Moore's powerful run midway through the half saw him blast just over the bar.

North Ferriby came into the game as the half progressed, but they were pegged back when Pinnock broke the deadlock with his first goal in a Rovers shirt.

**OCTOBER**

He got on the end of Noble's fantastic ball into the danger zone to produce a deft touch that was enough to find a way past Rory Watson in the host's goal.

North Ferriby's best chance of the half came just a minute after FGR had gone ahead. It fell to former Rovers man Stephen Brogan, whose left footed direct free kick only just inched past Sam Russell's left hand post.

Having struggled to score goals this season, North Ferriby tried their luck with two half chances early in the second half, although Vinny Mukendi couldn't get his headers on target.

And after substitute Doidge had seen his header comfortably saved down the other end, Darren Carter was forced to clear off the line as Mukendi's header down into the six yard box caused trouble.

From the resultant corner the home side saw a header scrape over the bar, but it was the wake-up call Mark Cooper's men needed, as they doubled their lead two minutes later.

It was another brilliant Noble delivery from a corner that provided the opportunity, as Clough rose highest to nod home.

The goal ended any hopes North Ferriby had to steal a point, and they conceded another in stoppage time, when Doidge was able to roll the ball home into an empty net after Elliott Frear's shot had slammed onto the post and bounced out to the forward.

### DESTINATION NORTH FERRIBY
*Rambling Man*

Just me and Mrs Rambling-Man this week. A relaxing Saturday morning passed pleasantly and I even had time to watch the dire first half of Tranmere v Wrexham courtesy of BT Sport.

We left at around 12.45 pm, much later than usual, rolling up at Elmore Court in good time for the start of the main event.

Lovely place Elmore Court, owned by the Guise family since 1262. They had come over with Willy the Conqueror. Since Brexit, not sure if that qualifies them for UK residency? Anyway, their pad is down by the Severn with impressive views of the river itself, Welsh Hills beyond to the north, and Cotswold scarps to the South.

The Guises were given the estate by one John De Burgh, whose dad was a mover and shaker in the court of Henry III. The rent was " ... the Clove of one Gilly-Flower' each year ... " which does not seem too excessive, unless the flower was extinct or highly valuable. The fine looking Cotswold stone building we see today dates from the Tudor 1540s, with characteristic multi-storey bay windows at the front.

Skipping a century or two, the splendidly named Berkeley Guise inherited all the estates in 1794 at the age of 20. Napoleon was on his bullying tour of Europe back then. Berkeley's younger brother went off to give that Jonny Foreigner a bloody nose whilst his senior stayed home to do some serious partying. Between foppish raves, he built the dining room. Exhausted, he died without children in 1834 when his soldier 'bro', now General John Wright Guise, inherited. He downsized the family property portfolio to pay off his late brother's predictable debts, but kept Elmore Court as the family's primary residence, as now. The classical Georgian side elevations are down to him. All of which made the wedding ceremony something memorable, set in the splendour of Elmore's Main Hall.

Now the sharpest of FGR's match day magazine readers will be thinking, "Elmore? The Severn? Welsh and Cotswold Hills? Wedding?! Isn't that a tad inconvenient for the North side of the Humber?" No fooling you.

Nope, I'd had to skip the journey to North Ferriby to celebrate with good friends as their younger son Jon tied the knot with the beautiful Tania. All went well but the party started in earnest when news of FGR's 3-0 triumph filtered through! Well, for me at any rate.

Glad to say that Foggy and Compo were not diverted from their duty. They related fine tales of the National League's 'junior village', warm hospitality from the local yeomen and a stadium that harked back to our own club a couple of decades ago. Also of a bumpy pitch and a stuttering Rovers' showing for whom a 3-0 victory was a little flattering.

Sadly, I gather I may have missed my chance of taking in football at North Ferriby. Compo says the club fears it cannot sustain National League football next term, regardless of league position, as its stadium may not meet requisite standards as to capacity. So, locals are making the most of 2016/17. My best wishes to them – may they vanquish our competitors!

## 3 GOALS 3 POINTS ROVERS PREVAIL AT THE TOP

*Jokerman*

On the road with Rovers. Kendo at the helm heading north. Lottery numbers today 5-42-1-18 and 62 lead the way to the east coast and North Ferriby. A first visit for Forest Green Rovers. Following a short reconnaissance trip towards the Humber Bridge, Kendo pulls in to this up-market village in the shadow of Hull City.

Tripping down the lane past the allotments one is confronted by a quintessential non-league ground. Heading for the beer dispensing

**O**
**C**
**T**
**O**
**B**
**E**
**R**

establishment fans are in time to see Wrexham present three points to Tranmere Rovers on the big screen. An hour is spent in the company of extremely friendly local supporters. Stories varied between female blacksmiths to club support. They viewed southern fans as friendly. This tranquil setting was disturbed when followers from the town where conveyors of WOMD are built, turned up. 'Funny' that.

Ferriby are struggling for points after reaching the pinnacle of non-league football. The Villagers, waiting for the miracle to come. Their situation will not be lost on today's visitors. Manager Mark Cooper will not allow Tuesday nights 'walk in the park' at Aldershot to instil any lack of application this afternoon.

Warm sunshine greets the teams on parade, Rovers in a late change of strip play in familiar green and black shirts due to a colour clash. Forest Green field an unchanged line-up that finished the game at Aldershot. It's a quiet start to the game and ten minutes in before any threat on goal when Robert raiding down the right picked out Murphy, whose shot with the outside of his foot sent the ball over the bar.

A similar result from Noble, after a clever exchange of passes with Robert on fifteen minutes. A Kiefer Moore shot from distance is off target and at the other end a mistake by Russell with a clearance presents the ball to Ferriby striker Mukendi, who fires it across the goalmouth. Fortunately he found no support. Ferriby were battling hard in mid-field to break up Rovers possession game and can claim some success, winning numerous free kicks in their opponents half. Relying on the high ball to Mukendi, Skelton and Thomson however presented few problems for Clough and company in the Rovers defence.

The first real goal threat came on 43mins when the visitors took the lead. A contentious free kick near the left touchline, where Carter was tripped jostling for position at a throw-in, saw Noble sweep in one of those 'impossible' to defend crosses over the six yard line and Pinnock, allegedly, lashed the ball past keeper Watson with his eyebrow.

Ferriby feeling hard done by won a free kick on the edge of the Rovers area. Ex-Rover Brogan stepped up and hit a fierce shot over the wall and only narrowly wide of the upright with Russell a spectator. The half ended with Traore shooting wide for Rovers.

The second half started in the same vein with Rovers finding it difficult to find a rhythm on an uneven surface, added to the home side scrapping gamely. Cooper had seen enough after fifty five minutes and exchanged Moore and Murphy for Keanu and Doidge. Doidge was soon involved, heading a Carter cross straight at Watson. Ferriby were sorely lacking a cutting edge but their chance came after seventy minutes. Following a melee in the left corner of the six yard box the ball was stabbed past Russell but Carter was on hand to hook the ball clear off the goal line. Not fully cleared it was crossed back in where Gray saw his header skim the bar when well placed.

It was a wake-up call for Forest Green who promptly put the game beyond doubt on 75mins. A Noble corner on the left was measured perfectly onto the head of Clough, making a run to the near post, and he glanced the ball across Watson and inside the right hand upright. Rovers dominated the closing stages and in time added Keanu slipped a pass to Frear in the box who leathered the ball from an acute angle past Watson, only to see it rebound off the far post into the path of the on rushing Doidge, who gleefully slammed it into the vacant net. It was a little harsh on Ferriby who had battled hard against more skilful opponents.

The facility Cooper has of being able to call on such a strong 'bench' was evident today. Add this to the significant signing of Dan Wishart and it is clear the club are making every effort to avoid the play-off debacle. The F.A. Cup trip to Sutton will be a welcome diversion from the prime target.

## Saturday 15.10.16
## Sutton United 2 FGR 1 (FA Cup)
## LATE GOAL ENDS ROVERS CUP AMBITIONS
*Richard Joyce*

Roarie Deacon's last gasp header denied Forest Green Rovers a place in the first round proper of the FA Cup.

Sutton sealed their progress into the next round by coming from behind to knock out an FGR side who had taken the lead in the first half through Liam Noble.

The two National League rivals fought out a tense encounter throughout, but a free kick from former Forest Green man Ross Stearn, and Deacon's dramatic late winner were the two goals that were enough to dump Mark Cooper's men out.

Stearn almost gave Sutton the lead after 12 minutes when his hit from a narrow angle was blocked by Sam Russell, and the hosts will have been disappointed to have not stuck the loose ball home in the six yard box.

Rovers' first chances were efforts from distance. Fabien Robert fired wide and Darren Carter's hit flew just over the bar.

After Dean Beckwith had almost stroked in for Sutton, Forest Green took the lead, as Noble found the back of the net with a well-executed finish following a quickly taken corner.

O
C
T
O
B
E
R

Robert almost followed up the opener with an ambitious overhead kick, but Sutton ensured they'd draw level ten minutes before half time with a free kick from distance. Stearn's right-footed effort flew into the back of the net to help the hosts equalise.

Noble tried his best to restore Rovers lead with a long range shot that was well saved by Ross Worner, while an excellent one-on-one stop from Russell a minute later down the other end prevented former Arsenal man Craig Eastmond from exploiting space that had been left open at the back.

Carter's long range effort in the first minute of the second half flew over the bar as FGR looked to make an early impact, and they nearly did on 51 minutes, when superb build up play ended with Elliott Frear crossing for Noble who couldn't hit the target.

Drissa Traore forced Worner into a save as chances continued to fall Rovers way, and Sutton missed a massive chance to take the lead when Beckwith headed wide from Nicky Bailey's brilliant ball into the box.

The chances were see-sawing between the sides, and Aarran Racine came just inches away from glancing home Noble's set piece delivery on 78 minutes, meanwhile Sutton substitute Chris Dickson forced a powerful effort that flew just wide.

Ethan Pinnock almost produced a moment of brilliance when his volley was tipped over by Worner as Forest Green looked for a late winner.

But after a key save from Russell had denied Dickson's powerful run down the left, the home side booked their first round place.

Deacon rose highest inside the area unmarked, and saw his header go in off the post, to complete the turnaround and send Sutton through.

## DESTINATION SUTTON
*Rambling Man*

A third of the way into the League Season and a break for t'Cup. The proper version, FA variety, the ornate one with big handles. Clegg was away, Foggy was travelling separately to meet family, and Deep-Throat had purchased tickets for the iron horse. Seemingly deserted, Compo and I welcomed a new buddy, Sir Tomcat. I picked him up from his crib near the Girls School then we rendezvous'd at the Glider where Compo's Beamer took over.

Quicker than you can say "Trump's groped an entire State" we'd arrived at Reading Services for a quick coffee. In good company we were, with Kendo's crew, and fans from Exeter City, Arsenal & Crystal Palace all there in numbers. As both the latter pair were at home, I think they must have taken the scenic route or got lost somewhere on the North Circular!

Compo hit the loud pedal and we were whisked to our second destination, The National Trust's Claremont Park near Esher. A park for some 300 years, the gardens have felt the full force of Sir John Vanbrugh, Charles Bridgeman, William Kent and 'Capability' Brown who all put their own distinctive stamp on the lake, terraced grass amphitheatre and woodland. A perfect place to take the air – in our case a circuit of the lake - and to mop up some hearty NT grub. Time did not permit inspection of 'Claremont Palace', commissioned for Clive of India, but I'm sure he won't mind if we go another time.

And so to Gander Green Lane, possibly the best address line of all National League clubs? Already impressed with the 3G Artificial Grass and Stadium at Maidstone, my first visit to Sutton United's 'The Borough Sports Ground' was eagerly awaited. It did not disappoint.

Unlike Maidstone, the stadium is not new. An off centre Grandstand sits well back from the pitch, opposite a smaller version. The small covered terraces at either end are reached by curves not corners. It has character, though you have to be at the border rails to feel close to the action. Then again, I've always liked grounds where you can have a wander and take in views from different spots.

Now I'm a sucker for all things archaeological and programmes like Baldrick's *Time Team*. My guess is that the curvy ends hark back to the hay-day of dog tracks. If I was directing a dig, I'd call in the JCB's to cut trenches across 2 of the curves, in the expectation of finding a fluffy mechanical hare and some dog biscuits. Maybe some rotting packets of steroids.

All the locals we encountered were proud of what the Club has achieved, hospitable and 'up for the cup' in line with United's tradition. And some of their older stagers were louder than the farming folk to be found at Hereford United, and that means decent volume.

On the pitch, the Amber clad home warriors were pretty *touchy feely* as Driss will attest when the bruises come out. But it was an entertaining encounter which Rovers largely dominated. Crucially though, they spurned many good chances, whereas Sutton took 2 of theirs, recovering well from Liam Noble's opener. For another year then, The FA Cup will be saved a journey to the Cotswolds.

**Saturday 22.10.16**
**FGR 3 Guiseley 0**
**HIGH FLYING ROVERS EASE PAST GUISELEY**
*Richard Joyce*
Powerful Forest Green swept aside Guiseley with a commanding performance to extend their lead at the top of the National League table,

**O
C
T
O
B
E
R**

Quality finishes from Darren Carter and Christian Doidge, plus a second half own goal from the unfortunate Jake Lawlor, handed Mark Cooper's men another three league points.

It's now six clean sheets on the bounce too for FGR, who have a four point lead at the top of the fifth tier heading into Tuesday's trip to Solihull Moors.

From as early as the fourth minute Rovers attacking intentions were clear when Liam Noble went close with an effort from just outside the area.

And the midfielders pin-point pass for Fabien Robert's clever forward run minutes later almost saw the Frenchman give FGR the lead when he broke into the Guiseley box.

It didn't take long for Carter to finally break the deadlock midway through the half. A brilliant strike from the former Birmingham City man was too far for Dan Atkinson in the Guiseley goal to reach.

The visitors, on a run of back-to-back league wins heading into the tie, struggled to threaten the FGR goal, and only a Jake Cassidy strike that went well over the bar from a cleverly worked corner kick was what the away side could show for their efforts.

They were thankful to their keeper, filling in for Jonny Maxted who is on loan with the Lions, for making a terrific save to prevent Kieffer Moore from nodding home Carter's cross.

Forest Green doubled their lead though straight after half time as Doidge netted for the fourth time this season.

Drissa Traore's pass into the feet of Moore was knocked onto Doidge, who turned excellently and then applied a superb finish for a deserved goal.

The third and final goal came just before the hour mark. On his home debut Dan Wishart produced a stinging low cross into a dangerous position that was too hot to handle for Lawlor in the Lions back line, and he helplessly touched the ball into his own net.

It was a goal that did enough to kill off the game in Rovers favour, and apart from Noble's fine strike on 85 minutes that hammered the post, FGR's work was done as a good crowd at The New Lawn celebrated another three points and an eleventh league win of the campaign.

## ROVERS' SPLAT CATS
*Jokerman*

It's been a week since Forest Green's FA Cup ranneth over and disappeared down the Gander Green Drain at Sutton. Manager Mark Cooper was not happy and even commentator Bob Hunt had to dodge verbal crockery at the post match interview. Today the attention turns to Guiseley, who held Lincoln away in the FA Cup on Saturday, so cannot be underestimated despite being twenty two places below Rovers in the league table.

The fallout from last week's reverse has been extra training and Rovers fans will be hoping for an emphatic victory this afternoon before embarking on a run of fixtures that in theory should see TNL attendance figures rocket. Nearly fifty 'Lions' fans have made the trip from Yorkshire and in The Green Man the food is always up for discussion and invites wry comments. They were even less happy on hearing FGR's 'no ferrets on the terrace' policy.

Cooper goes with Doidge and Moore in attack and Wishart returns after sitting out against his former club Sutton. The game kicks off in bright sunlight though the clouds would soon win that contest. Forest Green start well with Bennett who finds Noble but his shot is wide.

Nine minutes in and Noble hits a superb defence splitting pass to Robert inside the box, but he puts the ball wide of the left hand post. Guiseley are chasing and playing a spoiling game not allowing Rovers to get into their usual rhythm, resulting in more than usual aerial passes.

The visitors pose little threat and a through ball to Cassidy sees Russell quickly out to smother the danger. Despite the scrappy start Rovers take a deserved lead on 20mins. Robert and Bennett combine well on the right and the cross finds Carter on the edge of the 'D'. His touch is good and he hits a crisp shot high into the left hand corner of the net past keeper Atkinson.

The goal settles Rovers and they continue to press. Wishart is getting forward on the left to match Bennett on the right. He picks out Doidge, who is winning everything in the air, but can get no power on his effort. On the half hour mark Cassidy hits the ball out of the ground from a short corner. Rovers reply immediately when Wishart shows terrific control and cuts inside but his powerful shot finds the side netting.

On thirty six minutes Bennett is fouled by Purver in front of the dug outs. Cooper is not impressed and endeavours to convey some advice to the referee, fourth official and the roll of lino with the flag. This is met with disapproval and after much ado the referee has a quiet word and play resumes. Bennett recovers to cross for Moore who heads down to Doidge who is blocked on the six yard line. Traore and Carter then combine to set up Moore and his header is scrambled away for a corner which Noble crosses for Clough who heads the ball over the bar. The half ends with Rovers in the ascendancy.

**OCTOBER**

Quickly out of the blocks from the restart Forest Green double their advantage with a splendid move on 47mins. Down the centre Traore slots the ball to Carter, who flicks a short pass first time through to Doidge, who feints right spins left and strikes the ball into the top left hand corner with Atkinson helpless.

With daylight on the scoreboard Rovers start to freewheel. Their passing possession game kicks in and Guiseley have no answer. 58mins and the lead stretches to three when Carter sends Wishart down the left. The big man gets to the byline and fires low to Doidge running in at the near post, closely marked he jumps over the ball and the hapless Lawlor deflects the ball into his own net from point blank. Keanu and Murphy replaced Robert and Moore on the hour as the home side continued to torment the Guiseley defence for the duration. Noble came closest to a fourth goal on eighty four minutes when he hit a thunderous shot against the upright from twenty yards.

There was little response from the visitors. On a rare foray Purver burst through into the area only to find the rock steady Clough on hand, not only to time his block to perfection but to come away in possession. At the death as RJ announced Doidge as MoM, Noble hit a low forty yard pass across the area which the striker at full stretch could only direct wide of the post. It would have been a fitting end to the proceedings. In added time Traore had to be helped off after sustaining a painful ankle injury and looks doubtful for Tuesday's game.

Guiseley posed no threat to Rovers on reflection and it was a satisfactory day though Cooper will find plenty to work on no doubt, which is as it should be. Top of the League but no time to dwell on that. Solihull on Tuesday and surely two thousand plus for the Daggers on Saturday.

## FGR AMBASSADOR REPORT
*Isabelle Arris, Stroud High School*

Hi, I'm Isabelle Arris and I've just started my second year as an Ambassador. I really enjoyed my first year representing the club and getting to go to Wembley for the play offs. I have once again joined the Prediction League run by Mr Butterworth and my prediction for this match was 4-1 to FGR.

Today, Forest Green play Guiseley who are 23rd in the table. However, in their past two games, this Yorkshire team has secured 6 points; a run that may continue in this match. Forest Green also have a winning streak of 5 clean sheets in a row and a captain, Noble, with hair instead of a green mohawk or no hair at all!

After a few minutes, it became clear that Guiseley had a new found confidence as they came out gunning for another win to move them out of the relegation zone. The ball was put over the North Stand only 2 minutes in after a shot at the goal from Guiseley, another reason why we need a bigger stadium! Due to their strong beginning, their fans started singing 'We're gonna win the league!' which earned a laugh from our fans. In the 19th minute, a run from Bennett and a scuffle in the box saw Darren Carter put the ball calmly into the back of the net. The score stayed 1-0 at half time as the ball was cleared off the line to prevent Guiseley from getting an equalizer.

Just minutes after the second half began, Moore skilfully set up the second goal for Doidge making the score 2-0. Play continued through the second half and it was clear that Cooper's half time speech worked as we dominated play. After Guiseley made a double substitution in the 56th minute, FGR's new signing Wishart put the ball into the box trying to score his first goal. However, the ball was knocked past the young goalkeeper by one of Guiseley's own players, number 6. The own goal put us ahead by 3 goals, securing the win.

When the man of the match was announced as Christian Doidge by the Nailsworth Specsavers Branch, he nearly scored his 5th goal of the season – he really should've gone to Specsavers! The game ended minutes after Traore was supported off the pitch when he and a Guiseley player clashed ankles. The final score was a 3-0 win, increasing the clean sheet run to 6 games and giving us a 4 point lead. This win and the 1723 people who attended also made me top of the predictor league! Hopefully we can keep this up in the November matches as we come up against some of the toughest team yet.

**Tuesday 25.10.16**
**Solihull Moors 0 FGR 1**
**ROVERS POWER AHEAD WITH SOLIHULL WIN**
*Richard Joyce*

Eight league games unbeaten, four consecutive wins, and seven clean sheets on the bounce saw Forest Green Rovers continue their outstanding form to top the National League with another victory at Solihull Moors.

Liam Daly's second half own goal was the difference as Rovers continued their march at the top of the fifth tier by getting the job done on the road in midweek.

**O
C
T
O
B
E
R**

The difference between the two could have been greater had Forest Green taken more of their chances, but the defensive strength once again stood out, and FGR look powerfully strong in all areas.

Sam Russell was forced into action twice early on. He got down well to deny Jack Byrne and Joel Dielna's efforts from outside the area.

Down the other end after Liam Noble's tricky effort had been deflected away for a corner, Kieffer Moore forced Rovers first real opportunity, but his strong right footed hit was blocked away by Solihull's former Kidderminster stopper Danny Lewis.

The hosts were working hard to deny FGR opportunities in front of goal. But Dan Wishart did try his best, only to fire over, while Noble's dipping free kick was just about dealt with by Lewis scrambling across his goal.

With the clock ticking towards the interval, Solihull were denied a massive chance to open the scoring when Russell made a superb last ditch stop to stop Darryl Knights from finding the net when he had burst clean through.

All square at the break, another Noble free kick provided the first opportunity of the second half, although his curling effort drifted wide.

Keanu Marsh-Brown was then just inches away from opening the scoring when his brilliant strike went just over, but Mark Cooper's side didn't have to wait long to finally bag the opener.

A familiar Wishart run down the left ended with a fizzing low cross into the danger zone that Daly deflected past his own goalkeeper and into his own net.

Marsh-Brown tried his best to double the advantage with a long-range hit that was saved minutes later, while Solihull went close when Knights volley landed satisfyingly in the arms of Russell.

Moore continued FGR's search for a second goal when he had his right footed shot saved. And Noble almost added a second when on 75 minutes his low shot was somehow kept out.

Solihull were reduced to ten men on 78 minutes when Knights saw his night end early. A suggested stamp on Moore saw the experienced attacker make an early exit down the tunnel.

Marsh-Brown continued his assault on the Solihull goal in search of another strike, while Christian Doidge came incredibly close right at the death.

But without little pressure from the hosts, Rovers held on, to continue their excellent run of form ahead of a big clash with Dagenham & Redbridge on the weekend.

## DESTINATION SOLIHULL
*Rambling Man*

Not too many Tuesday nighters to brave this term. But in keeping with the National League's extraordinary approach to fixture planning, our nearest opponents cropped up as our next midweek fixture. A new venue for most of us – sustainably named Damson Park, home of Solihull Moors. Just 66 miles from The New Lawn according to RAC Route Planner. But that's for later.

Despite Foggy's temporary defection, we had a full squad on show. Clegg was at the wheel of one of Henry's specials, Compo at his side. New but distinguished companion Hunter joined for the evening. They picked me up from Stonehouse Court Hotel, thence to the congested M5 and M25.

Those of you who are devotees of *The Antiques Roadshow* – that's a BBC programme, not a description of Rambling Man's travelling mates – will have noticed that the last 2 weeks have featured Baddesley Clinton, a moated manor house near Solihull. So, that was bound to be the night's culture stop, right? Wrong. We were headed for Scandinavia.

You heard me correctly. Whilst Solihull does not scream Viking to most, it has a Scandi bar/restaurant called The Oktogon in a pretty little community called Knowle. And Knowle happens to be home for Ecotricity & FGR's Marketing Tsar, Chris Wintle. Oktogon boasts more craft beers that you can poke a smorgasbord at, and we were soon in sampling mode. Good thing Jokerman was not with us as Kendo would not have prised him away.

All too soon we had to leave for Damson Park though that turned out to be more welcoming still. A smart small ground with a discernible slope, covered at one end and with a flanking grandstand arrangement. A stadium where you can walk the circuit and chat to friendly locals who are justly proud of how this erstwhile combo of Solihull Borough & Moor Green has progressed.

Damson was full of hearty characters, none more so that the 'chef' of the burger van who served bacon and fried egg burger with onions to Clegg and me. "Vegan – 'course it is. Solid Quorn. Picked it m'self". I believed him, anyhow it barely touched the sides.

And the match was good fare too. Rovers have hit their straps of late in proper Mark Cooper style. Most teams try to respond by pushing up on our midfield, packing defence and leaving their speed merchants to live off the scraps. But Rovers have learned from early season reverses and seem better able to take this in their stride.

**OCTOBER**

Most of the game was one way traffic, though Moors were astute enough to cause occasional problems. But when they did, Sam was the equal. A goalless first period turned into a full blooded assault down the hill as the hosts defended desperately. They were eventually undone by a Wishart trademark low cross that provoked an own goal by a hapless defender, caught between a rock and a hard place.

Rovers fans seemed to make up at least a half of the 900 crowd. The EESI choir was relentless, noisy and funny. Highlight was Liam Noble surfing on them after Rovers' winning goal.

So, an emphatic win against over an impressive home club (in every sense of the word). And one that sets up a terrific encounter on Saturday versus the second placed team. The return of the Daggers!

**Saturday 29.10.16**
**FGR 1 Dagenham & Redbridge 1**
**FGR MARCH ON WITH A DAGGERS HOME POINT**
*Richard Joyce*

The National League's current top two sides couldn't be separated in an enthralling contest at The New Lawn.

Rhys Murphy's early second half strike had given Forest Green a second half lead, but Oliver Hawkins towering header earned Dagenham a point, in an entertaining afternoon that saw Rovers make it nine home games unbeaten this season.

Murphy was handed a place in the starting XI against his former club, and after Corey Whiteley's first minute chance had slipped just wide from the visitors, the forward made Daggers goalkeeper Elliot Justham pull off a great save when his left footed shot looked destined for the top corner.

Dagenham's former Luton keeper Justham then denied Murphy again with another great save midway through the half after Keanu Marsh-Brown had done well to create the opportunity.

A high tempo affair saw Rovers have a major shout for a penalty on 32 minutes. Defender Josh Staunton looked to have handled the bouncing ball in his own area, but referee Stephen Ross ignored Forest Green's protests, while shortly after the away side almost nosed in front.

Christian Doidge was on hand against his old side to make a vital goal line clearance after a free kick that had been lifted into the box ended up inches from being slammed home.

A long distance Doidge strike and counter attack that came to nothing ended an eventful first half, and the pacey tempo to proceedings continued after the interval when Mark Cooper's side went ahead.

Murphy linked up superbly in the box with Marsh-Brown and smashed in with a low hit past Justham to put some daylight between the two teams.

Now on seven goals for the season, Murphy almost doubled his and Rovers advantage in the minutes that followed, but he couldn't convert Dan Wishart's cross. Ten minutes later it was Marsh-Brown who tried to force the issue, only to see his powerful hit from outside the area deflect away for a corner.

Doidge was determined to become the second FGR player to score against his former employers. He saw his header on 64 minutes from a Liam Noble delivery just drop wide, while Hawkins down the other end blasted off target when he found space.

John Still's Dagenham would eventually level when leading marksman Hawkins found the back of the net with a terrific header.

He rose highest at the back post from a diagonal ball aimed towards the highly rated attacker, to head across goal in front of the travelling fans.

The visitors' goal scorer had another good chance with a header on 85 minutes to win it late on for his side, but he couldn't profit again from another good ball, and the division's two leading clubs shared the points.

## DAGGERS DRAWN
*Jokerman*

Today Forest Green Rovers face their sternest test of the season against nearest rivals Dagenham & Redbridge. Two for one but they were both 'rubbish' last season and relegation tracked them down. Manager John Still has been appointed with a view to an immediate return to the football league. Vastly experienced at this level he is from the same mould as Cheltenham's Gary Johnson. His side will be a true test for Mark Coopers League leaders.

Forest Green come in to today's game following a mid-week 1-0 victory at Solihull Moors, a game they dominated. A rock solid defence completed a run of seven clean sheets in league fixtures, a remarkable achievement. However on this occasion the statistics indicated a severe case of goal constipation amongst the strike force. Rovers fans will be hoping steps have been taken to relieve those symptoms this afternoon.

Having crossed the border into what historically has been a woollen stronghold today's visitors, for ease of prose will be referred to as the Daggs. Despite the overcast dismal conditions even The Green Man was buzzin' today in anticipation of this much awaited fixture. The team

**OCTOBER**

news named Keanu in place of the injured Robert and Murphy would partner Doidge in attack. The defence picked itself.

Two thousand two hundred fans greeted the teams, just under two hundred Daggs supporters had made the journey. The first chance of the game fell to the visitors. Following a poor clearance Whiteley rifled a shot past Russell's right hand post.

Rovers hit back on seven minutes when Murphy curled a shot towards the top left hand corner that Daggs keeper Justham pushed away for a corner. A break on ten minutes saw the Daggs have a three on two situation which ended when the imperious Clough put a foot in to clear the danger.

Soon after Widdowson, the Daggs full back, broke well down the left and crossed dangerously across the six yard box; fortunately for Rovers the ball eluded his strikers. Rovers then had a good spell of possession play and applied some real pressure on the Daggs defence.

Inter passing picked out Doidge in the box, his shot was blocked away for a corner that was wasted and then Keanu linked brilliantly with Doidge, whose flick found Murphy twelve yards out. The striker turned and smashed the ball goalwards only to be denied by Justham who made a splendid save to deflect it over the bar.

The keeper was in action again when Wishart went on the rampage down the left and forced him to save a firm low shot at his near post. The Daggs were not overawed and Whiteley had a clear site of goal from fifteen yards but could only hit a weak shot straight at Russell.

Thirty two minutes in and there was a massive appeal for a penalty from the Rovers players and officials as Staunton cut out a ball into the area. Cooper was incandescent but it was waved away by both Referee and his flag man. Soon after the Daggs almost took the lead. A free kick on the right near the by-line saw Drew put in a wicked cross that dropped into the six yard area between players. It was prodded goalwards and somehow Doidge and Murphy conspired to clear the ball as it rolled along the goal line. Another near miss for Rovers.

On half time Murphy forced the play in the Daggs box but Keanu was just beaten to the ball by Justham. Goalless at the break was a fair reflection on an entertaining half. Both sides were playing well in possession, just a lack of finishing the problem. Even more of a problem for Rovers was the referee's decision to send Cooper to the stand following the altercation over the penalty decision.

The second period could not have started better for Rovers. Three minutes in a good build up move culminated when a superb first time pass from Keanu split the defence and found Murphy in the six yard box, near the right hand post, who hit the ball, possibly with a deflection, past Justham into the net, to send the Forest Green fans behind the goal into mayhem.

Rovers were on the up and on fifty one minutes Murphy should have done better when Wishart set him up twelve yards out, but his shot was weak with Keanu waiting for the pass. Widdowson for the Daggs was overlapping well and Russell had to cut out yet another threatening cross on the hour mark. The home side then enjoyed another spell of good possession. Traore was dominant in mid-field and even overshadowed Noble and that takes some doing. The second goal however didn't arrive. Doidge put a header narrowly wide and Murphy was through on goal but a terrific block by Doe denied him.

The clean sheet record would not be extended. 73mins and Widdowson hit a deep diagonal cross to the back post, where the six foot plus Hawkins rose to plant a firm header back across goal and inside Russell's left hand post. The goal deflated Rovers and the final fifteen minutes saw the Daggs with the initiative.

Subs were made, Moore and Frear replaced Murphy and Keanu, but the sting had gone from the game. Both sides tired which was not surprising after a marvellous game of football which was a credit to all. There was a standing ovation at the final whistle for the combatants and well deserved. Forest Green Rovers remain top of the National League and performing as they are doing can progress without trepidation.

## FGR AMBASSADOR REPORT
*Charlie Smith, Rednock Secondary School, Dursley*
I'm one of two Forest Green Rovers' ambassadors at Rednock School, Dursley. I am in year nine and trying to build a following for the Rovers amongst my friends at the school. Our sports teacher is Alex Sykes, who used to play for FGR and now manages Shortwood F.C.

There was a big build up to this top of table clash with both teams fielding strong squads. The match didn't disappoint, only more goals should have been scored. The football was of high standard throughout with both teams cancelling each other out at times.

Rovers always looked like stretching their unbeaten run with many chances for Murphy in 1st half. Drissa Traore looked a class act all game but Daggers were well composed at the back. The big talking point was the penalty that was not given from what looked like handball.

O
C
T
O
B
E
R

Mark Cooper was sent off for this, as he told the referee what he thought of the linesman who must have seen the incident.

2nd half Rhys murphy scored early, followed by further Doidge and Noble chances. Then a brilliant header for Hawkins eventually levelled. Sadly this stopped Sam Russell from a record of minutes not conceding. A late chance from daggers on 85mins could of snatched the points. It had been a good game from two teams who look like fighting the promotion battle out for the rest of the season. The crowd had been a bumper one of 2268 and they were chanting majority of game."

It was all going so well! Two more wins to start the month – the second at Macclesfield Town in front of Sir Alex Ferguson – had established a 9 point lead at the top for Rovers. On 19th November, 2-0 up on 70 minutes at home to Lincoln, the win would have stretched the lead to 12 over their strongest challenger. But then the beautiful game did what it must do – reassert the priceless gift of unpredictability. Lincoln's last quarter recovery to snatch a 3-2 win cut everyone at FGR to the quick, a seminal result for the season. Rovers would not win again in the League until 2017.

*when the winner won't go in*
*when the main stand will not sing*
*when the late match nerves kick in*
*make some noise for Rovers*

(Excerpt from 'Make Some Noise for Rovers' Crispin Thomas "Football Poets" which summed up the sudden unease as Rovers hit the buffers)

Another post on the Fans Forum attempted to heal the wound through humour. The scribe will have to remain anonymous as I cannot track down the precise post, but it took its inspiration from Bogart and Bergman in Casablanca:

*"What about us? We'll always have the first twenty minutes v Tranmere"*

**Saturday 05.11.16**
**FGR 2 Aldershot Town 1**
**Doidge wins it late to extend Rovers lead**
*Richard Joyce*

Christian Doidge was the double goal scoring hero with a dramatic stoppage time winner as Forest Green Rovers went seven points clear at the top of the National League.

His brilliant late header was the perfect response to Aldershot's 89th minute Jake Gallagher equaliser, as Rovers took advantage of being one of the few teams not involved in FA Cup action to move further ahead at the top of the table.

Doidge had put FGR in front on 16 minutes, but Gallagher's low finish looked to have claimed a point for the visitors at the death, only for Doidge to bag his sixth goal of the season in front of a relieved and joyful New Lawn crowd.

**N
O
V
E
M
B
E
R**

Both teams tried their best to deal with the conditions in the opening exchanges, and after little action in front of goal Doidge broke the deadlock with a composed finish.

Liam Noble's terrific ball into the box was met on the chest by Doidge, and he had the confidence to take a number of touches before looping the ball past Jake Cole.

Within the next ten minutes the lead should have arguably been doubled. Matt Tubbs' burst and pass to Darren Carter was saved, while Dan Wishart's magnificent cross from the left was very nearly tucked in at the back post by Doidge.

It was then Aldershot's turn to go close. Shamir Fenelon's low shot was parried by Sam Russell, and Iffy Allen couldn't convert the follow up from within the six yard box.

A tentative second half was to come where both teams struggled to get hold of the ball.

Cheye Alexander forced Russell into action with a comfortable save, and substitute Keanu Marsh-Brown then came within inches of finding the net twice in quick succession as Mark Cooper's charges pushed for a second.

He slammed just past the post on two occasions after making a direct run down the right hand side.

After Shots replacement Matt McClure had tried his luck with two attempts, Noble became the latest FGR player to come just inches from scoring, but like Marsh-Brown his shot zipped just wide.

The pressure was on to hold onto the one goal lead, but former Welling United man Gallagher had other ideas, as he slotted into the bottom corner having seized upon Nick Arnold's through ball to level for the well-backed visitors.

It was a frustrating blow right at the end, but there was more drama to come, as Doidge headed the winner in stoppage time.

Substitute Rob Sinclair capped a wonderful return from injury by producing a pin-point ball into the area that saw Doidge get up well to glance home a memorable late winner.

## DOIDGE HEADS FOR GLORY
*Jokerman*

The F. A. Cup 1st Round plays out this afternoon, while here at TNL Forest Green Rovers and Aldershot Town, both failures in that respect, contest a re-arranged league fixture. Aldershot are only two points off the play-off places and Gary Waddock's team don't do 'sitting back' away from home. Rovers bested them a month ago but will need to be more ruthless in front of goal than of late to take all three points today.

Speculation regarding Ricky Miller should be all the incentive required for manager Mark Cooper's strikers to step up a gear. A fine game last week against close rivals Dagenham & Redbridge saw the points shared leaving Rovers clear at the top. A victory today would give them a psychological advantage ahead of the severe tests to come.

As the team news filtered into the ale house, a few eyebrows were raised on hearing Matt Tubbs was straight into the starting line-up on his return from a month's loan at Woking. Doidge and Murphy also start up front while Racine comes in for the suspended Bennett. A keen north wind bites the cheek as the teams take to the field.

Aldershot edged the opening minutes without troubling keeper Russell and Rovers fans had to wait until the thirteenth minute before any worthwhile attack on winning a corner. From then they turned the screw on Aldershot. On fifteen Noble arrowed a cross in to Doidge who was only inches away from connecting, the ball deflected behind and the corner cleared.

Forest Green then produced what has become their trade mark. Patient possession, probing and switching and bewildering their opponents. On this occasion it culminated in the 17th minute when Wishart and Noble combined on the left edge of the area. Noble lifted the ball into Doidge who controlled it skilfully on his chest before turning and lashing a left foot shot past Cole the Aldershot custodian. A goal of the finest making.

Rovers took command of the game and went in search of a second goal. Tubbs clear through the middle squared the ball instead of shooting and Carter could only manage a weak shot that Cole gathered. Carter and Wishart then linked well to cross hard and low for Doidge at the back post but the striker at full stretch put the ball wide of the upright. A buzzard circled ominously above the away end.

The goal would not come for Rovers and on thirty two minutes were fortunate not to concede. Fenelon raiding down the right, beat Pinnock and cut inside hitting a low shot that Russell could only parry across goal where Allen, at the back post, was slow to react and under pressure hit the side netting. A clear warning for the home side. They replied when Doidge set up Murphy who blasted the ball wide into the two hundred and fifty Shots fans behind the goal. They had been goading him from the start having been involved in the red card incident last month.

**N**
**O**
**V**
**E**
**M**
**B**
**E**
**R**

Traore was replaced by Sinclair on forty minutes after taking a knock earlier. Allen was booked for leaving a foot in on Noble just before the break. It looked nasty and a relief all round when the Rovers skipper resumed.

Ripping into the cake at half time the main consensus was that a second goal was a necessity. For the first fifteen minutes of the second half Aldershot effectively turned the tables on Rovers. They won the possession and began to pose a real threat. Although no clear cut chances were created, apart from a Russell save low down from a shot by Alexander, one could feel a sense of unease.

Just after the hour mark Cooper had seen enough and replaced Murphy and Carter with Keanu and Frear. It seemed a good move both players quickly involved. Keanu hit two identical shots past Cole from the right hand side of the area and both grazed the left hand post. So near yet so far. Frear made inroads down the left but could not make the final ball count.

A rare mistake by Noble on the left presented Aldershot sub McClure with a clear run into the box where he hit the ball past Russell, and agonisingly wide of the far post, much to the chagrin of their supporters. The same player again tested Russell with a low shot from distance that he was equal to. Noble replied with a diagonal shot inches wide but still the goal would not come. As the clock ran down Aldershot full back Arnold, who was having a fine game for the visitors, raced into the Rovers half and found the way opening before him. He arrowed a pass into the feet of Gallagher inside the box on the right who swept it past Russell at his near post. 88mins and the Shots fans went berserk as the players went over to celebrate with them. Rovers' fans were gutted but one goal was never going to be enough, as was the case last week.

Aldershot had been the better side in the second half and the board went up, four added minutes. Rovers went on a wing and a prayer looking for something. Sinclair had battled well since coming on and showed he had something to offer this team. 91mins Rovers swept downfield the ball played back to Wishart. He slips it to Sinclair in from the left touchline who hits a cross over the surging attackers and defenders in the area. Out of the maelstrom rose Doidge facing away from goal. He corkscrewed his body to direct a header past the flailing Cole and the ball dropped inside the right hand post. Magical. Cue pandemonium. Well it was palpable.

Aldershot fans were bringing up their breakfast. Football eh? You couldn't make it up!

## FGR AMBASSADOR REPORT
*Elsie Heslop, Sir William Romney Secondary School, Tetbury*

Elsie's FGR Experience. Hi, I'm Elsie and I'm 13 years old. As an ambassador I help promote the club by doing reports like these and they are published in the Avening Villager, Nailsworth News and the Gloucester Citizen. This is my second year being an ambassador and I have had lots of fun, especially as it gives my whole family time to spend together doing something we all enjoy. This is my second report for the FGR program this season and what a season it's been so far! Already we are top of the league and if we carry on our amazing run we could advance to league 2.

On Saturday the 5th of November Forest Green played against Aldershot Town who brought along an impressive 226 fans with them. However, they managed to bring in a red firework thing that covered the pitch in a thick layer of red smoke but the security took it swiftly out of the stadium. They were also very vocal ignoring the announcement that asked the stands to keep their swearing at a minimum because of all the children in the crowd.

Despite all that going on FGR managed to score a great goal in the 16th minute from Christian Doidge. After all that excitement, an Aldershot player got a yellow card and in the process Drissa Traore got injured meaning that a substitution was made: Drissa Traore came off for Rob Sinclair to come on.

In the second half now there were many, many chances created to score a goal which would have secured the win, but unfortunately as the game was about to end, Aldershot levelled in the 88th minute. The game wasn't over yet though and there was still a few minutes left and out of the blue Christian Doidge got his second goal in the 91st minute giving Forest Green Rovers the victory! The final whistle blew and Aarran Racine was named man of the match. It was a great game to watch despite the freezing weather but another 3 points towards promotion. Let's hope the Rovers can keep it up. Come on you Rovers!

### Saturday 12.11.16
### Macclesfield Town 0 FGR 1
### FGR GO FURTHER AHEAD WITH FINE AWAY WIN
*Richard Joyce*

Keanu Marsh-Brown's early first half goal earned Forest Green Rovers a magnificent three points on the road at Macclesfield Town.

Mark Cooper's side are now nine points clear at the top of the National League, after another superb defensive showing, which saw FGR extend their unbeaten run to eleven games.

**NOVEMBER**

A Macclesfield side away from home always prove to be tricky opponents, but FGR's away form has been the best in the division so far, and that showed no sign of stopping in front of a good backing of noisy travelling Forest Green supporters.

Manchester United and managerial legend Sir Alex Ferguson watched on as Marsh-Brown got the game underway in excellent fashion for Rovers, when he found the net after only two minutes.

He took advantage of a gaping hole in the Macclesfield back line to latch onto Christian Doidge's through ball to hammer home past Craig Ross.

FGR were enjoying some early joy in the Macclesfield defensive third, which continued when Marsh-Brown slammed across the face of goal following Daniel Wishart's bursting run, and Charlie Clough's header on the half hour mark from a Liam Noble corner was easily saved.

The Silkmen came into the game more towards the end of the half. Danny Whitaker's blast across goal slipped wide, while ex-Morecambe front man Jack Sampson forced Sam Russell into a stop low to his left.

Marsh-Brown tried to add a second before half time, but David Fitzpatrick got a vital touch on his volley, which was driven goalwards.

Elliott Frear provided an early tester for Ross at the start of the second half that the Silkmen keeper was equal to, and after Danny Rowe had fired wide down the other end, Ross was again called into action to deny Rob Sinclair's shot from 20 yards.

The Silkmen keeper was forced into a smart save when he kept out Frear's attempt at a finish after Marsh-Brown had done brilliantly down the right shortly after.

Russell was then called upon just past the hour mark when he plucked Mitch Hancox's rifled volley from distance out of the air.

Ross had been the busier of the two keepers, and the former Whitehawk man made a crucial save to keep the score line down to just the one goal when Noble fed Marsh-Brown on the right, for the attacker to see his slammed effort crucially saved.

The home team's search for an equaliser continued. They came close as the game ticked into the last ten minutes when Jack Mackreth's shot hit the side netting after he'd latched onto an excellent Rowe aerial ball.

It was the last chance John Askey's men would get, as Rovers held on to move nine points clear at the top of the division with a brilliant away result.

## DESTINATION MACCLESFIELD
*Rambling Man*

Some days are simply perfect. Doesn't happen often, leastways not to me, but on such rare occasions isn't life just dandy?

Perfection was the last thing on my mind on Saturday 12th November. To start with the destination for the day's match was Moss Rose – home to the Silkmen a k a Macclesfield Town – not a place I associate with pleasure. Results over the years for Rovers have been liquorice all-sorts and there's sometimes an element in the home support that is on the nasty side of abusive.

And Foggy and I had decided to give Compo moral support by accompanying him on the 40 strong Ambassadors coach. That was a big leap of faith for all concerned as I only have to sniff a coach to turn FGR green, as my stomach makes moves to reject its contents. In anticipation, I'd not eaten since the previous evening, took a placebo pill or two and packed enough chewing gum in my pockets to last a millennium.

Fears of pebble dashing the coach's smart interior were forgotten as we were lifted on a wave of noisy, good humoured optimism by the young ambassadors and their parent minders. The first part of the journey whizzed by as the M5/M6 traffic parted like the Red Sea and Compo kept everyone's brain occupied by a machine gun delivery of FGR general knowledge quizzes. Soon enough, we were stretching our limbs at Stratford Services.

During the course of our away trips, invariably we meet supporters of other teams, sometimes even the teams themselves. Exeter City, the Grecians, feature large in such impromptu gatherings, probably as they plough similar furrows up the M4 or M5/M6 to most of their away games. For the first time in my faulty memory, we were alone at rainy Stratford. An oddly curious feeling, not a scarf in sight save the green and black.

The trouble free onward journey meant we were at the Moss Rose by 1.30 pm as was Jokerman's Kendo Express carrying the core of hardened Rovers support. All in all some 120 souls. Much heel kicking as entrance to the ground did not begin until 2.00 pm.

Eventually, Foggy, Compo and I made our way to the Macclesfield Board Room where friendly, good old fashioned hospitality was afforded, and acquaintances renewed. At lunch, Chris Wintle nudged me – something about a guest behind me. As I turned my head (ever so subtle like) I think my eyes probably popped out of my head. Behind me was seated the prince of hairdryers – Sir Alex Ferguson, smiling and

**N**
**O**
**V**
**E**
**M**
**B**
**E**
**R**

enjoying chatting to his hosts and a number of youngsters who politely sought his autograph and some selfies.

Compo said I should get a picture with him and my book. No way – I couldn't do that. Oh, but I could! Usain Boult would have been trailing in my dash to get a copy from the coach. Then, as Sir Alex was temporarily without company, I moved in as Compo played paparazzi (or should that be paparazzo?). Either way, what a nice man Sir Alex is when confronted with a complete stranger thrusting a book! Why did I write it, what was it about and so on? Smile for the camera, handshakes, gift Sir Alex the book, all done. How was this day going to get any better?

Well, a loose ball in the match's second minute, then interplay between Darren Carter & Christian Doidge feeding Keanu Marsh-Brown was how. 0-1 and as it turned out, the winning goal. Throughout the match, Rovers supporters kept up a joyful din. Other results favoured Rovers too giving a decisive 9 point lead at the head of the table.

I'm told I was on the return trip of the coach. I don't remember it that way. Rather, I recall being hoovered into some sort of ethereal *Star Trek* teleporter and whooshed to my favourite sofa back home. One fantastic day.

## ROVERS ON THE STRETCH

*Jokerman*

A wet Saturday in November. The wipers swipe the windshield as Kendo guns the Express north to East Cheshire. For the Forest Green followers on board the weather surely cannot dampen the mood of excitement and optimism Mark Cooper's team has instilled this season. Following last Saturdays heart stopping climax against Aldershot, RJ's pronouncement was still echoing in the Nailsworth valley on Thursday. The victory lifted Rovers seven points clear at the summit of The National League.

It's destination Macclesfield this afternoon, home of the Hovis munchers and over seventy silk mills back in the day. The Silkmen demonstrated their rough side here last season crushing FGR 4-1. The travellers will be looking to readjust the balance today. The Moss Rose stadium has a scenic back drop of the surrounding hills, though this afternoon they are shrouded in dark storm clouds. Away fans are welcome to use the club lounge and over a pint or three the team sheets appear. Racine holds his place as Bennett is given the day off, Sinclair remains, Traore still on the injured list while Frear and Keanu both start.

The rain has ceased despite the threatening sky overhead as the Remembrance Day silence is held absolutely, prior to kick off. The game started in style for Forest Green. A sweeping move down field culminated in Doidge's tenacity winning a fifty-fifty ball and putting Keanu through on custodian Ross. He was never going to miss and fired the ball over him into the net. This triggered suitable acclaim from over a hundred away fans who were to give tremendous vocal support throughout to the accompaniment of a merciless drum.

Rovers soon settled into their possession game, Keanu shooting wide after clever interplay. There was little threat from Macclesfield as Rovers dominated, until an unfortunate clash between Noble and Lewis in a hard but fair challenge. Unfortunately for Lewis he was stretchered off with an ankle injury, Noble showing some anxiety for his opponent. Substitute Mackreth replaced Lewis and though Rovers continued to press, the reshuffled Macclesfield side began to give the visitors defence a sterner test.

Whitaker raced down the right but his low cross through the six yard box went unrewarded. Russell then played Russian roulette with a short goal kick, allowing Sampson possession, but his shot was weak and Russell recovered diving to his left. Winger Rowe was having some success against Wishart on the right and set up Halls but Clough was on hand to clear. Doidge replied for Rovers by playing in Keanu on the edge of the area but his goal bound shot was deflected away for a corner that was cleared.

Macclesfield finished the half strongly, Pinnock lashing the ball off McCombe's toe six yards out, while Carter was booked for a foul on Whitaker on the edge of the 'D'. The 'wall' stood strong and the danger was cleared as the half time whistle sounded.

Ground Hog Day for Rovers fans' discussion during the break. A single goal is always a nerve shredder. It was a slower start to the second half, Hancox hit a shot wide from distance for the home side while Sinclair with a rare opportunity powered a shot from the edge of the area, but it was a comfortable height for Ross to gather.

Forest Green were enjoying far less possession in the second period as Macclesfield sought a way back into the game. However although only attacking on the break they were creating the better chances. Keanu was out pacing his markers all afternoon and set up Frear with a cut back but his effort was blocked. Soon after Frear cut in from the left and his cross shot was fumbled over the bar by Ross. Hancox tested Russell from distance as the hour mark passed.

**N**
**O**
**V**
**E**
**M**
**B**
**E**
**R**

On seventy minutes Whitaker was booked for a foul on Noble. During the stoppage Kieffer Moore lined up, his footwear glowing all Halloween orange, to replace Doidge. The referee disallowed the change and restarted the game leaving the fourth official searching for a Geiger counter to check Moore's studs. Cooper protested but didn't risk a close encounter.

Rowe robbed Wishart on the right touchline and raced into the box, and from an acute angle forced Russell to beat the ball away for a corner that Clough cleared. Another Clough clearance found Noble who raced down the centre and slipped a pass to Keanu, on the overlap at full pace. He raced into the area and released a pile driver that Ross was equal to, saving with his legs.

It was Rovers last worthwhile effort and the final ten minutes they stood off and resisted the Macclesfield offence that ultimately lacked invention against the best defence in the division. Pinnock and especially Clough, whose physical prowess cannot be underestimated, gave fine performances.

It was still a relief to hear the final whistle for Forest Green fans and they were roundly applauded by their team for their vociferous encouragement. 20 games gone and Forest Green Rovers settle a score at Macclesfield.

## FGR AMBASSADOR REPORT
*Elsie Heslop, Sir William Romney Secondary School, Tetbury*
Elsie's inside view. On the 12th of November my dad and I went along with around 30 other ambassadors to go and support the Rovers up in Macclesfield. For me that's the furthest North I've ever been! Overall it took 3 and a ½ hours to get there and during our journey we were kept entertained by a variety of quizzes. Unfortunately we did absolutely rubbish, meaning that we didn't win any of the prizes; but oh well it was great fun anyway.

After that we had a quick pit stop in Stafford then we were back on the road again for the last hour. When we finally arrived there it was drizzling and we were kept standing outside of the stadium for 45 minutes before they let us in, which was a little bit rude; especially as they knew we were there. It's kind of hard to miss a large group of people wearing bright lime green clothing standing outside with a big drum. Eventually, we got in and I couldn't wait to have my portion of chips then when we got to the food area, there were none! So I settled for a sausage roll instead which was the wise decision as it was very tasty.

Of course the 12th of November is during the weekend of remembrance, for those who died in the war, and because of this there was a minutes silence before the game started. I thought everyone was very respectful as you could hear a pin drop, except from the traffic, but no-one was fidgeting either and it was the perfect way to start a game with total respect.

When the game started, we were instantly on the attack and after just 2 minutes a brilliant cross from Christian Doidge lead to Keanu Marsh-Brown scoring the first and only goal of the game. However, tension grew as Macclesfield were looking stronger but FGR put up some great shots too. Thankfully Macclesfield didn't score and our early goal lead us to victory.

This felt like the best game I have ever been too for me as I felt more involved and I just want to do it all over again. We were right next to the drum joining in with most of the singing and it felt great. Big thanks to Phil Butterworth who organised the whole thing, although it's made me want to go on more away games, which I will be begging my dad to do but we'll see. Obviously, the result was the icing on the cake and the players and manager coming over to thank the 125 fans who made the 3 and a ½ hour journey really topped it off: it was a great day out!

## Saturday 19.11.16
## FGR 2 Lincoln City 3
### LATE GOALS DENY ROVERS AT THE DEATH
*Richard Joyce*

Two late goals saw Forest Green's eleven match unbeaten run come to an abrupt end against second place Lincoln City at The New Lawn.

A lunchtime kick-off for the BT Sport cameras looked all but set to see Rovers extend their marvellous run at the top of the table after Christian Doidge and Keanu Marsh-Brown had put Mark Cooper's men two goals up.

However the Imps fought back to end their run of consecutive defeats against FGR. Alex Woodyard drew a goal back for them, and they then equalised on 89 minutes when Luke Waterfall blasted home.

And they capped their victory to silence The New Lawn crowd when Sean Raggett rose highest in the box to nod home in stoppage time.

It had been Forest Green who dominated the early exchanges with Darren Carter forcing two good opportunities that saw the former West Bromwich Albion man see his header saved by Paul Farman, and powerful strike go just over the bar.

**N
O
V
E
M
B
E
R**

After Lincoln's strike duo of Matt Rhead and Theo Robinson had combined for the latter to fire on the Rovers goal, the game's first goal saw Doidge head FGR in front.

He got on the end of Daniel Wishart's excellent delivery from the left hand side to open the scoring.

Waterfall attempted to equalise for the away side, only to see his effort tipped over by Russell, while at the opposite end of the pitch Farman pushed away Marsh-Brown's dangerous low free kick.

It was Forest Green who had dominated the first half, but Lincoln rose to the occasion in the second period and came out on top.

However that was after Marsh-Brown was involved in two huge opportunities at the start of the half. The first saw Bradley Wood's vital interception deny him the chance to set the ball on a plate for Elliott Frear, while the second saw him double the lead.

He drove home from 20 yards with an accurate strike into the bottom corner after Frear had laid the ball on for him on the edge of the area.

It looked like FGR were all set to add to their brilliant recent run, but Lincoln had other ideas, and Woodyard reacted to a rebound to fire a goal back.

Russell made a brilliant save to deny the visitors substitute Adam Marriott, but after Ethan Pinnock had been denied by a good stop himself, Lincoln equalised.

A touch from Rhead set the ball up nicely for Waterfall who hammered home inside the box.

With hardly any time to think, what looked set to be another three points were snatched away, when another set piece saw Lincoln score again to send their travelling fans home delighted.

Nathan Arnold's corner was headed home inside the six yard box by Raggett to inflict only Forest Green's third league defeat of the season, ahead of Tuesday's visit of Tranmere.

**FOREST FELLED**

*Jokerman*

Having failed to take all three points from near rivals Dagenham recently, Forest Green Rovers will look to be more decisive at home against their closest rivals Lincoln City this afternoon. The Bomber County boys are in good form and qualify along with Rovers as main contenders for the league title, bearing in mind, what the headline giveth the small print can taketh away.

These next two games are an opportunity for Forest Green to kick into touch the whispers that they are unable to see off the stronger teams. The car park full signs are up, the bars are rammed an hour before kick-off and BT cameras are in situ to broadcast what is beyond doubt the Match of the Day in Non-League football.

The man is here but he no longer brings his dog; things have changed. Manager Mark Cooper keeps the same starting eleven he picked for last week's win at Macclesfield, though Kieffer Moore has gone south for the winter. Traore and Bennett return to the bench. A cold northerly wind increases the chill factor as the teams take the field.

Forest Green start the brighter and a Noble free kick is headed on by Doidge to Carter whose header lacks power and Lincoln Keeper Farman gathers. On ten minutes Carter is again on target with a header saved but a minute later skims the bar with a powerful shot from the edge of the box after good build up play by Racine and Noble. Frear then drives the ball in to the near post, Farman blocks away with Doidge challenging. It's twenty four minutes before Lincoln can launch an attack when Power finds Robinson on the edge of the area. The striker hits the ball hard across Russell who makes a smart save diving to his right.

A minute later Rovers take a deserved lead. Noble hits a diagonal pass to Wishart on the left, he drives forward and hits an inch perfect cross to Doidge, unmarked, who heads past the exposed Farman from close range. The Rovers fans are up as the drummer gives it the stick. Good work by Frear sees his shot blocked out to Carter who sends a screamer just over the bar as Rovers continue to dominate. A free kick from a central position twenty five yards out by Keanu has Farman diving low to push the ball around the left hand post, and as the half ends Rovers fans are again thinking it should be more than a single goal lead.

Lincoln had to step it up after a poor first half and indeed they started the second period with some intent. Power living up to his name did just that in the first minute, racing through the entire Rovers defence into the area, where only a timely foot in by Sinclair averted the danger. Lincoln had subbed Anderson for Hawkridge to shake things up and the opening minutes put pressure on Rovers.

On fifty six minutes Clough broke up an attack and launched a terrific pass up field to Keanu who raced clear of the Lincoln defence into the area, but instead of striking at goal he tried to cut the ball back to Frear, but it was blocked away and the chance was gone. 65mins finally saw Rovers increase their lead.

**N O V E M B E R**

A corner by Noble on the right skimmed off Pinnock's head and came out wide to Frear on the left, who cut inside and played a precise pass to Keanu on the edge of the area. He took a touch and threaded a low shot inside the left hand post. The supporters behind the goal went into overdrive.

The 'daylight' lasted three minutes when Noble made a fatal error passing straight to Lincoln's Arnold, who rushed goalwards striking a shot that Pinnock did well to block, but the ball broke to Woodyard following in, and he duly struck the ball past Russell to put his side right back in the game.

The game became stretched and on seventy minutes Woodyard picked out Marriott in acres of space inside the box. He looked sure to score but Russell somehow scooped the ball out and it was blasted clear by his defence. Rovers were looking shaky. A Noble free kick then just eluded Pinnock as the home side fought back, but it was Lincoln who were looking the more dangerous and Whitehouse, free at the back post, was only denied by a terrific block from Clough.

Traore replaced Noble in an effort to steady the defence and calm things down. This appeared to be working and Pinnock placed a header that saw Farman slow to react. The ball was scrambled away to Traore, whose shot was beaten away as the clock ticked down. Keanu then tried to bend a shot past Farman with Carter on the edge of the area screaming for the pass.

Then came what was arguably a pivotal move. Bennett replaced Frear on eighty eight minutes in what looked like 'how many buses can we fit in?' It turned the Forest Green defence into a shambles, a minute later Lincoln were level. A throw on the right into the area found Waterfall unmarked, he turned and fired the ball past Russell inside the right hand post sending the three hundred Imps fans behind the goal wild. The board went up five added minutes, Lincoln only needed one. A corner again on the right, Habergham crossed the ball precisely to Raggett who bullets a header into the bottom right hand corner of the net unopposed. Understandably this sends Lincoln players and fans alike into dreamland. Rovers' fans turned a whiter shade of pale and found it difficult to get a grip on what just happened.

The referee blew the whistle on a game that saw Forest Green surrender a lead with few minutes remaining. The manner of the defeat and the mistakes made will make for a painful few days as Cooper works to restore confidence in time for Tuesdays encounter with Tranmere Rovers. The situation is far from desperate with Forest Green still clear at the top of the league. Tuesday evening presents the players with a quick opportunity to put things right and prevent the whispers getting louder.

## FGR AMBASSADOR REPORT
*Ethan Parry, Foxmoor Primary School, Stroud*
Hello, my name is Ethan Parry. I am 11 years old and I attend Foxmoor Primary School in Stroud.

I play football for Forest Green under 11's and since becoming School Ambassador for the club, I have enjoyed becoming more involved with Forest Green. As well as supporting Forest Green I also support Manchester City.

On Saturday 19th November Forest Green Rovers played Lincoln City at the New Lawn in an early kick off, televised match. Forest Green dominated in the first half and soon a brilliant goal from Christian Doidge put Forest Green ahead. Forest Green continued to mount on the pressure and it wasn't long before a great strike from Keanu Marsh-Brown put us two goals up.

However Lincoln City fought back and Alex Woodyard gave Lincoln a glimpse of hope with a rebound goal. As full time drew closer a second goal from Lincoln seemed inevitable with their constant pressure on Forest Green. Soon the equaliser came from a well set up goal, finished by Waterfall. A draw seemed a fair result however Lincoln had other ideas and in the 89th minute Raggett snatched the 3 points from Mark Cooper's Forest Green.

## Tuesday 22.11.16
## FGR 2 Tranmere Rovers 2
## DOIDGE AND NOBLE STRIKES CANCELLED OUT
*Richard Joyce*
A brilliant night of National League football saw Forest Green and Tranmere Rovers produce a superb 2-2 draw at The New Lawn.

Twice FGR led, but twice the visitors came back to earn a point on a wet Tuesday night in Gloucestershire, as two of the fifth tiers stand out sides came together for a entertaining midweek contest.

From as early as the third minute Mark Cooper's men led via Christian Doidge, but after Lois Maynard replied instantly, Liam Noble's sweet strike restored the Forest Green lead.

Former New Lawn favourite James Norwood spoiled the party in the second half though as he struck to earn Tranmere a share of the spoils.

It was Noble's excellent guided pass that allowed Doidge to open the scoring in a hectic opening, as the Welsh striker coolly slotted home.

**N
O
V
E
M
B
E
R**

But the Tranmere response was swift and Maynard rose highest at the back post to head the away side level just two minutes later.

A bright opening saw Darren Carter and Keanu Marsh-Brown denied soon after, while Tranmere keeper Scott Davies produced a stunning one handed stop on 14 minutes from Marsh-Brown's hit that looked destined for the net after Daniel Wishart had slammed a shot onto the post.

Forest Green's persistence in front of the Tranmere goal paid off near to the half hour mark when Noble steered his team into the lead again.

He picked up Doidge's lay-off on the edge of the area and guided the ball home triumphantly for what was a definite reward for FGR's attacking enthusiasm.

Noble had another terrific effort on 42 minutes that flew just wide at the end of a eye-catching opening 45 minutes.

Micky Mellon's Tranmere came into the tie more in the second half, and were it not for a vital block by Charlie Clough, Portsmouth loanee Ben Tollitt would have come close to drawing parity once again.

After substitute Norwood had teamed up with fellow ex-FGR man Andy Mangan for a shot that trickled wide, the former scored the only goal of the second half with a terrific finish, as he powered an effort into the bottom corner.

Keen to snatch back the lead, Forest Green hit the post again. This time it was Marsh-Brown who was denied by the upright after he had got on the end of a teasing Carter ball into the area.

Another huge chance minutes later saw Doidge fail to score his second when he came across Marsh-Brown's delivery into the danger zone, as the game opened up in the final quarter of an hour.

Noble blasted over, and at the other end Tollitt came close, with Mangan seeing another attempt blocked away for a corner.

Sam Russell was called upon to make two key saves at the death. He first denied former teammate Norwood, and then kept out Mangan's drive after the striker had burst through, to ensure both teams shared the points in what was an eventful and appealing encounter.

### ANOTHER GAME OF CARDIOLOGY AT THE NEW LAWN
*Jokerman*

It's been three days since Forest Green Rovers took their eye off the ball against Lincoln City. There can be few more stomach churning ways to lose a game than was witnessed on Saturday. From the positive point of view this is the finest squad of players ever assembled to represent the football club. The support has grown and in turn understandably the expectation. This season has confirmed their potential and the team deserve to be market leaders in the race for the title.

Tonight's game against Tranmere Rovers and the subsequent fixtures will define the character of Mark Cooper's team as they react to adversity. On a damp, cold but rain free evening the sprinkler system is redundant, the playing surface having been swamped in the past twenty four hours.

A crowd of over two thousand give the sides a rousing reception, three hundred and fifty have made the journey from The Wirral. In their white away strip Tranmere strike a physical presence, none more so than McNulty whose shirt could sail a yacht. Bennett replaces Frear in the starting line-up for Rovers,the only change from Saturday.

The game started at a hundred miles an hour and didn't really slow down for the duration. Sinclair gave the ball to Noble who hit the first of so many precision passes inside the defender to the overlapping Bennett. He hit a low cross in to Doidge, like quicksilver he flashed the ball into the net past keeper Davies.

Tranmere were stung but hit back immediately, winning a corner from the kick off that was headed down and forced Russell to tip the ball over the bar. The second kick played short to Ridehalgh who crossed for Maynard to place a deft header inside the right hand post. Two goals in 5mins.

Sixth minute a forty yard diagonal pass from Noble to the feet of Bennett and he crossed for Doidge who brought a magnificent save from Davies. The ball broke to Keanu but his shot was blocked away by some frantic defending. Rovers were relentless and opened up space for Noble who fired wide from the edge of the box. Doidge put a header over the bar from a Sinclair cross and Keanu tested Davies from range. Tranmere staged a brief raid when Maynard brought a comfortable save from Russell but Rovers continued the onslaught. Noble put Wishart down the left he drove into the area and smashed the ball past Davies only to see it rebound off the upright. Keanu was on hand and hit a scorcher goalwards only for Davies to again save his side from going behind with still only fifteen minutes on the clock.

Tranmere were only breaking in snatches as Rovers kept up the pressure winning the corner count with Pinnock heading one narrowly over the bar. On 29mins Forest Green took a deserved lead following a probing series of passes that culminated in Doidge slipping the ball to Noble on the edge of the area. He curled a delightful left foot strike into the top left hand corner of the net. A goal of quality that sent the home fans nuts. The same player zipped a shot just wide of the angle as the first

**N**
**O**
**V**
**E**
**M**
**B**
**E**
**R**

half ended. A breathless first half of attacking football from Rovers that saw Tranmere fans thankful to their custodian Davies for keeping them in the game.

Like Lincoln on Saturday Tranmere started the second half with a lot more energy and knocked Forest Green off their stride. They began to redress the balance of possession and aggression. Tollitt Tranmere's tall striker tested Russell early on and then, on fifty six minutes, looked sure to score only to be denied by a timely intervention by Clough. It was Rovers on the back foot now and on fifty seven minutes Tranmere manager Mellon replaced Cook with ex- FGR favourite Norwood. Another ex- Rovers striker Mangan put a shot wide from a good position on the hour mark.

Rovers replied when Keanu raced through but hit the ball wildly over the bar to the angst of the supporters behind the goal. On 66mins the same player was castigated when losing possession in his own half, which resulted in the ball being played across the edge of the area to Norwood, who struck a low shot into the net past Russell from fifteen yards. Nemesis. The travelling fans behind the goal stepped up a gear.

Three minutes later since being under the cosh for much of the second period Forest Green ripped the Tranmere defence open. Wishart and Carter attacked down the left channel drawing the defence. Carter then cut the ball back past the drifting iceberg McNulty to Keanu in oceans of space twelve yards out with the goal yawning. He nodded off and struck the ball against the post. Worse was to follow on seventy minutes, Bennett blazed down the right and hit a low cross through the six yard box to Doidge coming in on the back post. The striker three feet from the goal line allowed the ball to run under his foot and the swear box ranneth over.

Tranmere threatened to capitalise on their good fortune but the Rovers defence battled gamely. During four minutes of added time the visitors could have snatched the points when Mangan was through on Russell, but the big man denied him turning the ball over the bar. The referee blew the whistle to end a superb game of football that deserved a higher stage.

For Forest Green, Traore and Sinclair along with Noble were outstanding. Arguably this is Cooper's strongest eleven though many would prefer Moore and even Jefford to still be available. A point gained or two lost, whichever way you cut it, FGR are still top of the league. It is however five points lost in four days to their nearest rivals, whispers getting louder.

Time to kill some dragons.

## FGR AMBASSADOR REPORT
*Matthew Binns, Cam Everlands Primary School*

The mist rolled in over the New Lawn for an exciting evening kick off. The players came out of the changing room and the match was on. It couldn't have been a better start for Rovers, as a beautiful pass from Noble to Doidge turned into a goal. However, the crowd was quietened when 2 minutes later Maynard equalised for Tranmere. For the first 20 minutes, Forest Green were walloping shots at the Tranmere goal. Twenty nine minutes into the game, Noble put FGR back in-front with a curling shot over the defenders and into the net. When 2 minutes extra time was given, Steven McNulty was awarded a yellow card. Twenty minutes into the second half, Tranmere's sub Norwood (the ex FGR player) equalised again for Tranmere. This match left us with a 2-2 draw and an outstanding attendance of 2389 with a strong Tranmere presence of 349 fans. Carlsberg named Drissa Traore man of the match in this action packed game, which most of the fans will agree with. With things getting closer at the top, the next few matches are crucial for our League winner ambitions.

## Saturday 26.11.16
## Wrexham 3 FGR 1
## WREXHAM HOLD ON TO FRUSTRATE ROVERS
*Richard Joyce*

A patient Wrexham side executed their game plan perfectly to inflict a rare defeat on Forest Green Rovers at the Racecourse Ground.

Although FGR were dominant throughout, Wrexham saw a surprising first half lead give them a huge advantage, as Darren Carter's early penalty miss denied Forest Green the chance to secure an early lead.

And despite the midfielders second half header, FGR couldn't break down a robust North Wales side whose on loan goalkeeper Luke Coddington played his part in helping them to victory as Gerry McDonagh netted in stoppage time.

Having controlled possession against a side happy to sit back and soak up pressure from the start, Rovers were handed the ideal opportunity to score early on with a penalty on eight minutes.

Coddington's diving save denied Carter though from 12 yards, and it lifted the home support, who took the lead on 15 minutes when a rare foray forward saw Shaun Harrad glance a good header past Sam Russell.

**N
O
V
E
M
B
E
R**

Huddersfield loanee Coddington made a fantastic reaction save midway through the half to keep his side ahead when Liam Noble's shot flew low towards his goal.

And the hosts doubled their advantage on the half hour mark as McDonagh had the simple task of finishing from close range after FGR failed to clear the ball inside the six-yard box.

Wrexham's game plan had worked excellently up to the break, but with a new system first introduced towards the end of the opening 45 minutes, Mark Cooper's men kept up the pressure into the second period.

Debutant Manny Monthe saw his header from a corner shortly after coming on go wide, and after Charlie Clough had nodded off target, Carter got a deserved goal back.

He found the net with a header from close range after Monthe's aerial effort himself had flashed across the face of goal.

The final quarter of an hour promised a huge 15 minutes for FGR. Carter saw a shot slip wide, while Coddington made another tremendous stop to stretch and keep out Matt Tubbs' effort towards the bottom corner.

Carter came within inches of scoring with another header from Keanu Marsh-Brown's corner, as McDonagh almost added to the home team's tally with a right footed shot that was blasted off target.

Another Coddington save prevented Ethan Pinnock from levelling the affair in Forest Green's final chance in stoppage time.

But there was to be still one more goal – and it went to the hosts. With FGR bodies stranded high up the pitch, Wrexham broke clear, and McDonagh kept his cool brilliantly to round Russell and fire into an empty net.

### DESTINATION WREXHAM
*Rambling Man*

We keyboard warriors are not usually slow to point out when our players are perceived to be out of form. In fairness, I've rarely known Rovers fans to 'get after' a player at matches. We tend to be quiet, sometimes prone to the odd moan, though even that is usually in sadness rather than anger. It is the excellent Forum that dissects players' ratings.

But that begs the question, do supporters lose their form? If so, who does what to remedy the situation? Does Coops take the person aside and tell him (or her) he's to be rested for the next game, or in the worst case, tell him that he will not stand in the way of his support being transferred to a new club. "Where is this going R M?" editor Rich is thinking.

Glad he asked. The fact is, I've been a tad jaded of late. Too many games, too much book flogging, trauma sparked by the Lincoln City nightmare? Who knows? Certainly, when I look back over recent games there have been worrying symptoms: no appetite for Em's lovely grub, out of time with my clapping, forgetting words to familiar chants. I needed time away from 'the lads'.

So I self-prescribed a long weekend in Antibes with Mrs R M, to visit first born and her *young man*, who have lived in that picturesque Napoleonic town for 4 years. That would still involve some additional sacrifice though. SFS (Support Fatigue Syndrome) needs the patient to go cold turkey. Easier said than done.

Despite nearby Monaco and Nice being first and second in French League 1, and having home games on Saturday & Sunday respectively, and local derbies to boot (v Marseilles & Bastia), I resolutely stayed off the footy. Nor did I tune in to Bob Hunt's dulcet tones on the valve radio.

Instead the four of us drove inland to take in local Provencal villages, supped the local wines and ales and guzzled copious amounts of bar food. I can honestly say that I did not pick up the football results until Sunday, due in no small part to the complimentary Brandy *monsieur le patron* insisted we drink after our Saturday night meal, and just possibly the after effects of Antibes' infamous Absinthe Bar. So, I was granted a stay of execution in respect of Rovers' reverse at Wrexham.

A sufferer of SFS does not welcome news of unexpected defeat, certainly not one who is hung over. For the second time this season, Compo, Foggy & Clegg had failed to do as they'd promised – look after my team in my absence (Dover being the other occasion).

Strangely however, I felt serene and at peace. Sure it was not welcome to hear that Rovers had missed a 7th minute penalty and succumbed to a Wrexham team on a miserable trot. Yet I told myself that there was nothing to concern me and that I was in a safe place, well removed from footballing depression in the Five Valleys. More than that, I would return and work a change of fortunes for my team, no danger. Clearly the prescription had worked.

After all, Absinthe makes the heart grow fonder.

## FGR PULL UP LAME AT THE RACECOURSE

*Jokerman*

Statistics do not favour Forest Green when they have crossed the dyke to take on the Celts. As those on board Kendo's express head north to the border crossing they are under no illusion that it will be easy to contain and fleece the natives. Wrexham are underachievers at this level and have become unpredictable, such have been their form fluctuations.

One point from six has not impressed Forest Green manager Mark Cooper. With loanee Kieffer Moore scoring goals for fun on the south coast your man immediately signs a central defender, ships out keeper Maxted to Guiseley and is in discussions with an unnamed striker. A mover and shaker extraordinaire he keeps his squad on that hot tin roof though to some it must feel like the burning deck.

Plenty for fans to speculate over as Kendo reels off the miles. The early cloud retreated to leave clear blue sky for much of the journey and the sun was shining as the coach pulled in to The Racecourse car park. In contrast the club's bar is housed in a windowless dungeon beneath the stand where Real Ale is noticeable by its absence, though prices are favourable.

The team news announces a similar line-up for Rovers that drew with Tranmere on Tuesday and recent signing Manny Monthe is on the bench. A crowd of nearly three and a half thousand were present as the game kicked off with the sun blinding the sixty plus Rovers supporters in the away corner of the ancient stand. What should have been a dream start for the visitors quickly turned into a nightmare when, eight minutes in, Noble was impeded in the area and the referee had no hesitation pointing to the spot. Up stepped Carter to face Wrexham keeper Coddington. Carter hit the ball low to the right, Coddington guessed correctly and blocked the ball over the bar.

For the Forest Green supporters those heart murmurings started all over again. Rovers kept the pressure on and Keanu blazed the ball over the bar following a cross from Bennett. 15mins saw the first worthwhile attack from Wrexham and Rovers wilted. A loose ball in the box was not dealt with and cleared out only as far as Rooney, who whipped in a cross from the right hand corner of the area that skimmed off Harrad's head and flew low into the left hand corner of the net.

Forest Green were stung and went about levelling things up. They came closest when Noble struck a ferocious shot from distance that forced Coddington to make a fine save. Keanu then ended some good build up play by hitting the ball the wrong side of the right hand post from twenty yards.

Wrexham, lifted by their goal, were defying recent form and certainly not lying down in the face of their opponents' superior ball retention ability. On 30mins they delivered another sucker punch. A ball crossed into the box fell to Evans on the six yard line. He seemed sure to score, but his shot was brilliantly saved by Russell who blocked his shot away, but McDonagh was on hand to slam the loose ball past him into the net. As Russell retrieved the ball the empty disused derelict gloom of the terrace behind him was apt.

Rovers were now suitably stunned and anxiously seeking a way back into the game. On thirty eight minutes a newsletter appeared from the touchline and was relayed eventually to Carter. At that stage of proceedings it was probably to phone a friend. A promising move ended with Noble creating an opening but Doidge was fractionally offside. The half time break left Rovers fans to reflect on a missed penalty and despite their clever interplay there was nothing to show. Wrexham had exposed defensive frailties and left Cooper to face an uncomfortable dressing room for his team talk.

He had to gamble and Tubbs replaced Sinclair for the restart. It was Wrexham who started the quicker and it was left to Pinnock, who started as he meant to go on, with a tremendous block inside the box to deny a killer blow.

Rovers dominated possession for the second period without success and around the hour Mark Cooper replaced Wishart with new signing Monthe. He made an immediate impact leaping to put a free header wide inside the area from a Keanu cross. Rovers then won a series of corners and it seemed all were wasted to the frustration of the Fans. It must be said the Drum Troop were giving fantastic unwavering support throughout.

The breakthrough came on 68mins. Noble hit a cross from the right to the back post where Monthe headed back across goal to Carter, who duly nodded the ball inside the right hand post from close range. Rovers went all out on the offensive with Noble everywhere orchestrating the attacks. Wrexham were attacking on the break as Rovers pressed for the second goal, but they were thwarted time and again by Pinnock, who was having a tremendous game. He also added to the attack and was injured when denied by a desperate block.

Robert replaced the tiring Doidge and had a shot well saved by Coddrington and Tubbs thought he had scored with a turn and shot only for the keeper to fingertip the ball round the post. Throwing the whole kitchen at Wrexham and camped in their half they were always prone to the counter and so it proved in time added on. 93mins McDonagh went clear with Rovers defence in desperate pursuit. He carved his way into the penalty area and easily beat Russell to bring the curtain down.

**N**
**O**
**V**
**E**
**M**
**B**
**E**
**R**

Starved of success the home fans were delirious with joy. The third goal was harsh on Rovers defence who had done well in the second half.

For all their dominance it's goals that win matches and Rovers came up short. It was disappointing for the magnificent few that travelled and one from nine means Forest Green's tenure at the top hangs by a thread until Tuesday. Form will always slip, it is avoiding the landslide that is key. With cup games intruding it will be three weeks before the next league fixture. Three weeks for Mark Cooper to put his players back on track to regain the initiative that has been lost.

A strangely football starved month saw only 2 League games plus FA Trophy success over Truro City after a replay. Off the pitch, Coops had decided to ring the changes with more players going and coming than you could shake a stick at. Most notably, club captain Aarran Racine was shipped out on loan and Charlie Clough sold to Barnet, as the iconic centre back partnership was consigned to New Lawn history. Loanees joined the fight, including 19 year old manager's son Charlie. Rovers ended the year in a gloomy place with a chaotic 4-3 defeat at Torquay United on Boxing Day, probably their season's lowest ebb. Since 27th August, 3rd position was as low as Rovers had slipped, yet for all the angst played out amongst concerned supporters, 3rd was as low as the team would go all season. The truth is, Rovers would be haunted by the Lincoln City home defeat and the 'what ifs' it posed, all season long.

*But how am I supposed to feel*
*With all the games we just can't steal.*
*And I can't thank my lucky stars*
*Cause we're not as good as we like to think we are.*

(Excerpt of Voodoobluesman catching the mood with his reworking of Dean Friedman's 'Lucky Stars')

**Saturday 10.12.16**
**FGR 1 Truro City 1 (FA Trophy 1st round)**
**TRURO HIT BACK TO MAKE IT TROPHY STALEMATE**
*Richard Joyce*
Keanu Marsh-Brown's early second half goal wasn't enough for Forest Green to see off Truro City in the FA Trophy, and Rovers will travel to Cornwall on Tuesday for a replay in search of a place in the second round.

Marsh-Brown's finish after the break had given Mark Cooper's men the lead in a game FGR dominated, although Andrew Neal's equaliser from a corner ensured sixth tier Truro secured a draw and another opportunity on home turf in midweek.

A first half littered with FGR chances couldn't see Rovers break through. Early on Christian Doidge's header was saved by Martin Rice in the Truro goal, while the former Torquay stopper did well again to save from Marsh-Brown after he had cut inside.

**D**
**E**
**C**
**E**
**M**
**B**
**E**
**R**

Speculative long range strikes from Darren Carter failed to threaten before Rob Sinclair's back-to-back corners kicks were very nearly forced home by Ethan Pinnock and Charlie Clough.

Truro centre back Aaron Bentley made a vital clearance from off the line on 37 minutes to ensure his side maintained their clean sheet to deny Fabien Robert who had stooped to head at goal.

Despite having limited opportunities in the half, Truro almost took the lead shortly before the break.

Danger man Niall Thompson latched onto Neale's forward pass and saw his driving run end with a right footed shot that hammered the foot of Sam Russell's right hand post.

Patient Forest Green didn't take long to go in front after half time as Marsh-Brown broke the deadlock.

Sinclair's brilliant mazy run saw him work the ball to the forward, who finished confidently to give his side the lead.

Rovers' lead was almost doubled not long after when another Doidge header from a Sinclair corner was saved well by Rice.

The deficit was however halved on 73 minutes. A Truro corner, whipped into the near post, was glanced in by Neale to draw the visitors level.

Having dominated for so long it was suddenly FGR who were on the back foot for the final ten minutes as Truro sensed an opportunity to secure a late win.

Zane Sole saw his strike blocked away, while Neale missed a massive opportunity to break FGR hearts on 90 minutes as he blasted over Thompson's terrific pull back.

Another big opening fell the way of the Cornish team's goal scorer in stoppage time. But again he couldn't take advantage on a soggy pitch as FGR held on for another crack at progressing in the competition on Tuesday evening.

## ROVERS HANG ON FOR A DRAW

*Jokerman*

Since the winds of fortune have shifted at Forest Green, and the advent of two promotion places, for at least half the clubs in The National League the FA Trophy has become a sideshow to the rush for the play-offs. Its fixture-crunching format near seasons end, plus the FA lumping it with The Vase as a BOGOF event, has arguably not added to its appeal.

Be that as it may FGR manager Mark Cooper has a pedigree in this competition and the 'double' is not beyond the potential of his squad. In today's 1st Round Truro City from National League South arrive at TNL hoping to cause an upset. The weather forecast for an extremely wet day proved correct and this lop-sided fixture against lower league opposition led many to opt for Christmas shopping instead. There was certainly no crush at the bar in The Green Man.

It would be difficult for Cooper to pick anything other than a strong side from his squad and only Robert for Traore was a change from the usual suspects. Doidge led the attack supported by Keanu. Recent loan signing Charlie Cooper was on the bench.

The rain clouds were swirling like smoke over the stands as the teams paraded, underfoot going would be testing. Predictably Forest Green bossed the game from the first whistle. An early corner ended with Sinclair blasting the ball over the bar as the fog thickened.

It was ten minutes before Rovers had an effort on target when Noble crossed to the back post to Robert, whose header was gathered under the bar by Truro keeper Rice. Carter's shot was too high from distance and a good run by Wishart down the left ended with Keanu forcing Rice to save his shot low down.

On twenty minutes Carter again blazed the ball high into the mist which seemed to take the hint and began to lift. A good quick exchange on the edge of the box between Doidge and Noble was saved by Rice as the Rovers skipper failed to find enough power on his effort. Clough had a shot blocked and Rice was stranded when a shot from Doidge went just wide of the left hand post. For all their possession, as half time approached Rovers could easily have gone in at half time a goal down.

A rare break away by Neal through the middle caught Rovers flat. He slipped an inch perfect ball to Thompson who raced into the box and beat Russell with a cross shot that struck the foot of the left hand post. It was the nearest either side had come to scoring as the half time whistle sounded. Rovers build up had been lethargic in the final third leaving the six hundred fans disgruntled over the interval.

Five minutes into the second half they finally made the break through. Sinclair weaved his way along the eighteen yard line before threading a pass to Keanu inside the area left side. He took a touch and hit the ball low through the legs of Rice into the net. The FGR fans behind the goal finally woke up.

Rovers went close to a second on fifty eight minutes when a Sinclair corner was met by Doidge whose downward header was well saved by Rice on the goal line. It was around the hour mark when conditions began to deteriorate rapidly as the incessant rain began to take its toll with surface water appearing all over the pitch.

**D
E
C
E
M
B
E
R**

It turned the contest into a war of attrition and Rovers did not win it. Kelly and Cooper replaced Carter and Wishart on sixty seven minutes. Truro began to look dangerous with their breakaway attacks and began to win corners from which they profited. 72mins a corner from the left saw the visitors level. Sole dropped the ball into a melee on the six yard line and diminutive striker Neal flicked the ball past Russell. The fifty Truro fans behind the goal were duly rewarded for their loyalty and Forest Green were embarrassed.

Keanu replied by hitting the side netting from an acute angle but Truro had the better chances as the game entered the closing stages. Sole was picked out with a cross only twelve yards out but his shot was deflected away for a corner with five minutes remaining. And on ninety minutes Thompson, set up Neal on the penalty spot with his back to goal. He managed to turn but thundered the ball miles over the bar when a cool head would have won the game. The same player in added time took a pass from Allen and with only Russell to beat from the edge of the box, he lost his footing in the by now atrocious conditions and the chance was lost.

The game ended with the rain still pouring down. Not a good afternoon for those who braved it all as they headed home into the gloom. Mark Cooper will persevere with his style of play which has taken his team into contention. Recent flaws in the final third will need to be hammered out and supporters must hope the answer lies with his recent signings as the Dover game looms.

**Tuesday 13.12.16**
**Truro City 0 FGR 1 (FA Trophy 1st round replay)**
**CARTER STUNNER EARNS FGR TROPHY PROGRESS**
*Richard Joyce*
Darren Carter came off the bench to score in extra time with an exquisite strike to send Forest Green into the next round of the FA Trophy

Rovers will advance to face league rivals Chester next month after a gruelling first round replay with National League South Truro City who pushed Mark Cooper's men all the way.

Following Saturday's stalemate at The New Lawn, FGR made the lengthy midweek journey south, and were rewarded for their persistence when Carter slammed home with a rocket of a strike.

Dale Bennett saw red at the death in a tense affair which means Forest Green will now travel to the Lookers Vauxhall Stadium in mid-January, after Chester earned a late replay win themselves on the same night against Witton Albion.

Man of the match Charlie Cooper earned his first start since joining on loan from Birmingham, and the 19-year-old set Christian Doidge up for a header that was cleared off the line in the first half.

Cooper's swooping cross was then almost headed home at a difficult angle by Ethan Pinnock, meanwhile the half ended with Keanu Marsh-Brown blasting over from Charlie Clough's low cross.

Immediately after the interval Rovers had the ball in the back of the net. Doidge's shot was however ruled out by the linesman who deemed him to be in an offside position.

After Jamie Richards had gone close for the hosts, Ollie Knowles saw big opportunities go amiss for the sixth tier side, as Doidge fired wide on 72 minutes following a speedy breakaway involving Liam Noble.

The relatively quiet Sam Russell was called into action to make a good save to his left to prevent Niall Thompson's deflected strike from finding the bottom corner, and the same players right footed shot minutes later was straight at the FGR goalkeeper.

As the game edged nearer an additional 30 minutes, Rovers tried to win it late on. Clough was denied by Martin Rice's block, Manny Monthe's header was then also blocked, while Richards's late attempt from a Zane Sole corner for Truro went just over.

The beginning of extra time saw substitute Elliott Frear force an early effort on the home team's goal. And they themselves hit the bar on 95 minutes.

Doidge and Marcus Kelly saw efforts go close at the end of the first half of extra time, but it didn't take long for the deadlock to be broken on 108 minutes.

Cooper's pass into the path of Carter was hammered home outstandingly by the experienced midfielder for the game's first and only goal.

Truro upped their urgency as they chased a leveller. Courageous FGR defending denied them though, although there was to be one late twist, as Bennett was sent off right at the end by referee Wayne Barratt.

**Saturday 17.12.16**
**FGR 1 Dover Athletic 1**
**MOORE STRIKES LATE ON TO EARN HOME POINT**
*Richard Joyce*
Kieffer Moore marked his first game back at Forest Green following a return from his loan spell at Torquay United with a stoppage time equaliser on an eventful day at The New Lawn,

**D
E
C
E
M
B
E
R**

The towering forward notched his tenth goal of the season late on to earn a point as he turned home Shamir Mullings knock down at the death.

Moses Emmanuel's header earlier in the second half had given Dover the lead, but Mark Cooper's men fought back in the Nailsworth fog to draw.

The fog made life difficult for both teams, but the game itself was called into question, when during the warm up a local grid connected power cut delayed kick-off for 45 minutes with the floodlights out and power down in the stadium.

When things did getting going however it was FGR who worked the first opportunity, but Charlie Clough was unable to get a good connection on Charlie Cooper's delivery from a corner.

Debutant Shamir Mullings blasted wide just before the half hour mark, while shortly after Cooper made a brilliant block to prevent Dover's Aswad Thomas from hammering in at the back post.

Mullings, making his first appearance since signing from Chelmsford, almost marked his first game with a goal when he saw his header from a dinked Darren Carter cross well-defended.

And fellow new addition Manny Monthe almost hit the net himself a minute later, but his header was defended as effectively.

The opportunity of the first half came the way of Dover's leading marksman Ricky Miller. Sam Russell's brilliant push over the bar denied the attackers fabulous long distance strike though.

Another fine save this time by former FGR keeper Steve Arnold just before the break denied Moore who had managed to get clear only to see his effort smothered.

Following half time Emmanuel almost cleverly steered home Miller's low cross for the visitors, while Arnold's fantastic block denied Mullings who had done well to latch onto Cooper's similar delivery into the box from the right.

After Russell had saved well from Thomas and Ross Lafayette, Dover finally found a way through, and it was Emmanuel who broke the deadlock. He headed in Ricky Modeste's cross to put the Kent side in front.

The Forest Green response was almost immediate. Liam Noble's cross to Moore saw the striker spin brilliantly on the ball before powering a low shot just wide of the post.

In the final ten minutes Mark Cooper's men upped the ante in the search for an equaliser.

Arnold kept his side in front when he denied Ethan Pinnock's header and Richard Orlu then made a brilliant hooked clearance off the line for the visitors to prevent Moore from finding the net.

Clough saw two strikes go close when looking to cause chaos in the Dover box, but the leveller would come for Rovers, as Moore's persistence in front of goal earned him a reward.

Mullings' header back into the busy bodies in the box was turned home past Arnold by Moore to ensure the spoils were shared as part of a last gasp finale.

## AT THE DEATH MOORE STAYS THE REAPER'S BLADE
*Jokerman*

Lincoln, Tranmere and Wrexham, an unholy trinity that exposed a vulnerable weakness in Mark Coopers Forest Green Rovers team that had topped the table as the mid-season point approached. Having raised questions for the first time in his tenure, the manager reacted. Abandoning the scalpel he reached for the chainsaw, scattering bark and sap to the four winds and gathering in new growth. Set-backs test both character and faith, Cooper lacks neither in his beliefs and management skills. Those too quick to judge should beware the face full of yolk.

Wrexham seems eons ago. Since then there has been an aquatic nightmare and a prolonged card-fest at the ends of the earth that few wanted. Cooper was full of praise for his team following their FA Trophy replay win at Truro on Tuesday night. However it is understandable that supporters are quaffing ale like it was going out of fashion in an effort to fill the void of apprehension before today's encounter with Dover at TNL.

As the team news broke, darkness descended when the spark on which all human life now depends disappeared. As the hour of kick-off past the anxious crowd of eighteen hundred were calmed as Ray Mears survival guides were handed out and quick start up sheets on cave painting and smoke signals were available on request.

The Greater Power soon relented and a start time of 3.45pm was set. Cooper launched new signing Mullings into the starting line-up to play alongside Moore, Kelly was in for the suspended Bennett while Monthe kept his place ahead of Wishart. As the game kicked off the mist surrounding the stadium began to swirl in over the stands creating an eerie atmosphere, the players appearing ghostlike at times throughout the afternoon.

All that had been held dear with possession play was defenestrated, mid-field bypassed and the ball played long to the two big men up front.

**D**
**E**
**C**
**E**
**M**
**B**
**E**
**R**

For half an hour it was dire, both sides showing a distinct lack of quality in their play. Dover did look the more likely side with Miller featuring prominently in attack. On thirty minutes a Dover free kick was crossed to the back post and fell invitingly for Thomas up in support. About to pull the trigger from six yards, Cooper nicked the ball off his toe to much relief of the Rovers support behind the goal. Russell then saved well from a deflected shot by Emmanuel and set up a quick break ending in Carter having a shot deflected over the bar.

Rovers applied pressure with a series of corners the second of which saw Mullings come close to scoring. The tall striker had looked well off the pace on his introduction to this level but rose to head Carters cross goalwards, only to see his effort cleared off the line.

Miller demonstrated his credentials on forty minutes with a ferocious shot from all of thirty yards which had Russell stretching to palm away from the top right hand corner. From the resulting kick Magri's half volley cleared the bar. Home hopes were raised when Noble threaded a pass to Moore in the clear but Arnold was quickly off his line to smother the danger. As the half ended there was much to ponder for the Rovers manager during the break.

The first chance of the second half fell to Rovers when the exceptional Sinclair, raiding down the right, picked out Cooper who hit a low cross to the near post which Mullings guided goalwards, but was thwarted by an excellent save by Arnold. Around the hour mark Dover applied pressure which saw Russell saving first from Thomas and then getting down low to grab a powerful shot from Lafayette at the second attempt.

On sixty four minutes Cooper changed tack, Keanu and Frear replaced Carter and Kelly. This sparked Rovers and they appeared to be gaining the upper hand in this second period but the gods were not smiling on them. 70mins and on a break up field the home defence were caught short. Miller on the right, side footed the ball to Modeste, and his perfect cross was met by Emmanuel, unmarked, who headed the ball past Russell from six yards.

A minute later Moore might well have levelled the score when he turned and fired the ball past Arnold, who could only watch as it went inches wide. Traore replaced Sinclair with fifteen minutes remaining.

Rovers laid siege on the Dover goal and an undercurrent of temper and frustrations surfaced a little, not helped by the referee who had a propensity to hand out cards like a salesman on speed. Entering the final minutes, another series of corners from Rovers culminated in the excellent Pinnock rising above everyone, only to head the ball straight into the grateful arms of Arnold. A ghost in the fog then crossed from the right and Moore, at full stretch, stabbed the ball past Arnold from close range, but Orlu on the goal line hooked it clear.

In the final minute of normal time it was Moore again desperately trying to pull the game out of the fire. He brilliantly controlled a pass on his chest and laid it into the path of Clough, up in support, who beat Arnold but again the ball rolled wide. Fans and players alike were bereft as Frear hit an angled shot straight at Arnold.

The board signalled four extra minutes, Rovers poured it on. A corner on the left went out for a corner on the right. The ball fell to Mullings who headed it down into the ruck six yards out. Moore was quickest. With players in front of him, he hit the ball on the turn and smashed it through the bodies into the back of the net. It is no more than he or his team deserved for a battling second half performance as they struggled with an unfamiliar line-up.

Some frustration mixed with relief for Rovers fans at the end. There is much to do but Forest Green are still in touch and have exceptional talent in their squad. If that fat bloke in red is listening, a win or preferably two over the festive period would not go amiss, and would keep the knife grinder redundant to boot.

## FGR AMBASSADOR REPORT
*Tyler Hinchcliffe, Leonard Stanley Primary School*

My name is Tyler Hinchliffe and I am the ambassador for Leonard Stanley School. I play for Leonard Stanley Sharks football team. Here is my report on the game against Dover Athletic on Saturday 17th December 2016.

The match started later than we all expected due to a power cut across the area and the stadium that delayed the game for about an hour. This was just the start of the drama for this match. The game started off competitively with Charlie Clough being booked within the first few minutes for a challenge against Ricky Miller – this was the first of 6 yellow cards awarded in the game. The match became hard to watch because of a thick fog which stayed around for the full 90 minutes. This made it difficult for the players to get any flow into their play early on and Forest Green had some good attacking drives forward from the midfield but were not able to find the back of the net.

The second half saw Rovers dominating and then against the run of play Dover went ahead when Moses Emmanuel headed in from an accurate cross by Ricky Modeste. Rovers came back with a number of attacks that

**D**
**E**
**C**
**E**
**M**
**B**
**E**
**R**

saw Kiefer Moore fire wide and then have a shot spectacularly cleared off the line by Richard Orlu. The home crowd became more vocal and then Rovers' determination finally paid off in stoppage time when Moore got onto the end of a Charlie Cooper corner to secure a point and prevent Dover doing the double over us this season. Man of the Match was Liam Noble.

**Monday 26.12.16**
**Torquay United 4 FGR 3**
**PLAINMOOR COMEBACK NOT ENOUGH FOR FGR**
*Richard Joyce*

A second half thriller saw Forest Green come out on the wrong side of the club's final game of 2016 at Plainmoor.

Opponents Torquay United raced into an unexpected 3-0 lead after the interval, but Rovers looked all set to secure the most incredible of comebacks, when in the space of four minutes they found the net three times to draw level.

The Gulls provided one final twist though when they reclaimed their lead which this time FGR couldn't wrestle away from them.

In the early exchanges both sides threatened with minor opportunities on goal, but it was on 21 minutes when Brendan Moore had to produce the matches first notable save when he denied Liam Noble after good work by Shamir Mullings.

The home team's American goalkeeper then tipped over Kieffer Moore's superb turn and shot shortly after, while after Dan Sparkes had been denied at the other end by Sam Russell, Moore again made a vital stop to deny his namesake in the Rovers front line after he had latched brilliantly onto Noble's clever through ball.

A stalemate at the break, there was plenty of drama to come, and after Nathan Blissett had spurned two good openings for the hosts, he finally took another chance on 55 minutes when he broke the deadlock by getting on the end of Sparkes's low ball.

Within the next ten minutes Noble and Moore went close for FGR, but Torquay's advantage was doubled, as David Fitzpatrick slotted confidently.

And just 60 seconds later it was three. Sean McGinty nodded home at the back post to provide the Plainmoor crowd with the festive cheer they had enjoyed similarly 12 months before.

Their joy would soon be short-lived as Mark Cooper's charges began a stunning comeback. It started as substitute Christian Doidge headed in from a Keanu Marsh-Brown cross on 74 minutes.

Two minutes later it was Charlie Clough who would draw another goal back as he pushed the ball into the net from close range.

And the stunning comeback was complete when on 78 minutes Ethan Pinnock forced home at the back post.

The game had been turned on its head in the most unpredictable of circumstances, but there was another twist to come, as Torquay extinguished any ambitions Forest Green had to win the game when Gerring headed home the winner.

Gerring provided relief for the home support when he was left unmarked and nodded in the afternoon's final goal.

There was still time for FGR to try and draw parity again, although Elliott Frear's shot on his right foot was saved, and Mullings couldn't get an effort from a Marsh-Brown cross on target with Torquay doing enough to hang on for three points.

## DESTINATION TORQUAY
*Rambling Man*

Having missed the Wrexham reverse a month ago, Torquay would be my first Rovers away league fixture since Macclesfield on 12th November. And since the giddy heights of Moss Rose, Rovers fortunes have nose-dived.

Season by season, the National League programme becomes increasingly random. This is only Rovers' second league game in what is usually a fixture congested month. Boxing Day 2015 also saw Rovers travel to Torquay. So, in the name of fairness, surely the Gulls might have been asked to make a tour of the Cotswolds this term? Ever get the feeling persons in authority are extracting the Michael?

So it was that Foggy, me and new companion TJ met at the Stonehouse Court Hotel at 10.00 sharp. Mrs Foggy was up north and had allowed him the rare privilege of piloting their gleaming new scarlet Vauxhall Astra. "Don't bend it" was her terse instruction which was obeyed (by and large).

The journey was uneventful and surprisingly short. Though there was a fair amount of traffic about, free of roadworks the M5 did what it was designed for, and we had reached the English Riviera by noon. Of course, being a Vauxhall, we were kept on our toes by the constant fear of our chariot bursting into flames, but lady luck was on our side, at least until mid-afternoon.

With plenty of time in hand, we parked up near the harbour and joined the throngs doing their post-Christmas perambulation on a cold, clear

**D
E
C
E
M
B
E
R**

winter day. Shame most the water front cafes were shut-up, but eventually we found an open one and whiled away a pleasing early afternoon. Even so, we still parked at Plainmoor with the thick end of 2 hours before kick-off.

Ushered into the main restaurant, we joined other Rovers supporters in an excellent seasonal meal. Before we left, we were treated to an address by the Chair of the newly reconstituted Torquay United Supporters Club and a question and answer session by its President, Gulls & Gas legend Robin Stubbs.

Sadly, that is where our hosts' generosity terminated. On the pitch a bizarre Rovers formation was disassembled by a buccaneering home team. Fortunate to be level at half time, Rovers were soon 3-0 down in the second period. On trooped Doidge, Frear & Keanu Marsh-Brown (who most around us thought should have been in the starting line-up) and within minutes it was 3-3. Still time for Rovers to miss sitters as the hosts were rocking, before yet more chaos in defence saw Rovers surrender all 3 points.

All that meant a glum and frustrating return blast up the M5. The shape and fortunes of the current team are a country mile away from Moss Rose. 2 points from 15 and a suddenly leaky defence leaves the Manager much to do to restore faith around The New Lawn.

### GULLS DISEMBOWEL THE PHOENIX
*Jokerman*

As the annual turkey carcass heads for the soup kitchen, Forest Green Rovers supporters, keen to avoid the leftovers, heed the call to journey south aboard the Kendo Express heading for the coast. Twelve months ago to the day this same trip and match against Torquay United did not go well. Rovers recent hunger for points has produced an anorexic diet and retribution for the thumping a year since would not go amiss this afternoon.

The club house bar was doing a roaring trade prior to kick-off and, 'Tribute' a rare decent ale amongst the dross was spotted as the team news came through. Wishart replaced the injured Monthe and Bennett returned from suspension. Eyebrows were raised as Mullings continued up front with Moore. Over two hundred FGR fans were body searched for explosive devices, knuckle dusters and knives before entering the away end of the ground. The war goes on. A crowd of over two and a half thousand greeted the teams in bright sunshine that blinded the visiting support behind the goal for the first half duration.

From the kick-off Rovers appeared to have returned to their possession game but did not dominate the home side. On twenty minutes Rovers had their first real chance when a cross from Cooper was knocked down by Mullings to Noble, who was denied by a fine save from Moore the Torquay keeper. A long diagonal ball from Clough found Moore on the edge of the box, his turn and shot forced the keeper to fist the ball over the bar. Torquay replied with a pass inside Clough that saw Sparkes through on Russell, who saved with his legs at the near post.

Mullings was being bullied off the ball despite his physical presence as Torquay sought an edge in attack, but it was Rovers who created the better chances. On half time Noble put Moore through on the keeper but his flick with the outside of his right foot failed to beat his namesake. Honours even at the break and the peepers were relieved as the earth turned away from the sun.

Torquay were fast out of the blocks as the second half got under way. The giant Blissett raced into the area and hit a fierce drive across Russell but wide of the far post. Mullings replied in kind at the other end, but it was the home side that took the game by the throat.

55mins a raid down the left by Sparkes, who crossed low to the near post where Blissett arrived first and slid the ball into the net from close range. The crowd were up and Rovers on the back foot.

Manager Mark Cooper changed it, sacrificing Traore for Doidge on the hour and Frear for Wishart soon after. Before the changes could make an impact Torquay turned the screw on the Forest Green defence. On 65mins Fitzpatrick was played into the clear on the right side of the area, and fairly lashed the ball past an exposed Russell. And before the crowd had finished celebrating, a cross to the back post was headed back across goal for McGinty to head the ball home from close in. 67mins 3-0 down, some Rovers fans had heard the fire alarm.

Cooper played his last card, Keanu replacing Cooper on seventy one minutes. It takes three minutes as Doidge gives Mullings a master class on what is required at this level. This starts after Russell foils Sparkes with his legs in a one on one.

Rovers go on the rampage having no other choice. 74mins as the ball zips across the Torquay box Keanu, on the right edge, dinks it across the six yard line where Doidge throws himself between two defenders and plants his downward header into the net. Two minutes later, Keanu pinpoints a corner from the right into Doidge whose header is only parried by keeper Moore on the goal line, and Clough following up smashes the ball into the net. Another two minutes and a Noble corner from the left

**D
E
C
E
M
B
E
R**

has Pinnock rising above all others to place a firm header down and inside the right hand post. 78mins 3-3 and emotions are running high all round the ground.

Then the defining two acts are played. Straight back on attack Moore bursts through the desperate Torquay defence into the area, and as the keeper comes out to challenge he dithers, with Frear waiting for the ball that never comes and the chance is gone. As Moore retreats he is confronted by his skipper Noble and berated, the two almost come to blows.

Amid this mayhem Torquay gain possession and attack through the ever dangerous Sparkes who is denied a goal chance by a terrific block from Clough. From the resulting corner the ball is played to the back post, nodded across the face and Gerring, unmarked, heads a simple goal on 82mins. The stadium erupts. It was a cruel blow for Forest Green who had staged a spectacular recovery.

They made desperate efforts to save the game. Frear struck a shot into the keeper's midriff and Mullings skimmed a header wide, but despite six added minutes Torquay's fourth goal proved to be a step too far.

At the final whistle Forest Green fans were staggered and their players shattered. Credit must be given to Torquay for exploiting Rovers fragile confidence. The promotion hopefuls appear a little confused and certainly spoilt for choice in the selection department just now. As the Kendo Liner glided into the night, somewhere in the distance the wolves began to howl.

FGR Team photo August 2016. Back row to front row, left to right.
Harry Hickford, Ethan Pinnock, Aarran Racine, Sam Russell, Simon Lefebvre, Jonny Maxted, Charlie Clough, Dale Bennett, Jon Moran.
Steve Hale, McGrory, Elliott Frear, Sam Wedgbury, Drissa Traore, Marcus Kelly, Ben Jefford, Joe Stokes, Tim Grigg.
Ian Weston, Olly Mehew, Keanu Marsh-Brown, Rob Sinclair, Liam Noble, Mo Chemlal, Darren Carter, Blake Davies, Tom Huelin.
Joe Baker, Kieffer Moore, Matt Tubbs, Mark Cooper, Dale Vince, Scott Lindsey, Rhys Murphy, Christian Doidge, Scott Bartlett.

With compo at Wembley Way before the Play Off Final 14.05.17.

FGR & Tranmere stride onto the pitch at the Wembley Final 14.05.17.

Shamir Mullings.

Mark Ellis.

Omar Bugiel.

Kaiyne Woolery.

Curtis Tilt.

Fabian Robert.

Dan Wishart.

Manny Monthe.

Charlie Cooper.

High summer football – ice cream cart at Boreham Wood 06.08.16.

High summer at Maidstone – Liam Noble & Rhys Murphy cool off with Maidstone players 27.08.16.

Tatton Park ideas hut with Foggy & Compo en route Chester 03.09.16.

At Cressing Barns local serf prepares noose for
The Iron's Jamie Day – sadly the ex-FGR coach was
sacked after the game 24.09.16.

Foggy, Compo & Cleggy trying their hands at
Cressing Barns en route Braintree 24.09.16.

Book launch CG with Dale & Jilly v Guiseley
22.10.16.

An amazing privilege – presenting my 1st book to
Sir Alex Ferguson before Macclesfield v FGR 12.11.16.

Reg Cobb GDA with Dean Holdsworth, FGR's
Chris Wintle & GDA's Deaf Football Team before
FGR v Barrow 01.10.16.

Foggy gets to grips with latest phone technology at
Polesden Lacey en route Bromley 07.01.17.

Foggy & Compo at Waddesdon Manor 06.08.16.

Beautiful ballroom at Polesden Lacey en route Bromley 07.01.17.

Breathtaking wall painting at Little Moreton Hall en route Tranmere 11.04.17.

Elizabeth I's favourite hang-out Hatfield House en route Daggers 04.05.17.

Gloriously wonky Little Moreton Hall en route Tranmere 11.04.17.

Iconic Liverpool waterfront 29.02.17.

Restored Wellington bomber at Brooklands
Museum before Sutton v FGR 14.03.17.

Sumptious 4 poster bed at Riddlesden Hall en
route Guiseley 08.04.17.

# THE GREEN DEVIL

SUPPORTING FOREST GREEN ROVERS AT EASTINGTON SCHOOL

FOREST GREEN ROVERS FGR 1889

Student Ambassador Evie Urquhart with Rob Sinclair.

## IT WAS ALL GOING OUR WAY!
### (NOT ANY MORE)

Okay, Lincoln may have beat us, but we had terrific wins against Macclesfield Town, Sutton United, Wrexham and Solihull Moors! Then it all ended when Lincoln City beat FGR 3-1 at Sincil Bank. This was a must win game so automatic promotion to the football league now looks unlikely, to make matters even worse, the match was live on BT Sport.

The following Saturday we had a chance to put things right when bottom of the league North Ferriby Utd visited the New Lawn and what happened? They only went and beat us. Both teams played well throughout both halves of the game but Rovers should have won it. Well done to the 20 North Ferriby fans who made the 400 mile round trip to The New Lawn. Our automatic promotion hopes are fading away rapidly. FGR are still to play Tranmere Rovers away, so if we can't beat a team at the bottom of the league, it will be difficult to beat a team one place below us. I still think we will qualify for the play-offs, so lets hope we can get another trip to Wembley and fight for promotion that way.

## Instagram

If you aren't already, why not follow me on Instagram at:

**fgr_at_eastington_school**

for all the latest FGR news and results.

### STAR PLAYER — OMAR BUGIEL

| | |
|---|---|
| Age: | 22 |
| Birthday: | Sept. 25th 1994 |
| Place of birth: | Germany |
| Height: | 6ft 2in |
| Position: | Striker |
| Previous clubs: | Worthing Town |
| Joined FGR | February 2017 |
| Appearances | 6 |
| Goals so far | 3 |

## WIN ONE OF THESE EASTER EGGS BY NAMING THE FGR EASTER BUNNIES

Go to the FGR website to find the identity of the bunnies below. Please get your entries to Tyler by the end of school on Thursday ( 06.04.17) **Good Luck!**

R____ S_____     D____ T_____     M____ C_____

L____ N_____     M____ E_____     K____ M____ B____

Your name _____ Class_____

### Vanarama National League
#### Top 5 - 3rd April 2017

| | P | W | D | L | PTS |
|---|---|---|---|---|---|
| Lincoln.C | 38 | 24 | 7 | 7 | 79 |
| Tranmere | 39 | 24 | 7 | 8 | 79 |
| Forest Green | 40 | 22 | 9 | 9 | 75 |
| Dag & Red | 40 | 23 | 4 | 13 | 73 |
| Aldershot | 41 | 20 | 11 | 10 | 71 |

### TOP GOAL SCORERS

| | | |
|---|---|---|
| 1 | Christian Doidge | 23 |
| 2 | Keanu Marsh-Brown | 9 |
| 3 | Liam Noble | 6 |
| 4 | Darren Carter | 4 |
| 5 | Omar Bugiel | 3 |
| 6 | Ethan Pinnock | 3 |
| 7 | Fabien Robert | 3 |

www.forestgreenroversfc.com

Student Ambassador Seth Tiley at York.

*Green Devil* edition 8 by FGR Ambassador Tyler Watson, Eastington School.

FGR squad with the student ambassadors 01.09.2016.

Shouldn't a mascot take more interest? Folkestone Invicta 1 Havant & Waterlooville 3 28.01.17.

Jilly Cooper 80 – Jilly shows off her birthday present from FGR at the home game v North Ferriby United 01.04.17.

Jilly Cooper 80 rear view.

The Green Army in fine voice at Sincil Bank 25.03.17.

300 of the finest from the 5 Valleys packed a corner of the Victoria Road Stadium 04.05.17.

Memorable FGR Special to York arranged by Pathfinder Tours 29.04.17.

My 2016/17 favourite stadium 'The Gallagher' despite the plastic surface 27.08.16.

Before the 1st half rout, the teams walk out at Aldershot's Electrical Services Stadium 04.10.16.

Bromley's Hayes Lane a characterful stadium yet again prey to the expanding tunnel salemen 07.01.17.

Christian Doidge puts Rovers 1-0 up at a packed Sincil Bank but it did not last 25.03.17.

Least favourite stadium, The Gateshead International where FGR slumped to a 3-1 defeat.

Foggy & Compo at the Macron for Bolton v Bristol Rovers after FGR's match at Tranmere was rained off 28.02.17.

While FGR was at Barrow I spotted this double rainbow at Folkestone Invicta's Fullicks Stadium.

Welcoming Nethermoor Park home to Guiseley FC. Ex-FGR custodian Jonny Maxted on his toes 08.04.17.

A famous victory at Prenton Park, where the home fans are as impressive as the stadium 11.04.17.

Live on BT Sport a packed Bootham Crescent expected but a 2-2 draw meant relegation for York City 29.04.17.

The New Lawn celebrates reaching Wembley again after FGR 2 Daggers 0 07.05.17.

Woolery 1-0! at Wembley Final 14.05.17.

Half time dreamland Wembley Final 14.05.17.

We've done it! Green Army in raptures Wembley Final 14.05.17.

And now you're gonna believe us! Wembley Final 14.05.17.

Victorious, FGR players allowing victory to sink in Wembley Final 14.05.17.

Team & supporters on cloud 9 Wembley Final 14.05.17.

Dale & Kate Vince take it all in Wembley Final 14.05.17.

Mr & Mrs Compo Wembley Final 14.05.17.

Manny Monthe's family & friends go potty! Wembley Final 14.05.17.

Trophy celebrations Wembley Final 14.05.17.

FGR on-pitch celebrations on the rostrum for the cameras 14.05.17.

FGR on-pitch celebrations continue with Shamir exiting left on hands and knees! 14.05.17.

Team picture in front of supporters Wembley Final 14.05.17.

oooh Sam! Trophy in grasp Wembley Final 14.05.17.

Getting the party started at The New Lawn 16.05.17.

FGR's Organic Lager by Stroud Brewery.

Chef Em's famous FGR Q-Pie.

Helen Taylor receives FGR's SLC Award for Best Menu 2016 from Mark Durden-Smith.

FGR Chef Em Franklin proudly displaying the Sports & Leisure Catering Magazine Award for Menu of the Year 2016.

## BREAK FOR REFRESHMENTS: CHEF EM'S FAMOUS FGR RECIPE – 'Q' PIE

A few years ago, Dale Vince made headlines by exercising owner's prerogative in deciding that all food served at The New Lawn, including to FGR's players and coaches, would be vegan. The reaction of journalists and supporters was mixed to put it mildly. Oh how we were teased by other clubs and their supporters!

Yet outside the caldron of Gloucestershire opinion, there was a more level headed appreciation that a football club taking diet seriously was long overdue, as was closer interest in players own diet plans. Professional footballers were arguably the last professional athletes to adopt bespoke dietary advice.

Dale's move spawned a plethora of national and international media reporting. Our very own Bob Hunt was the latest to indulge as he commentated joyously at the conclusion of the 2017 Play-Off Final "Let me tell you this: Cheltenham, Swindon, Newport – you're going to eat hummus at the New Lawn next season because Forest Green Rovers are in the Football League!"

Truth be told, the publicity was as welcome as it was inevitable. Principle mixed with marketing.

Ignoring the headlines, there is a genuine hero in the story, the chef who turned the hype into an appreciation that FGR was not just dishing out *vegan food*. Simply, if you are lucky enough to eat and drink at The New Lawn you will be consuming good value, good food. *That* is the story.

So, enter Chef 'Em' Franklin. FGR's resident Chef and well known to those who frequent Stroud's Star Anise cafe/restaurant. To enjoy the best of her fare, you will need to join the 1,800 season ticket holders or guests of the stadium's East Stand. Before, during and after the game, the throng in the Carole Embrey bar/restaurant and all the hospitality lounges choose from a varied and changing menu.

The staple however is the now famous 'Q-Pie'. So, for your half time refreshments after your valiant efforts in getting this far in my book, I invite you to take some time off and make 'Q-Pie'. Thanks to Em and Forest Green Rovers FC, I am able to disclose the recipe below:

### Q-Pie Recipe by Em Franklin. Serving Size: 2

Ingredients:
1 tablespoon Light Soya Sauce
280g Vegan Quorn Cubes
1/2 a small leak, 80g Fresh Leek, washed
1/2 a small onion Onion, finely diced

H
A
L
F

T
I
M
E

3 stems Fresh Thyme, leaves only
1 Bay Leaf
For Bechamel Sauce
1 rounded tablespoon/15g Plain White Flour
1 tablespoon/15ml Vegetable Oil
1/2 Vegetable Stock Cube
Salt
Ground White Pepper
1/4 cup Sweetened Soya Milk, For Glaze
Shop Bought Pastry. For simplicity this recipe uses shop bought vegan pastry. If you prefer to make vegan pastry yourself, a recipe is set out at the end of this section.
120g Puff Pastry
150g Shortcrust Pastry
2 Single Portion Pie Tins, or triple the recipe to make 1 Large 6" Pie. Cooking instructions remain the same.

Directions:

1 If you are making your pastry make it now and place in the fridge to chill. If using shop bought, ensure it is defrosted and at room temperature. Place quorn pieces in a bowl and add soy sauce to season. Set aside.

2 Remove leaves from each thyme stem by holding narrowest tip in one hand and with the other hand pinch lightly between finger and thumb and run this hand down to stem base.

3 Finely slice the Onion and fry in a small amount of the vegetable oil with the fresh thyme leaves, bay leaf on low heat until opaque.

4 Wash the leeks and slice into 1cm 'rounds'

5 Blanch the leeks in boiling, salted, water for approx 5 minutes, until bright green and softened.

6 Drain leeks in a sieve (retain water for gravy, don't loose it down the sink!) Allow leeks to steam 'dry' whilst you continue.

7 To make your white sauce (Bechamel). Heat the oil in a non stick pan, add the flour and mix into a loose paste. Still on the heat, gradually add soya milk, whisking continuously until you have a 'creamy, thick sauce.

8 Remove from the heat, add vegetable stock, salt & peer to taste. Combine leeks, onions, quorn, white sauce, taste again for seasoning. Set aside, covered with cling film.

9 Have your sweetened soya milk and pastry brush ready in a bowl/cup.

10  Halve your puff pastry and with a rolling pin roll to 1/2 cm thickness. Place an upturned bowl onto one pastry sheet as a 'lid template' and cut a circle 1.5 times larger than the rim of you pie case. Set aside and cover with a clean tea towel. Repeat with shortcrust pastry, your base pastry, to a larger size round, 2 times the diameter of your small pie tin.

11  Now you are going to build your pie! Lightly grease your pie tin. Line the tin with shortcrust pastry ensuring it touches, but isn't forced, right to the base of tin. The pastry should come over the top of the tin wall.

12  Divide the filling between the 2 tins, ensuring it is central to the pie well, it will spread evenly on heating.

13  Brush one side of your pastry lid with sweetened soya milk. Place milk side down on top of filling. Gently bring lid & base edges together and pinch together to form a 'crimped edge'. Trim any excess pastry with a knife or scissors and discard excess. Brush top of pies with sweetened soya milk. Prick each lid twice, with a small, sharp knife to allow steam to escape and air to enter on baking.

14  Place on a baking sheet and bake for 1 hr at 180°C.

15  Leave to rest for 5 minutes before removing from tin and eating!

### Em's Vegan Shortcrust Pastry Recipe

Ingredients:
300g Self-raising Flour
1/4 tea spoon Fine Salt
6 Tablespoons Sunflower/Vegetable Oil
6 Tablespoons Aquafaba. (Aquafaba is chick pea juice, pour straight from a can of tinned chick peas)

Directions:
1  Sieve your flour into a bowl and add salt.
2  Add oil to flour and combine with your finger tips to make a fine 'breadcrumb' mix.
3  Add Aquafaba enough to form a soft ball. Do not knead or over work.
4  You can use immediately or for best results chill in your fridge for an hour before rolling for use.
5  Cooking time for rolled pastry 25–30 mins at 180°C.

Reader, if you have made and consumed Q-Pie you are ready for anything. So start by ploughing on with the book!

Personnel changes were ongoing in Coops' post-Lincoln revolution, yet a pattern was beginning to emerge. What was happening on the pitch was more like we'd expected at the season's start – more goals scored, more conceded and less predictable performances. It confused and confounded in equal measure but the much changed team was beginning to pick up the scent. Wins were being notched up and Christian Doidge had resumed his crusade to score relentlessly, targeting a personal tally of 25-30. Boring it was not!

*Ethan, may I introduce Charlie, he is to be a friend of yours*
*Charlie, this is Dale and he'll also be your chum*
*And this is Dan who may occasionally be close by*
*You will come together and gesticulate after the opposition scores*
*But don't look blue or feel too glum*
*It's part of my dastardly plan to make friends and foe as bemused as I*

(Excerpt from 'Passing Strangers – a new panto for FGR' by The Farmcotian, a combination of seasonal humour, irony and panic!)

**Sunday 01.01.17**
**FGR 5 Torquay United 5**
**2017 STARTS OFF WITH A BANG AT THE NEW LAWN**
*Richard Joyce*
A sensational afternoon of football saw Forest Green Rovers begin 2017 with an incredible ten goal thriller at The New Lawn.

Throughout the game Rovers led, fought back from being behind, and almost came within a whisker of claiming maximum points, as Boxing Day opponents Torquay United once again contributed to a brilliant entertaining clash.

The two teams last meeting six days ago saw the Gulls claim the points in a dramatic 4-3 win, however Mark Cooper's men ensured they secured a share of the spoils with two late goals in front of a good New Year's Day crowd.

Keanu Marsh-Brown and Christian Doidge both scored twice, and it was the former who opened the scoring on four minutes, when he finished accurately following Darren Carter's terrific dummy from a Liam Noble pass.

It didn't take long for the visitors to equalise, and on 15 minutes they did so when Dan Sparkes slid home at the back post from the first of David Fitzpatrick's four assists.

And Fitzpatrick again turned provided for Sparkes a short while later, as a near identical goal saw the Gulls go in front.

This time it was FGR's turn to fight their way back into the contest and they did so successfully just before the half hour mark.

Marsh-Brown grabbed his second of the afternoon as he pounced upon Dale Bennett's excellent cut back.

A Forest Green counter attack as half time approached almost saw Doidge turn in Kieffer Moore's low ball into the box, while before the half time whistle there was still time for Torquay to retake the lead.

Fitzpatrick's free kick from the right hand side was curled in towards the near post where Aman Verma was on hand to head home.

It got worse for Rovers immediately after the break. Another driving run forward from Fitzpatrick saw his pacey cross turned home by the unfortunate Ethan Pinnock.

Defender Ben Gerring very nearly extended Torquay's advantage, but it would be Rovers who'd score next, as Doidge netted his first by finishing off Elliott Frear's soft header.

The Gulls two-goal lead was restored when Fitzpatrick crowned a wonderful afternoon for the AFC Wimbledon loanee by finding the net with a free kick to make it five for the visitors.

But Forest Green were not to be beaten, and they launched an epic comeback that saw Doidge claim another goal on 83 minutes.

The Welshman forced the ball over the line after Frear's fine work on the left had seen him force Brendan Moore to parry his shot into the path of the striker.

And there was to be one final crucial goal to come before the 90 minute mark when Moore, under pressure from Shamir Mullings, pushed the ball into his own net for the afternoon's second own goal and FGR's much sought after equaliser.

## ROVERS ON TENTERHOOKS

*Jokerman*

Day one and game one of the New Year. Time to banish the previous five league games to the dustbin of history. Six days ago Torquay United prevailed in an extraordinary encounter to prolong Forest Greens lean spell. The season of good will to all men was quite lost on several emotionally incontinent Rovers fans who vented their spleens at team boss Mark Cooper. The very nature of the defeat against the same opposition this afternoon, should see both players and supporters highly charged to exact retribution and begin a twenty one game all-out assault for the title. This would go some way to assuaging all the doom mongers that a small fan base can ill afford.

The packed Green Man bar was testament to a large following of Torquay supporters who were in good voice. The team sheet appeared and as expected Doidge was paired with Moore in attack and Keanu also made the starting line-up. Mullings and Cooper dropped to the bench. Over two thousand three hundred fans greeted the teams on a wet, windy and cold afternoon.

Torquay elected to defend the home end in the first half. This gave Forest Green the breeze on their backs and after three minutes forced as many corners. The third of which was cleared to half way, where Noble hit a low pass down the centre, which Carter dummied and let the ball run to Keanu, who burst through and curled the ball past Moore, the Torquay custodian, into the net via the foot of the post on 4mins.

Rovers dominated until the 15min when Torquay launched their first meaningful attack. Fitzpatrick sprinted clear on the right and crossed low into the penalty area, void of defence, to Sparkes racing in to fire the ball past Russell from six yards. This woke their fans up and urged the visitors on. They pressed Rovers and Fitzpatrick put a shot wide from a great position on twenty minutes. A minute later he did better with an action replay of his side's first goal, again crossing from the right for Sparkes again to gleefully fire the visitors in front. This triggered wild celebrations from the four hundred Gulls fans behind the goal.

This stung Rovers. Bennett at least gave that impression on 29mins when he went careering down the right and pulled the ball back to Keanu, just inside the box, who controlled and struck it fiercely low past Moore. Relief for Rovers fans who then witnessed Kieffer Moore put a free header wide at the back post from a cross by Wishart.

Sinclair then conceded a free kick on the left edge of the area on 40mins. The ball was struck towards the near post, where Verma stepped in front of his marker and glanced a header inside the post with Russell helpless. As the half time whistle sounded to the away cheers it left Forest Green fans somewhat bemused at their sides inability to defend.

Things did not improve after the break. In the first minute Reid found himself with space in the Rovers box but side footed the ball wide. Then on 50mins, a crushing blow. Fitzpatrick on the break down the right hit a cross that struck Pinnocks shin, as he attempted to block, and the ball flew high into the net past Russell. Body language told the tale.

Frear replaced Carter. There was not an immediate improvement as Torquay continued to press and a free kick from the right of the area was slid into Gerring, up in attack, but he side footed wide from a yard out when a fifth goal looked certain.

Two goals behind Rovers were in all-out attack mode and on 62mins were rewarded, when a high cross from the right by Bennett to the back post, was knocked down by Frear to Doidge, who scored from point blank. It was game on and Frear raced down the left and hit a vicious shot across the keeper but wide.

On 66mins a highly contentious free kick was awarded to the visitors in a central position twenty yards from goal. Fitzpatrick curled the ball low around the wall where Russell moved towards it with hands pointing to the heavens, no problem going wide, whoops, 3-5. 'Can we play you every week' echoed from the other end.

Mullings was now on in place of Moore and blasted an effort wide from distance as Forest Green chased the game. Frear was making an impact and on 83mins he went on a defence splitting run down the left, cut into the box and unleashed a thunderous shot that was too hot for keeper Moore and Doidge was on hand to smash the rebound past him into the net.

The Gulls fans were hushed as Rovers were clearly on top now. They were pounding the Torquay goal and the crowd sensed there was still time. 88mins and Bennett, always a threat on the right overlap, crossed to Keanu whose mistimed strike lofted the ball goalwards. As the ball dropped keeper Moore and Mullings, amongst others, were enveloped in an almighty scramble, he dropped the ball and it rolled over the goal line. The referee signalled the goal amidst a storm of protests from the Torquay players. The Gulls fans behind the goal were going bananas Rovers fans didn't give a monkeys.

Five added minutes the atmosphere was electric as Rovers went for the kill. A frantic goalmouth scramble led to a corner on the right. Sinclair crossed perfectly for Doidge, but his bullet header crashed against the cross bar and was cleared for another corner, which Doidge nodded down for Mullings, whose volley was brilliantly saved by Moore. It wasn't to be and the referee brought this breathtaking game to an end.

There will be much discussion and no doubt fair comments mixed with the nonsensical remarks on the forum following this lean time. It is however plain to see this Forest Green side do not lack spirit and the will to fight for the cause. And when the going gets tough we should stick together.

**JANUARY**

### FGR AMBASSADOR REPORT
*Milo Mullarkey, Randwick Primary School*

I'm Milo Mullarkey and I'm 9 years old and I have been the Forest Green Rovers school ambassador for Randwick primary for 2 years. I have 3 favourite players Keanu Marsh-Brown, Ethan Pinnock and Dale Bennett. I was lucky enough to go to Wembley for the play off final last year however the best game I've been too was the play off semi against Dover FC last season.

FGR Match Report. It was Sunday the 1st of January 2017 and there was a match at the New Lawn. Forest Green Rovers were playing Torquay united, it might have been freezing but that did not stop the fans from coming. Rovers started brightly and after 3 corners Marsh-Brown scored with a shot in off the post in the 4th minute. After 11 minutes Dan Sparkes scored for Torquay after they broke quickly down the right hand side of the pitch. 6 minutes later he scored again with a goal almost identical to his first. The game was very open and Dale Bennett put a good cross in for Marsh-Brown and scored another goal for FGR in the 29th minute. Then out of the blue verma scored a goal witch made it 3-2 half time.

Rovers couldn't have got off to a worst start in the 2nd half when Pinnock scored an own goal after a good cross from Torquay. Chrisian Doidge pulled one back for Rovers to make it 4-3 but then Torquay went 5-3 up when Fitzpatrick scored from a free kick from just outside the box. Mark Cooper made a few changes as Rovers applied the pressure. Doidge scored again in the 83rd minute and a late own goal for the Torquay keeper made it 5-5. At the end of the match it was very dramatic both teams had a few chances to win the game. However this terrific game of football played on New year's day finished 5-5 at the New Lawn.

### Saturday 07.01.17
### Bromley 1 FGR 5
### MAGNIFICENT ROVERS SHINE AT BROMLEY
*Richard Joyce*

The goals continued to flow for Forest Green on the road at Bromley, as for a second consecutive game Rovers registered five times, claiming a superb away win.

Whereas Forest Green's New Year's Day clash with Torquay had ended all square, this time it was three points for Rovers, as Mark Cooper's men got back in form with a tremendous showing.

Christian Doidge extended his place as the leader in the goal scoring charts with two goals, while further contributions from Ethan Pinnock, Elliott Frear and Keanu Marsh-Brown added to the emphatic nature of the score line.

Frear was causing Bromley problems from as early as the fourth minute. The Ravens goalkeeper Alan Julian produced an excellent save to deny his low hit that looked destined for the bottom corner.

Two good chances followed from corners as Charlie Clough and Pinnock saw aerial attempts go just wide.

But FGR's dominance rewarded when on 28 minutes Frear broke the deadlock with a good finish.

Rob Sinclair did brilliantly to win the ball in the middle of the park, and he set Frear into space on the left, with the wide man executing a brilliant shot into the bottom corner.

Bromley had failed to get going despite their recent impressive home record, but their danger man Blair Turgott forced Sam Russell into an excellent save just before FGR doubled their lead.

Liam Noble's fine work saw him play in Frear on the left, and his pin-point low ball into the danger zone was turned home by Doidge for his first.

Forest Green were in full control at the break, however their lead was halved shortly into the second half, when Swaine was left free and headed in.

But within a minute the two goal lead was restored. Marsh-Brown added to his New Year's Day brace with a tremendous angled finish on the right hand side.

Three minutes later there was another goal. Frear's wonderful delivery from a free kick saw Pinnock rise highest in the box to glance home.

Bromley's experienced goalkeeper Julian had been beaten four times, but the former Stevenage man produced a number of crucial saves to keep the score down, and he made a fantastic stop almost immediately after conceding a fourth to deny Frear.

He made another good stop from Doidge, and Bromley then saw two decent efforts saved by Russell, who did well to prevent Turgott and Adam Cunnington from firing in from distance.

Substitute Shamir Mullings got in down the middle in the final ten minutes but saw Julian push away his strong volley, with Bromley reduced to ten men shortly after.

Swaine headed for an early exit after he hacked down Doidge who had burst clear on the left.

The match had slowed down in the final stages but there was still time for Forest Green to extend their lead in stoppage time.

Noble's instrumental performance from midfield saw him edge the ball to Doidge who opened up his body and executed another finish for his second and Rovers fifth, as his side stylishly wrapped up the three points on an entertaining and positive afternoon in south London.

## DESTINATION BROMLEY
*Rambling Man*

Bromley, Kent provided Rovers' first away outing of 2017. In fact, Kent seems to be an area growing in football influence at our modest level during the 2000s, witness our tussles with Welling, Dover, Ebbsfleet, Maidstone & Margate.

Since mid-November, Rovers form has been as confusing as the chaotic National League fixture list. Some hard talking was needed with my regular companions to decide how, as supporters, we would manage a 'Fleetwood Mac'. (Break the Chain – *common, keep up!*).

As self-appointed Dictator, it fell to me to identify the causes of success this term, before the rot had set in. We would return to basics and three key aspects shone out:

1 Travelling in my venerable Passat
2 Making time for pre-match cultural destinations
3 My cream jumper – unbeaten in all competitions

The course was obvious. For Rovers to prevail, some of these items, if not all three, had to be present.

I confess that in recent weeks, my support has been open to criticism, due to clashing family stuff. Take the Torquay 5-5 extravaganza. Whilst that was playing out, I was strolling in the grounds of Versailles Palace with Mrs R-M and our French domiciled daughter and her boyfriend. The astonishing gardens resembled something out of Narnia with 2 inches of hoar frost coating everything. When my mobile 'chirruped' to tell me Rovers led 1-0, I was set to relax amid the frozen splendour. 9 chirrups later, I was a gibbering wreck. Clearly, culture not linked to match attendance will not bring on-pitch success.

Back to reality. Foggy, Compo & I met at the Glider with me doing my Shaun the Sheep impersonation, clad in my legendary cream jumper. The SatNav was set for Kent, via The National Trust's Polesden Lacey. The Passat's power plant emitted its contented tug boat chuggings.

Polesden Lacey is an Edwardian house and estate located on the North Downs at Great Bookham, near Dorking, close enough to M25 Junction 9. The current house has Regency origins, built from 1824, replacing a much earlier mansion. It was extensively remodelled in 1906 at the hands of Margaret Greville an Edwardian hostess and socialite. There are grounds of 1,400 acres including walled gardens, landscaped, lawns and ancient woodland. All in all, not too shabby.

What made Polesden fascinating for me was that its Edwardian presentation is tantalisingly close history. The fixtures and fittings bring childhood memories of the things my Grandparents used or had around them; even the smell was evocative. Maybe it's just me getting old, but I revelled in the 90 minutes we spent there.

An hour's drive from Polesden Lacey took us to the Hayes Lane stadium, a first for me. The car park was next to a paddock where horses frolicked happily in the mud. Hayes Lane is yet another neat, distinctive National League venue, full of good people who know how to welcome strangers in the football fraternity. The playing surface is not so hot though, unsurprising as it also hosts Cray Wanderers and a Ladies XI.

In the manner of Ian Botham, Coops set up his charges to attack their way to form. He and they were rewarded for their bravery with an impressive 5-1 trouncing. Smiles and 5 star entertainment aplenty. Just one cloud on the horizon, as the snivels with which I awoke that day developed into triple man-flu by our arrival home. A fitness test would be needed for Eastleigh on Tuesday.

### ROVERS FILL THEIR BOOTS ON THE TURNIP FIELD
*Jokerman*

Forest Green Rovers are enduring testing times at the mid-way stage of the season. Shambolic defending has led to a shedding of fifteen points recently. That they are still in touch in third place says much for the competitive nature of The National League and the degree of difficulty to make the step up.

Dull the weather may be but it is not a word that applies to FGR, having witnessed seventeen goals in two games against Torquay, surely a record of sorts. Supporters aboard the Kendo Express eastbound for Bromley will be hoping the team find a way to defend the indefensible. Easing past the stables and grazing pastures into the car park fans were in good time to seek out the beer establishment and rip into the excellent Cornish pasties on offer.

The keenly awaited team news was broadly welcomed. Monthe returned at the back and Frear started with Doidge and Keanu up front, Carter dropping to the bench. Heavy low clouds hung over the arena but crucially no rain. The teams shook hands on a surface that mirrored the adjacent equine paddocks. A case for 'plastic' right there.

Rovers were given a good reception by over seventy travelling fans and rewarded them by starting on the front foot. Frear was seeing plenty of the ball and had an early shot blocked away for a corner. He was given space from a Doidge header but his attempted chip over Julian in the Bromley goal was wide. Julian, a legend in his own lunchtime of non-league football was getting friendly banter from the Rovers fans behind his goal.

There was a warning from the home side on ten minutes when Martin, finding room down the left, crossed for Turgott at full stretch, but the ball eluded him. It was the visitors who were impressing with good build up play despite the heavy going. The corner count was building and from one such Clough put a diving header wide.

It was no surprise when Rovers took the lead on 28mins. The hard working Sinclair was the instigator. Rushing forward he dispossessed Swaine, raced to the edge of the area and slipped a pass to his left for Frear to strike the ball low inside the left hand post. There was little reply from Bromley as Rovers continued to dominate, with Noble and Sinclair spraying passes all over the allotment. Even Keanu was seen helping out in defence.

Bromley did stir themselves around the forty minute mark when Anderson raided down the left and picked out Turgott, clear inside the area, but Russell was equal to his fierce shot diving low to his right. Encouraged, they pressed and had a big penalty shout waved away when Wishart challenged Dennis in the box, and another one soon after which woke the home fans up.

On 43mins Rovers hit back with a 'stiletto' through the heart of the Bromley defence. Noble struck a slide rule pass twenty five yards inside the defender, for Frear to one touch sideways to Doidge, who similarly fired the ball past Julian. A goal to savour. Bromley had a spell prior to the half time whistle but Rovers defence looked strong, with Monthe making his presence felt and Bennett heading a crucial clearance.

Having no doubt been given a good talking to at the break the home side came out with more purpose as the second half got under way.

Dennis weaved his way through the Rovers defence inside the area but fluffed his chance. He did better on 50mins, when hitting a great diagonal pass wide to Higgs on the right edge of the box. It stretched the defence and the cross was met by Swaine up in support, who headed firmly past Russell.

Forest Green's response was immediate. From the kick off Noble again hit a precision pass into the path of Keanu, ghosting in on the right side of the area. With unerring accuracy he fizzed the ball low across Julian and into the net, via the foot of the left hand upright.

The Rovers fans behind the goal gave it the vocals and it knocked the compost out of Bromley. Two minutes later a Rovers free kick near the right touch line saw Noble leave it for Frear to cross left footed with pace, the ball curling in over the 'D'. Pinnock soars, Pinnock scores, skimming a header past Julian's right hand. Rovers' fans exultant.

Frear had an effort blocked before being replaced by Robert, having taken a knock earlier. Although wilting Bromley fought on, and a good build up and cross from the left saw substitute Minshull head over from six yards, when he should have reduced the arrears. Trying to prevent this move Keanu was laid low and went off to be replaced by Cooper. He was soon in action and set up Noble, who in turn found Doidge on a double, but Julian denied him with a magnificent save.

Sinclair received a standing ovation from Rovers fans as he was replaced by Mullings on seventy minutes. The tall striker nearly opened his account on eighty minutes, when a high ball was flicked on to him by Doidge. He hit a thunderbolt on the volley only to bring out the save of the day from Julian.

Russell was accused of time wasting, when he needed the penalty area removed from his eye after diving into the mire to save a free kick from Turgott. To compound Bromley's misery Swaine received a very harsh second yellow on eighty five minutes.

Rovers laid siege to the Bromley goal in the closing stages and in time added Doidge finally scored his second, courtesy of Noble who set him up, to hit the ball through the brave Julian. He celebrated with the fans along with the rest of the team. A fitting finale.

This was the performance manager Mark Cooper had demanded and his players had delivered. A similar show of belief at Eastleigh, on Tuesday night, will build the momentum to chase down the leaders and quell the doubters.

**Tuesday 10.01.17**
**Eastleigh 1 FGR 1**
**FOREST GREEN HELD DOWN AT THE SPITFIRES**
*Richard Joyce*

Christian Doidge saw his first half header cancelled out as Forest Green and Eastleigh once again couldn't be separated at the Silverlake Stadium.

As was the case at The New Lawn earlier in the season, it was a goal apiece and a point each as the Spitfires fought back with the two goals coming in the first half.

Doidge's excellent header had put FGR in front in Hampshire. However Eastleigh levelled when they scored from a tricky corner.

An uneventful opening saw neither side make any mark on the game, but an FGR attack on 24 minutes proved to be the goal the game needed to spark into life, and it was Doidge who secured it.

Keanu Marsh-Brown's excellent cross from the right was met by the Welsh forward for goal number 14 of the campaign.

Eastleigh were almost gifted the chance to level straight away. The ball was stolen from Manny Monthe in the box, and former Sunderland striker Mikael Mandron was foiled by a terrific Sam Russell save.

Liam Noble's audacious 45-yard chip almost caught out Eastleigh's former Arsenal stopper Graham Stack shortly after down the other end before the hosts drew level from a corner.

A dangerous Luke Coulson corner caused havoc for the FGR bodies looking to get the ball clear in the box, and the ball squeezed in under the bar.

The Forest Green reply was almost instant. Marsh-Brown, cutting in from the left, had Stack at full stretch to push away his corner bound effort.

From the subsequent corner, Eastleigh won the ball and broke quickly, but saw Dale Bennett's perfectly timed lunge deny Hakeem Odoffin who had been set up with a clear shot on goal.

On the stroke of the interval Charlie Cooper came close to slamming in his first goal in Rovers colours, but courageous defending denied him, and Doidge's follow up was also blocked.

Again in the second half the match took time to get going, but after Cooper's header had been cleared, Dan Wishart forced Stack into action with a well-produced volley that was pushed out for a corner.

Marsh-Brown was thwarted just past the hour mark, and at the other end Ben Strevens missed a big opportunity for the hosts, as his diving header fizzed wide after he had done well to meet Coulson's cross.

Eastleigh debutant Darius Henderson headed over in the final ten minutes, as his second half strike partner Mandron spurned a massive opportunity minutes later, drilling a low shot wide.

Time was running out in the hunt for a winner. But it was FGR who very nearly claimed one.

Shamir Mullings met Marcus Kelly's wonderful cross from the left, although couldn't direct his attempt when sliding in on target with the goal gaping.

Doidge saw a stoppage time header scrape over the crossbar as Rovers looked to win it at the death but for the second time this season both teams shared the points.

## DESTINATION EASTLEIGH
*Rambling Man*

The first *Tuesday-nighter* for quite a while. Originally fixed for Saturday 3rd December, the match was lost due to the Hampshire club's impressive FA Cup exploits for the second season running.

The previous Saturday's results were a mirror image for today's adversaries. Rovers had notched 5 again, at Bromley, this time suffering just 1 in reply. In the FA Cup, Eastleigh went down to a 5-1 spanking at Championship Brentford. A harsh reality check. Given the unpredictability of football, a nil-nil seemed certain!

Rover's thumping win at Bromley had restored much bruised confidence, not least of its supporters. A win at Eastleigh would put them level on points with Lincoln at the summit albeit having played 2 games more. The sun was peeping through the clouds.

Eastleigh has underachieved again this season, despite continuous high profile player investment. But 3 managers between August and December tells its own story, as does one of the League's worst playing surfaces. 10 points behind Rovers, the hosts needed a win to revive any play-off ambitions, as badly as Rovers needed the points to put Lincoln & Tranmere under pressure.

The Bromley triumph had come at a cost. The rampaging Elliott Frear had not recovered from a 'dead leg'. More importantly, I had contracted raging man-flu, the deadliest illness known to the human species. That deprived Rovers of the positive input of my lucky cream jumper, a car with a winning record and an invigorating pre-match cultural visit which usually heralds success. So, whilst the Grim Reaper patrolled my door, Foggy and Compo ventured to darkest Hampshire, passing up the blessing of a cultural destination (as I'd feared).

The Silverlake Stadium or Ten Acres - neither name does justice to an uninviting location. Trapped within the coils of the A335 and the M27 it is bare of anything resembling a hostelry, within easy walking distance, and is a nightmare to enter or leave by car.

So many National League Clubs have grounds of real character irrespective of their resources and often pitches that boast a thick, striped turf. Not so Silverlake. A narrow, tall main stand sits uneasily opposite a long low shed. At the ends, the preferred 'home shed' faces a 2000 seater Meccano cast-off from Exeter Rugby, boasting 2 whacking columns that obscure spectators' view. That is where away supporters are directed. Refreshment facilities are minimal and the pitch owes more to agriculture that the beautiful game. In short the stadium falls well short of its club's ambition and is not popular with away fans.

The game ended with honours shared at 1-1. Probably more satisfying to Mark Cooper as Rovers edged into second place on goal difference above Tranmere. Also, his team largely rebuffed an energised aerial assault in the Silverlake mud and created the better chances. Important progress considering the many goals conceded so easily in preceding games.

Over the last few seasons, January and February have seen good times for FGR. Hopefully, the same will be true of 2017. We faithful live in hope.

### Saturday 14.01.17
### Chester 0 FGR 2 (FA Trophy 2nd round)
### KELLY DOUBLE EARNS FGR TROPHY VICTORY
*Richard Joyce*

Marcus Kelly's fantastic brace helped Forest Green make it into the third round of the FA Trophy for the first time in eight years.

The midfielders' double helped FGR make it eight consecutive wins against Chester, as Rovers capped a busy week on the road with another good result.

Mark Cooper made a series of changes to his side who ensured they made it a second win at the Lookers Vauxhall Stadium this season with a dominant display, and after nine months out injured, fans favourite Sam Wedgbury made a welcome return at the end.

The tie took time to get going, and after Dan Wishart had fired wide and Christian Doidge had seen a header saved, Rovers edged closer to the opener.

Alex Lynch produced a superb reaction save for the hosts to prevent Fabien Robert from powering home, but the young Welsh stopper couldn't prevent Kelly from breaking the deadlock.

Patient Rovers build up play saw the ball worked to Kelly on the right hand side of the box, and he produced a sublime finish to put his team a goal up.

After half time Chester were offered a huge opportunity to earn a much needed equaliser. A ball to the back post fell into the path of Tom Shaw, but Sam Russell did brilliantly to thwart him with a block.

Rovers put themselves in the driving seat on 56 minutes when Kelly doubled his and the team's tally.

It was a carbon copy of his first half strike, as he planted the ball past Lynch for the second time in the afternoon.

The goal added to Forest Green's control of the tie, although Chester had some half chances as they attempted to fight back, with former FGR loanee James Alabi and Kane Richards both trying their luck.

They couldn't find a way through though, and after Robert had powered a shot over the bar at the death, Wedgbury's late introduction as a substitute crowned a good week on the road for Rovers, who will now eagerly await Monday's third round draw.

## DESTINATION CHESTER
*Rambling Man*

Still languishing with rampant man-flu, contracted after the Bromley victory, the Chester match was out of the question. I had at least made the trip for the 2-1 League win, earlier in the season. Compo has also succumbed to my germs and his wife duly wrote him a note. And that just left Foggy, an English Yeoman fashioned from the finest oak and dismissive of illness.

By all accounts he had a good day too, along with the FGR travelling support. In the September encounter, we had found a more confident club at the Diva than for several seasons. Supporters and Directors whose glasses were half full now, a friendly young manager grooming a good young team and a sense of optimism about the place. We might have won that day, but soon after, Chester's fortunes improved consistently and they have steadily climbed the table.

Foggy was pleased to make the acquaintance of Chester Director Brian, a former player who did not hang up his boots until in his 40s and is now delighted to have contributed to the current Fan-Run structure of the club. He epitomised a club on the rise.

According to all the publicity, the hosts were well up for the visit of inconsistent Rovers and for a dash at the FA Trophy. Rovers' followers would have been wondering which team would turn up and probably pessimistic given our poor record in the Trophy over several seasons.

**J**
**A**
**N**
**U**
**A**
**R**
**Y**

As it turned out, they should not have worried. Rovers have beaten Chester home and away ever since they regained their National League status. They must dread any fixture with FGR. Yet again, Rovers left with the spoils. Foggy reported a classy performance where passes found their targets, possession was held effectively and Marcus Kelly scored two crackers.

On and off the pitch, Marcus is one of the most popular faces at The New Lawn and one of our longest serving players. He has danced to the tune of 4 managers in positions as diverse as left midfield, left back, left wing and support striker. He has held the post of club captain and been voted player of the year on multiple occasions. And I doubt if any FGR player has had more selfies with Ambassadors! Truly, one of football's nice guys.

Boss Mark Cooper is known to be a fan of this fleet footed, pass & move left-kicker, though opportunities have been limited so far this term given the number of options in his favoured position. Yet, as we approach the business end of the season, no better time to emerge into the sunlight.

Days later, as I bravely overcame man-flu, I decided that I was due some hours in the FGR gym. Writing a book is all very well, but it does little for your quads. I was in good company too as I put an hour or so in every day. Sam Russell, Aarran Raccine, Simon Lefebvre, Mo Chemlal, Louis McGrory, Rhys Murphy & Elliott Frear made frequent appearances directed by our fitness coaches. They are all good lads and a welcome sight any day of the week. Funniest incident was Simon being put through his paces on the treadmill, quite mercilessly. As he collapsed after, the rest of us had corpsed too. Back in the day, a keeper would not have been fitness tested to destruction!

And that brings me to my final thoughts. The rumour mill is linking one or two of the above mentioned with a move away from FGR. That is the nature of being a professional footballer as you negotiate a 10-15 year playing career. All I know is that I like and respect them all, not least because they have given their best for my club. Should any move on, they will be fondly remembered hereabouts.

**Saturday 21.01.17**
**FGR 1 Braintree Town 1**
**ROVERS HELD AT HOME BY THE IRONS**
*Richard Joyce*
Christian Doidge's ruled out late header ensured Forest Green picked up just a point in a frustrating afternoon at The New Lawn against Braintree Town.

The Welsh striker's stoppage-time header was judged to be offside, despite video evidence showing otherwise, as Mark Cooper's men were held to a draw against the Irons.

In form Michael Cheek had given Braintree the lead in the first half. But Charlie Clough's second half header saw FGR deservedly equalise, and arguably Rovers would have been left disappointed not to have claimed all three points.

New loan arrival Jake Gosling and Kaiyne Woolery were named in the matchday squad as Forest Green made a bright start. Keanu Marsh-Brown and Doidge both saw early attempts saved by Sam Beasant in the Braintree goal.

Cheek had scored a hat-trick in Braintree's FA Trophy victory last week, and the forward continued his fine goal scoring form by knocking his side in front when he finished a Jerome Okimo cross off a quarter of an hour in.

The goal had been against the run of play, and despite good efforts from Liam Noble and Marsh-Brown in an attempt to get back on level terms Rovers couldn't find a way through, and former Welling midfielder Sam Corne almost extended Braintree's lead albeit for Sam Russell's push over the bar.

Beasant, son of former Wimbledon great Dave, maintained his team's clean sheet with two fantastic saves before half time. He denied Marsh-Brown's thumping strike, and then kept out Rob Sinclair's hit from outside the box.

Immediately after the interval Russell demonstrated his qualities with a sublime save as he kept out Cheek's header, which looked destined to ripple the back of the net with a wonderful stop.

Russell was called into action again shortly after when he denied Chez Isaac's run and shot, and his two early second half saves proved crucial, as Forest Green drew parity on the hour mark.

Noble's perfect free kick from the left hand side was met with an unstoppable header from Clough as FGR snapped up the goal their afternoon deserved.

And they almost took the lead five minutes later. A Charlie Cooper corner caused chaos in the box, and after a number of chances, Doidge finally scooped over the bar.

Beasant continued to play a part in earning his team a very important point. His top drawer save from Noble's pin-point free kick on 69 minutes was another outstanding moment for one of the game's two goalkeepers.

The momentum was very much with FGR as they continued to scrap for a late winner. Debutant Woolery on as a substitute saw his powerful smash blocked by Beasant, and Cooper's follow up was deflected wide.

And after the away side almost snatched something at the end when Okimo headed over, Woolery again saw an effort in seven minutes of stoppage time go close, a couple of minutes before the days controversial moment right at the death.

Another excellent Noble free kick saw Doidge head in to give the home crowd the late finish they savoured, however the linesman had his flag up, to deny Rovers maximum points as Braintree claimed a much sought after point on the road.

## WARNING – TIES CAN CHOKE
### Jokerman

Last week's win away to Chester, in the FA Trophy, came on the back of a bonding session, following announcements that Kieffer Moore was transferring to Ipswich Town and Elliot Frear's departure was imminent. The performance reflected a fine response in attitude and determination.

Jake Gosling has since been signed on loan from Bristol Rovers for the duration to replace Frear, and Kaiyne Woolery brought in from Wigan to boost the attack. Both will need to impress to allay misgivings regarding the departures.

This afternoon's return to league football against Braintree Town must surely bring a positive outcome for a side with pretensions of promotion. On a bright but freezing day a crowd of over seventeen hundred greeted the sides, under fifty having made the journey from Essex. Noble, Pinnock and Keanu returned to the side having been rested at Chester, both new signings are on the bench.

For the first dozen minutes Braintree hardly touched the ball as Rovers took control. Keanu had an early strike and a Cooper corner provided Doidge with a header that was easily gathered by Beasant the Braintree keeper. 14mins and Bennett, attacking down the right, slipped over the ball on the edge of the box, and the defence cleared it to halfway and taking a quick throw to release Okimo on the left wing. Rovers defence was nowhere as his cross picked out Cheek, who controlled the ball on his chest, and beat Russell from close range. Forest Green were chasing the game and their fans were loosening the dandruff.

Noble replied with a twenty yard shot that Beasant blocked with his legs and Keanu hit the ball wide from the edge of the box. But the home side's domination had disappeared and a looping header from Corne had

Russell scrambling the ball over the bar. Both keepers were in action in the run up to half time. Sinclair saw his curled effort palmed away for a corner by Beasant while Russell was at full stretch to deny Midson's fierce cross shot. Much muttering at the break through mouthfuls of fruit cake.

Many fans may well have missed the opening minute of the second half, which saw Russell bring off the finest of saves. Straight on the offensive, Braintree streaked down the right and Midson crossed to the back post, where Cheek headed the ball forcefully down inside the left hand post, only for Russell to throw himself to his right and trap the ball on the goal line with his hand. Cheek could only applaud. After Hensall again gave Russell work to do, Rovers boss Cooper had seen enough and replaced Keanu and Monthe with new signings Gosling and Woolery on fifty five minutes.

This improved things for Rovers and they began to look the better side once again. They began to apply real pressure on the Braintree defence and Doidge beat himself up after hitting the ball wide from twelve yards. But a minute later his side were level. 59mins and a superbly flighted free kick by Noble from deep was headed home strongly by Clough.

The goal triggered sustained attacks that included a couple of almighty scrambles in the Braintree penalty area, but the second goal was proving elusive. On sixty eight minutes Noble struck a free kick from twenty five yards to the top right angle, but Beasant emulated his father with a brilliant one handed save. Gosling was prominent on the left and Woolery also worked hard on the opposite flank, but they met a stubborn Braintree rearguard. Both Woolery and Cooper had shots blocked and a splendidly floated free kick from Kelly went unrewarded, as the clock ticked down.

Braintree, only attacking in breakaways, went close to taking the points on eighty nine minutes, when a rare corner was headed narrowly over the bar by Okimo. Seven added minutes gave Rovers time and Gosling won a free kick out on the left. Noble again hit a precise cross that Doidge met and headed the ball past Beasant. Rovers' celebrations were abruptly deflated as the linesman flagged for an offside infringement. It was not to be for Rovers and the game ended all square.

The team could not be faulted for lack of endeavour. They worked hard but a better understanding is key.

Many fans will be disappointed despite the unbeaten run. There is much football still to play, nothing is settled, but there is no escaping the fact that recent events indicate this also applies to the playing squad. For the team and the intrepid supporters making the long trek north to the burial chamber Barrow next week, best ensure Lazarus is on the bench.

## FGR AMBASSADOR REPORT
*Oliver Sykes, Eastcombe Primary School*

My name is Olly Sykes and I am the Forest Green Rovers ambassador for Eastcombe primary school. I am in year 6 and my aim is to raise the profile of Forest Green in the school and get as many of my friends as possible to come and watch the Rovers.

Here is my report on the match against Braintree FC. It was a cold and bright day and the crowd of 1711 with 47 away fans that were looking forward to a great game of football, with two debutants for FGR number 3 Emannuel Monthe and number 31 Jake Gosling

Kick off starts at 3:00 and the game starts well for FGR it was only 3 minutes into the game when a corner from noble found the head of Christian Doidge who tamely headed straight at the goalkeeper. Then the pressure got to Rovers and a break from Braintree lead to a cross from the left and a shot that was unsaveable from Michael Cheek. Though throughout the rest of the half Rovers created many chances they couldn't beat the Braintree goalkeeper and Braintree were always dangerous on the break.

The second half started with Braintree on the attack a cross from the right lead to a crunching header which was going in to the FGR goal before a superb right handed save from Sam Russell pushed it away. The game then settled down with chances at both ends and Christian Doidge put a shot wide when he should have scored. A free kick from Noble in the 59th minute was floated into the box and Charlie Clough scored with a great header. Surely we would win from here, Rovers piled on the pressure a great free kick from Noble was saved and lots of other chances were missed and then in the final minutes of added time a free kick from Noble was headed in by Christian Doidge the crowd cheered only for the linesman to have his flag up for offside. A disappointing draw in a game I think we should have won but we are still looking at promotion. Come on you Rovers!

**Saturday 28.01.17**
**Barrow 2 FGR 3**
**HARDY ROVERS WIN IT LATE ON AT BARROW**
*Richard Joyce*

Manny Monthe's stoppage time header helped Forest Green become only the second team this season to win at Barrow's Holker Street.

The powerful substitute glanced home the impressive Liam Noble's late corner to help Rovers move within a point of the league leaders.

Noble's early free kick had given FGR a great advantage at the start. But having been repeatedly pegged back, goals from Christian Doidge and Monthe got the job done right at the death.

Noble's sixth minute free kick marked the perfect opening for Forest Green. After Rob Sinclair had been brought down the Rovers skipper stepped up and curled a wonderful effort past the reach of former Cheltenham Town goalkeeper Jon Flatt to break the deadlock early on.

A cautioned tackle from Alex Ray-Harvey brought the two teams to blows midway through a quiet half that saw the hosts work an impressive first opportunity on the half hour mark – Akil Wright saw his volley from Danny Livesey's cross fall wide though.

The hosts would draw parity shortly after. Ray-Harvey whipped a dangerous free kick into the box, and Richie Bennett got a final deft touch to send the ball into the back of the net.

Barrow's goal scorer looked to score again before half time, but his strike from distance bounced wide, while Kaiyne Woolery's dash down the middle when latching onto a long ball ended with the Wigan loanee lobbing the ball over.

The second half similarly to the opening 45 minutes lacked spark. Dan Wishart's run forward on 55 minutes ended in his shot going out for a corner, and Noble's volley from the subsequent set piece was deflected away by Livesey.

Neither team looked close to finding the game's next goal, but it would come, and it came the way of FGR when midway through the half Doidge bagged his 15th of the campaign.

Noble's inch perfect free kick from the right was swooped wonderfully into the Barrow box where Doidge was on hand to stoop and head in.

Wright tried to hit back for Barrow with a shot that went wide, but the hosts were struggling to develop opportunities.

They did get handed a good chance on 82 minutes when they were awarded a free kick just outside the Forest Green area. However substitute Andy Haworth's effort was pushed away by Sam Russell.

They would however level when a dubiously awarded penalty towards the end handed the home side a late opportunity to claim a point.

Hannah stepped up from 12 yards, but saw his effort saved by Russell, however the follow up landed centrally in the six-yard box and he knocked in the rebound.

The late drama did not end there. Monthe became the hero as a stoppage time corner saw the three points fall into the hands of FGR.

Noble claimed his second assist of the day with his corner that saw Monthe plant the winning goal past Flatt to wrap up a fine day on the road for Mark Cooper's men.

## DESTINATION BARROW
*Rambling Man*

Like the fixture list, my availability this term has been chaotic. End of January/Start of February is the traditional slaking of my thirst for skiing. So, whilst Cumbrian hospitality at Barrow awaited, I was sneaking south to the French Alps.

During the previous week, multiple player departures and acquisitions had turned the The New Lawn Reception's sliding doors into revolving ones. Fond goodbyes were offered to Aarran Racine and Elliott Frear bound for the opposite ends of the universe – Torquay & Motherwell. But the welcome mat was laid for Jake Gosling, Kaiyne Woolery and Mark Ellis.

Though I was AWOL, Compo and Foggy were present and correct, the latter driving them up on Friday with an overnight stay booked in. They must have had a sinking feeling before the match, as Barrow had consigned triumphant Lincoln to a 3-0 defeat on Tuesday night. And in previous matches FGR's defence under aerial assault – the Cumbrian speciality – had been as water tight as a string vest.

Both reported that they watched a terrific 'blood and thunder' game, with Rovers' last gasp 3-2 win fully merited. Liam Noble had put Rovers 1-0 up, Christian Doidge made it 2-1 and Manny Monthe plundered the 3 points in 94+1 for his first strike for FGR. With Tranmere losing at home to Daggers, and Lincoln stacking up fixtures (whilst taking time out to thrash Brighton in the FA Cup), suddenly it's game on at the top of the League. Does not take long to change a mood from suicidal to euphoric?

Of course I missed all that. My overnight stay was Folkestone, but I got there early enough to sniff out the beautiful game. I needed something to rid myself of the repulsive sight of Trump and May holding hands. Dover v Chester? No, that seemed like a betrayal. I went for Folkestone Invicta. a mid-table outfit facing title chasing Havant & Waterlooville, in the Ryman Premier. The venue was the Fullicks Stadium, a good old fashioned non-league ground with the chalk Downs as back drop, otherwise sandwiched between Folkestone CC and a Bowls rink, with Morrisons handily placed. Just 378 miles drive south of Barrow. I was not disappointed by the entertainment that followed.

For the record, Havant won 3-1, a deserved win in front of an impressive 400+ men, women & canines of Kent & Hampshire. They were cruising at 2-0 close to half time when a Liam-like free kick gave Invicta a lifeline. During a break, a double rainbow shone – perhaps signifying that a pot of gold awaited the home team. But after mounting useful pressure, Havant notched a third and that was that.

In all honesty, I was as busy taking in the surroundings as much as the on-pitch display. I started with a tea, a competitive 90 pence at the Wild Armoury Suite cafe. Deciding on a perambulation of the ground I passed a motorbike with a pannier advert for a Canadian 'Greasy Spoon': "I stop for pies". Next came the Brian Merriman (all seater) Stand next to which I met Ari, an impressive mutt clad in the black and old gold of Invicta. He looked bored and sat with his back to the play.

Still thirsty, I had another tea at the Seasider Cafe & Bar, this time £1 for an identical brew! The popular end is the Remland Stand, a hugely over-engineered Medieval Tythe barn of a structure supported by no less than 27 thick, square profiled oak columns. I continued to the toilet block facing the Brian Merriman, but despite nature's call, was dissuaded by the 4-foot-high stalls; think the building was nicked from a primary school? Lastly, I chatted to a guy I can only call 'ladder man'. As ball after ball is belted towards Folkestone CC, this gallant gent grabs his aluminium ladder to negotiate the perilous drop to reclaim the pig's bladder.

All in all I had a fine time. Not sure what the French Alps can throw up to replace Macclesfield v FGR in the FAT come Saturday. Maybe Ice Hockey?

The roller coaster continued. February started with defeat at Macclesfield in the FA Trophy, but wins in 2 out of 3 league games. It seemed that Lincoln City could do little wrong including an amazing FA Cup run for which they were not accorded the credit deserved. Yet if Rovers could put a winning run together as in summer and early autumn, the champions elect might feel the pressure of their deficit of League games. Elliot Frear was sold to Motherwell.

*Oh me Oh my Omar*
*Methinks this lad will go far*
*Attacking from the very start*
*Raising spirits, playing with skill and heart*

(Excerpt from 'A Clarion Call' by The Farmcotian in response to a dramatic debut by Omar Bugiel)

### Saturday 04.02.16
### Macclesfield 1 FGR 0 (FA Trophy 3rd round)
### FIRST HALF GOAL ENDS TROPHY AMBITIONS
*Richard Joyce*

A heavily deflected first half strike was enough to dump Forest Green Rovers out of the FA Trophy at Moss Rose.

Danny Whitehead's deflected effort helped National League counterparts Macclesfield Town claim a place in the quarter-finals of this year's competition.

Mark Cooper's men dominated throughout in Cheshire but couldn't find a way past the Silkmen's experienced goalkeeper Scott Flinders who kept a clean sheet as Rovers were denied a place in the last eight of the competition yet again since they last achieved the feat in 2009.

Liam Noble's fantastic deliveries had contributed to a significant win at Barrow last weekend. He was looking to make an impact with the dead ball again from as early as the second minute a week later, as his terrific free kick was headed onto the post by Christian Doidge to almost hand FGR a lead right at the start.

Rovers dominated in the minutes after but a freak deflection was enough to see the Silkmen go in front. Whitehead's strike from outside the area hit an FGR man on the way through to wrong foot Sam Russell and put the home side a goal up.

Flinders was called upon by the hosts to make two good saves to deny Forest Green the chance to draw level.

He kept out Ethan Pinnock's left footed shot after a positive run by the centre back, and then produced a diving save to keep out Dan Wishart's header from another dangerous Noble delivery.

Jake Gosling's free kick on 27 minutes almost crept in under the bar after Kaiyne Woolery had been brought down, but despite FGR's dominance, Macclesfield almost doubled their lead ten minutes before the break.

A shot from distance by former Birmingham City youngster Mitch Hancox was parried by Russell, and Whitehead saw his follow up hit the post.

Immediately after the break Hancox tried to double his team's lead however he fired over and it proved to be a rare opening for Macclesfield in a second half that saw Rovers continuously attack the hosts in search for an equaliser.

Chances were hard to create against a sea of defensive bodies, however Mark Ellis drove a long-range strike wide and substitute Keanu Marsh-Brown went close after turning well.

Noble's sweetly struck free kick on 75 minutes fell just the wrong way of Flinders left hand post, while another free kick from the number 15 was headed just wide by Pinnock shortly after.

Macclesfield finally secured a big opportunity to enhance their lead right at the end. Russell did brilliantly well though to foil Chris Holroyd who had got in.

There were still late opportunities as the game entered stoppage time. Flinders though was on hand to stop Charlie Cooper's hooked attempt and the Silkmen stopper again proved to be a barrier to confirm his side's progress when he reached to save Pinnock's glancing nod on goal.

## Saturday 11.02.17
## FGR 2 Boreham Wood 0
## PATIENT ROVERS EARN BOREHAM WOOD REWARD
*Richard Joyce*

Debutant Omar Bugiel came on as a late second half substitute and claimed an assist and a goal as Forest Green kept up their unbeaten league form in 2017.

The striker, signed from Worthing less than 24 hours before, set up Christian Doidge to break the deadlock in the final ten minutes and then added a goal himself minutes later.

Bugiel made the impact needed when coming off the bench but it was an afternoon that required patience against a Boreham Wood side that

**F
E
B
R
U
A
R
Y**

like so many that visit The New Lawn set up solidly and are hard to break down.

There were chances for both sides early on. Doidge's header from a Liam Noble cross was saved by Grant Smith while Angelo Balanta tested Sam Russell with a low effort after he found a way through in the FGR box.

Loan pair Kaiyne Woolery and Charlie Cooper both tried their luck with shots, and after Noble's long distance free kick had flown past the post, former QPR attacker Bruno Andrade hit the side netting for the visitors.

Five minutes before half time Cooper went close again. Patient build up play saw Dale Bennett draw the ball back for the former who curled a shot just off target.

After the break Smith had to desperately scatter along his line to ensure Matt Paine's touch from a Noble cross didn't end up in the back of his own net. Meanwhile at the opposite end Russell saved from Balanta again after Ricky Shakes' initial effort had been blocked.

Former Bognor Regis stopper Smith was kept busy in the second half to keep his clean sheet intact. He produced an excellent save on the hour mark to deny Doidge's header from Cooper's fine cross, and then followed that up with another key save to prevent Noble from nodding past him.

And after he had kept out Keanu Marsh-Brown's long range hit, Bugiel was introduced for the first time in the afternoon, and would go onto play a big part in the victory.

Before that however Russell had to make a strong stop to deny Andrade who had got in for the away side.

On 83 minutes the goal the home faithful yearned for finally came. Noble's fizzing pass into Bugiel saw the number 11 slip the ball into the patch of Doidge, and the Welsh hit man netted his 16th goal of the campaign past the on rushing Smith.

The score line was doubled as Rovers confirmed their win five minutes later. Noble's powerful strike was too hot to handle for Smith, and Bugiel had the instinct to follow up the goalkeepers spill, as he slotted home in front of the fans in the South Stand.

Boreham Wood had little to offer in response with only a few minutes left to make a difference in stoppage time, which ensured FGR snapped up all the points to make it six league matches unbeaten in the New Year.

## WOOD BURNS AS OMAR IGNITES FOREST FIRE

*Jokerman*

It's all over in The Trophy, no more distractions, all straight forward now. Lincoln can still implode following their inevitable exit from the FA Cup but Forest Green have to start winning at home to have a chance of reeling them in. It gives today's game against Boreham Wood added significance. The heavens are throwing down a mixture of rain, sleet and snow, and the air temperature is in low single figures as supporters seek refuge in the bars prior to kick-off. One topic concerns the Friday signing of Omar Bugiel from Worthing.

Team news finds him on the bench alongside Keanu. Mullings is on the sick, but fans were relieved to find Doidge present in an unchanged team that were hard done by at Macclesfield last week. A crowd of nearly sixteen hundred were shivering as the teams paraded. An early cross by Woolery won a corner for Rovers that Noble sent in to Doidge, whose downward header was collected by Boreham keeper Smith.

In reply Ferrier and Balanta combined well. Balanta had a clear sight of goal and a relieved Russell was not stretched to save his effort. It was an even first half with both sides having spells of pressure and both defences protecting their keepers with timely blocks. More frustrating for the home fans as their sides passing game failed to prise an opening.

As the half time whistle blew the cold was into the flesh reaching for the bone. The vegan dodgers were ripping into the cake and wondering where a goal would come from.

Soon after the restart Boreham nearly handed Rovers a goal, when a slip by Goodliffe allowed Gosling to cross dangerously. Paine, under pressure from Doidge, headed the ball down towards his own goal, forcing Smith to save on the line. Rovers began to look far more likely and after Balanta again shot straight at Russell from a good position, they took charge of the game.

Ellis was solid at the back and although Wishart and Cooper were not at their best, they persevered ably supported by Bennett, Pinnock and Sinclair. Noble, playing a more forward role, always wanted the ball, and tested Smith from the edge of the box, as the hour mark approached.

Keanu replaced Woolery on fifty eight minutes. Rovers began in earnest to break the deadlock. Smith in the Boreham goal was busy. He saved from Doidge and gathered a stooped header from Noble, following a cross from Gosling. He did even better on sixty seven minutes when he

**FEBRUARY**

blocked out a thunderbolt from Keanu. Doidge, following up, seemed sure to score but he failed to connect and the chance was lost.

The cold was now seeking the marrow. Twelve minutes left and Cooper sent on Bugiel in place of his offspring. He looked keen from the off. The eighty second minute was a key moment when Andrade, in space fifteen yards out, gave the thirty travelling supporters behind the goal a glimpse of what might have been, only to see Russell at his best to deny the striker with a great save.

83mins and Rovers finally took a deserved lead. Noble on the left curved a pass into Bugiel on the edge of the box. Under pressure, he slipped the ball through to Doidge. As Smith came out to block, Doidge's shot defied his valiant effort and the ball spun over him into the net.

The Rovers army behind the goal were impressed. Rovers were rampant now and on 88mins sealed victory. Twenty five yards from goal, Noble hit a shot of such ferocity that Smith knew little about. The ball struck him and rebounded to about the penalty spot. Bugiel's anticipation was something to behold, as he struck the loose ball with precision into the back of the net. Skipper Noble's celebration with his new team mate was significant. It was game over.

Bugiel? Well one swallow doesn't slake a thirst and all that kinda stuff, but he certainly put a smile on faces this afternoon and restored some 'warmth'. With fifteen games to play Forest Green can still win the title. The players certainly believe this and supporters who would settle for the play-offs could be considered losers. Nothing is real until it has happened. For the hardy souls who make the dire journey next week they must believe and endure and bring home the points.

## FGR AMBASSADOR REPORT

*Evie Urquhart, Rednock Secondary School, Dursley*

My name is Evie, I am the FGR ambassador for Rednock School. I've been one of their ambassadors for nearly half a year. As part of my ambassadorial role, I have done many things to promote the club in and out of school. For example, for the ambassador's match away at Macclesfield Town, I created a documentary giving an ambassador's view about FGR and the game. I live down the road where the 'old' Lawn used to be, around about the halfway line. I've been going to matches since I was five and now I'm twelve.

Match Report. It was a cold and snowy start with not much initial excitement, but we earned a corner five minutes into the game, unfortunately not resulting in a goal. Seconds later, Boreham Wood's midfielder came running up the wing, taking his chances, luckily Sam Russell safely gathers it up in his big hands. Soon after we earn ourselves a free kick, but unfortunately it was nowhere near! At 17mins Pinnock uses his head to keep out Boreham Woods shot on goal, they've had the stronger 5 minutes. FGR didn't take their multiple chances in the first half and kept passing the ball backwards far too much. Bennett was working his socks off getting free and his team mates finally passed to him raising a big cheer from the crowd. 33 minutes had passed and we still hadn't improved, I thought it was a bit like ping pong. As soon as Rob gets hold of the ball he shoots but here we go disappointment again, straight over the cross bar. I think to myself and tell my mum, they'll be needing a shooting practice tomorrow! What looks like a two footed tackle to me turns into a yellow card for Cooper at 37 minutes. At the end of the first half there must have been at least 10 chances of a goal but nothing to show for it.

At the start of the second half we actually played like we did at the start of the season passing quickly and with confidence, it looked a bit more promising. At 76 minutes Dan Wishart is running up the wing looking like he might score, but he ruins his chances by passing it to another player instead of shooting which quickly gets stolen by a Boreham wood player. At 78 minutes Charlie Cooper is substituted after having a poor match and Bugiel on his debut comes on. This change made a massive impact on the second half, we like the look of him tall and aggressive. Bugiel passes, Noble shoots, Doidge scores after 82 minutes of waiting, now we have to defend excellently to stop any of our opponents from scoring. A couple of minutes later it could have been a penalty but it was a free kick just outside the box. Only 6 minutes after our last goal we have another goal scored by Bugiel, could he be our new Frear or Moore replacement? The man of the match as we correctly predicted was the superb Rob Sinclair, the end result was FGR 2 Boreham Wood 0, thank goodness!

**Saturday 18.02.17**
**Gateshead 3 FGR 1**
**UNBEATEN FGR PEGGED BACK BY THE HEED**
*Richard Joyce*
For the first time in 2017 Forest Green tasted defeat in the National League on the long trip north to Gateshead.

A Danny Johnson brace and Wes York stunner condemned Rovers to defeat despite Kaiyne Woolery's first goal for the club in the second half.

**FEBRUARY**

Forest Green did hit the post on three occasions but couldn't recover from going two goals down in the opening 45 minutes.

Gateshead threatened from the start as FGR struggled to find their feet in the early stages. York forced an early effort wide for the hosts after the ball had dropped to him outside the area.

And after a quiet period they did eventually have the ball in the back of the net on 21 minutes when Johnson fired in low under Sam Russell. He latched onto York's through ball and drove the home side into the lead.

The scores were almost levelled immediately. Jake Gosling received the ball in space in the Gateshead area and fired a low shot that Heed goalkeeper James Montgomery pushed onto the post.

Johnson grabbed his and Gateshead's second on the half hour mark to further their advantage.

The former Cardiff City front man was allowed to tuck inside onto his dangerous left foot and he slotted into the bottom corner.

For the second time in the half Rovers hit the post just before the break. Montgomery rushed out of his goal and allowed Christian Doidge the chance to fire from a difficult angle at goal, but his shot was curving away and clipped the woodwork before being cleared.

Major improvements would be needed after half time if FGR were to find a way back into the game - and Mark Cooper's men got off to the best possible start.

Omar Bugiel's shot from distance was parried by Montgomery into the path of Woolery, and the attacker kept his composure to find the net.

It was the lifeline that was needed, although Gateshead responded by restoring their two goal advantage with a stunning strike from York on 56 minutes. Ethan Pinnock's clearance from a corner dropped to the ex-Nuneaton attacker who smashed home emphatically from distance.

The hosts had the ball in the back of the net again minutes later. However Paddy McLaughlin's effort was ruled out as he was caught offside having latched onto Johnson's tremendous low shot that had slammed onto the post.

Keanu Marsh-Brown forced Montgomery into action after coming on as a substitute when his low hit after Forest Green had worked the ball well across the Gateshead box almost crept in.

The lively York continued to threaten for the home side in search of an opportunity to extend his team's lead. He saw Russell get down low to save his strong near post shot as time began to dwindle away in the search for an FGR comeback.

Yet again the woodwork denied Rovers as Doidge was prevented from scoring by the post. He beat Montgomery but not the frame of the goal after being put through by Shamir Mullings.

And Pinnock almost notched with a goal his performance deserved in the final minute of normal time. The centre back saw his left footed hit just skip past the post though.

It was FGR who were on top in the latter stages, although on the break Gateshead almost added to their lead. Russell stood tall to deny York after he had run onto Montgomery's clearance.

And the Gateshead keeper then made a good save himself in stoppage time to prevent Ellis from heading in at the far post from a Marsh-Brown corner as Gateshead held on to claim all three points.

## DESTINATION GATESHEAD
*Rambling Man*

How to get to Geordie central? My usual travelling companions, Compo & Foggy were taking a few days 'up north' taking in the sights and visiting family, so would go direct to the Heed from their hotels.

Family was my hurdle. France domiciled first born had returned for 10 days. She'd booked intensive driving lessons, and the Test itself on her final day before flying back. She needed ferrying around to the lesson venues. That should not have been a problem.

However, Mrs R-M had endured an innocuous fall on the slopes in our last day in the Alps, a week or so back. On our return, the shoulder pain forced a visit to Stroud Hospital then Gloucester Hospital X-Ray. Diagnosis: broken scapula. Hence slings, and for me, arrows of outrageous fortune. Despite my protests, she was strictly off driving.

Just for good measure, Main Road Whiteshill, *chez les R-M*, had become a builders' compound to enable the reconstruction of the series of potholes that comprised the carriageway. The bus service that generally passes our door is suspended for the duration. So, whereas I'd fancied a day or two contemplating Hadrian's Wall and photogenic Northumbrian coastal towns, my leave card was withdrawn and replaced by week day taxi duty.

Nothing for it but to clamber aboard Sir Tomcat's Tours with 37 other stout souls. Now I have nothing against the FGR supporters' coach. However, since an infant, my stomach has rejected coaches and generally rejects its contents when presented with this means of travel. Still, Rovers cannot do without me (or so I tell myself) so I was at The New Lawn, ready and waiting, as Ken's stage coach rumbled in. Tablets taken, check;

**FEBRUARY**

a year's supply of chewing gum, check; containers of tea, check; and absolutely no reading matter. Clegg had chosen the coach too, and sat beside me to monitor the colour of my face.

Thankfully, there is nothing intestinal to report. My stomach rumbled and quaked but did not erupt. A walk about midway at Woodall Services allowed ablutions and a reset. Therefore, I thank Sir Tomcat and his doughty helpers for delivering me safely and for providing such good company. By 1.15 pm we disembarked at the Gateshead International Stadium and I was up for the contest.

Now usually I drone on about the complete unsuitability of this stadium to host football. The stands being so remote from the pitch that you barely feel connected to the action. Not this time. I'd remembered my National Trust complimentary binoculars and was able to put them to good use. Also, our hosts were friendly and gracious. Reunited with Compo, Foggy, Morse and their wives, Clegg and I enjoyed a hearty meal before the gladiators appeared.

In retrospect, I wish I'd been wearing a bag over my head. Rovers' generosity more than matched that of The Heed's Club hosts. Contrary to hope and expectation, FGR crashed to a damaging 3-1 defeat, with Woolery's first goal the only bright spot. This despite the support of a remarkable 160 from the 5 Valleys. Erratic finishing saw the Heed's woodwork struck no fewer than 4 times, but in truth they were well worth the win. The clinching 3rd goal was a veritable rocket for which Sam will be thankful to have been a spectator.

The loss means championship chances are all but gone, though a play-off spot is still attainable if consistent good form returns.

My return trip was made in Foggy's red Vauxhall (soon to be Peugeot?) with him and Mrs F sharing the piloting. Good of them to offer and I'm grateful to them for their peerless driving. It was though a sombre, reflective 270 mile trip.

**Tuesday 25.02.17**
**FGR 4 Woking 3**
**BUGIEL STRIKES LATE AGAIN TO EARN WOKING WIN**
*Richard Joyce*
Two late goals from German forward Omar Bugiel helped Forest Green Rovers edge to victory in a seven-goal encounter with Woking at The New Lawn.

The striker came off the bench for only his second home appearance, and repeated his debut heroics, with a huge contribution to help FGR claim all three points.

Keanu Marsh-Brown had given Rovers the lead, but after a scorcher of a strike from Joey Jones, FGR had to fight back from falling behind to Gozie Ugwu's early second half header, before Christian Doidge and Bugiel's double confirmed a much needed victory in response to last weekend's defeat at Gateshead.

The tone of the occasion was set from the first minute. Within the opening 60 seconds Michael Poke was called into action to deny Doidge's low drive, and Woking's bright start saw Fabio Saraiva's powerful free kick fly just wide in the opening quarter of an hour.

Keanu Marsh-Brown did well to round Poke on an FGR break forward, but couldn't draw the ball back, while the end-to-end opening continued when Sam Russell had to save Woking's Colchester United loanee Macauley Bonne's low effort.

Doidge had the ball in the back of the net for the first of two disallowed goals midway through the half. The ball had cannoned off his arm into the net after Poke had struggled to deal with a cross from the left and was ruled out.

Doidge's strike partner Marsh-Brown edged closer to breaking the deadlock when his smash on the half hour mark flew wide, and he eventually did notch his tenth goal of the campaign when he powered in from close range.

A terrific set piece delivery from Liam Noble fell into the path of the Rovers number nine via the knees of Poke, and he put FGR ahead with ease.

Woking would hit back in stunning circumstances just before half time. Jones drove forward and unleashed a sensational strike from 40 yards that slammed in on the underside of the bar to draw the visitors level with a contender for goal of the season.

A tasty opening 45 minutes was repeated in the second half. After Ugwu had seen his early shot stopped by Russell, Poke made a fantastic double save minutes later as he pushed away Noble's strike and then got up quickly to keep out Mark Ellis' follow up.

The visitors turned it around to take the lead when Ugwu added to his tally for the campaign when he demonstrated his aerial prowess with a good header past the helpless Russell.

Immediately FGR set about trying to find a way of getting back on level terms, but Poke stood tall when Marsh-Brown burst through, although Mark Cooper's men were level on 56 minutes.

Darren Carter's deep corner kick towards the back post was met by Doidge who nodded in.

A formation change saw Woking's positive style switch to a more defensive minded approach. It allowed FGR the chance to flood forward

**F**
**E**
**B**
**R**
**U**
**A**
**R**
**Y**

and Charlie Cooper almost blasted in from the right hand side as Forest Green aimed to regain the lead.

The Birmingham City loanee was then brought down on 66 minutes to hand his side a major opportunity from the penalty spot. It was a chance that couldn't be taken though as Poke guessed right to save Carter's effort from 12 yards.

Despite the missed opportunity from the spot Forest Green's attacking optimism was growing, and Ellis saw a header from a difficult angle cleared off the line, and Doidge saw his header on 74 minutes disallowed once again by the officials.

With the clock ticking for a second consecutive home game new addition Bugiel was introduced from off the bench, and the German scored the goal the home supporters craved near the death with a marvellous finish from a fantastic move.

Noble's sprayed pass was inch perfect for Wedgbury, whose brilliant cross was equally turned home emphatically by Bugiel to send The New Lawn supporters to their feet.

And it was a Bugiel double when his solo effort in stoppage time cemented his impact as a substitute. He picked the ball up in his own half and went on a driving run that ended with a tidy bottom corner finish past the outstretched arms of Poke.

The late flurry of goals didn't finish there. Woking hit back for the afternoon's seventh.

Charlton Athletic loanee Terell Thomas headed in late on, but it was all too late for the Surrey side, who saw Forest Green do the double over them in an afternoon of National League drama.

### CARDINALS MARTYRED ON THE LAWN
*Jokerman*

The hardy supporters who endured the pointless journey to Tyneside last weekend deserved better. Reading reports there appeared to be a lack of cohesion in the performance. Maybe as disjointed as the Flowerpot Men, listening to manager Mark Cooper in the aftermath. It is to be hoped he pulls the right strings to put his team back on track against Woking this afternoon.

The threatened rain duly arrives, as fans head for the preferred option to soak up the ale in The Green Man. For many, expectations have been lowered following recent results but all things are still possible. The team sheet shows yet another changed line-up. Wedgbury and Carter start, Sinclair returning after injury. Keanu partners Doidge in attack while Bennett, Gosling, Woolery and Bugiel return to the bench.

A stiff breeze is blowing into the away end and Woking choose to play in the same direction for the first half. From the kick-off Rovers launch an attack down the left and Wishart picks out Doidge, whose cross shot is palmed out for a corner by Woking keeper Poke.

The visitors soon hit back forcing Rovers to concede possession, although not causing Russell any concern. On fourteen minutes, against the run of play Rovers break and Noble puts Keanu through. He takes the ball past Poke but fails to beat the covering defence. His first touch lets him down minutes later, from an even better position.

A series of four corners follow for Woking, and their first effort on goal comes when Bonne tests Russell low down at his near post. On twenty two minutes Wishart crossed to Doidge who bundled the ball past Poke, but the referee after indicating the goal, sees the assistant's flag raised for offside.

The reply from Woking is an overhead kick by Bonne from a corner, that goes high and wide. Doidge puts Keanu in, who rifles a shot over the bar, and when he returns the favour Doidge rounds Poke and then falls over, as he slices the ball out for a goal kick with the net unguarded.

37mins and Rovers put things right. A free kick central and mid-way in the Woking half is fired goalwards by Noble. Poke dives low to save, but under pressure from Doidge he spills the ball and Keanu powers it into the back of the net. A minute later it could have been two when Carter failed to connect with a squared pass from Keanu inside the area.

With half time approaching Jones, the Woking mid-fielder stunned the crowd and probably the hundred visiting fans behind the goal. Taking the ball all of thirty five yards out, he struck a shot that propelled it like a missile that Russell's outstretched hand was unable to prevent the ball ripping into the roof of the net. Wind assisted but even the home fans had to admit it was a cracker. The half time cake still went down well as FGR usually improve in the second half.

Ugwu brought an early save from Russell but Rovers should have gone in front when Noble's shot from the edge of the area was fumbled by Poke, this time it rolled to Ellis up in support, but his low shot struck the keepers legs and was cleared.

Rovers looked to be gaining the upper hand, when on 54mins Woking broke down the right and Caprice put in a terrific cross that eluded Ellis, and Ugwu was on hand to flash the ball past Russell, into the left hand side of the goal.

Straight from the kick-off Rovers went at the Woking defence. Keanu was put through on Poke who blocked the ball away for a corner on the right. Carter crossed to the back post where the imperious Doidge

**FEBRUARY**

bounced a header down that Poke somehow allowed past him into the net. A relief for the home side to even things up so quickly and regain the initiative.

Rovers were in charge and pressed their advantage on sixty six minutes, when Cooper was bundled over in the box and the referee was in no doubt pointing to the spot. Noble grabbed the ball away from Keanu and handed it to Carter. He in turn proceeded to half hit the ball too close to Poke who only had to fall on it to save. Keanu was suitably unimpressed.

The swear box overfloweth. Tremendous pressure on Woking then ensued as Rovers tried to make amends. Thomas cleared off the line and a free kick from Carter was put into the net by Doidge but it was ruled out for handball.

Seventy five minutes, Bugiel replaced Keanu and soon after Gosling came on for Carter. As the clock ran down Rovers kept up the pressure and on 88mins Ellis picked out Wedgbury, who was getting plenty of room on the right wing. He hit a dangerous cross over the penalty spot, where Bugiel beat his marker and acrobatically powered the ball into the bottom right hand corner of the net. He was ecstatic as were team mates and supporters.

Woking tried to retrieve the situation immediately winning a corner that Doidge was on hand to clear. Five minutes of added time was indicated. Fans became a little anxious as Woking pressed but a clearance up field was collected by Bugiel, who raced away to the left corner of the area, cut back on his right foot and hit the ball low across Poke into the right hand side of the goal. The whole place went up in smoke. He raced towards the bench and was duly swamped by his team mates.

Yet still Woking were not finished as they scored within a minute, with the last action of the match. Thomas rose above the Rovers defence to skim a header past Russell, following a cross from the right. Quite a game. A fighting second half display from Forest Green and a deserved victory. A trip to The Wirral on Tuesday evening will sort out the men from the boys. It's going to be interesting.

### FGR AMBASSADOR REPORT
*Tom Ratcliffe, Beaudesert School, Minchinhampton*
Hi, my name is Tom, I live in Amberley and attend Beaudesert School up on Minchinhampton Common. This is my first season as a Forest Green Rovers ambassador and it is a pleasure to be able to report on this fixture.

In all the matches that I have ever watched, this one against Woking was the best. Incredible goals scored at unexpected times. Amazing defence and amazing saves. It was very tense at all times.

The atmosphere in the stadium was electric, the Woking–FGR rivalry resulting in a 7-goal thriller. After last year's defeat we had to win (my grandad's smug face was unbearable – he's from Woking).

We had a strong start. A chance on goal in the first two minutes. We passed strongly in midfield for the duration of the match. The first half Woking had us under a lot of pressure. Including four consecutive corners in which two had goal scoring opportunities, but safely picked up by keeper Sam Russell. In the 22nd minute a Wishart cross came in and Doidge picked up the keepers error but handballed it into the back of the net. Carter being yellow carded in the 24th minute made no difference to the free kick of Noble into the goalie who made a mistake giving Keanu Marsh-Brown a ball to hammer into the back of the net resulting in a 1-0 lead to FGR in the 36th minute. But Woking didn't give up and 6 minutes later Joey Jones scored with a 30 yard curling and dipping shot that came out of the blue.

After a slow restart from FGR, 9 minutes into the 2nd half number Ugwu scored for Woking from an incredible right hand side attack adding pressure with a 2-1 lead. But no dampened hearts for FGR coming back in the same minute. But a wasted one on one for Keanu Marsh Brown. With a missed opportunity we all thought we were on the way down, but no a bouncing ball came in for Doidge in the 56th minute at waist height heading it in for 2-2.

We had an edge now and in the 58th minute Cooper just missed high and wide. When he was pushed in the penalty box 7 minutes later Carter took the resulting penalty but placed it right by the goalkeepers left leg resulting for an easy save.

Then in the 75th minute, Bugiel came on for Marsh-Brown. When Cooper zipped in a cross from the right in 87 minute Bugiel took a beautiful header to gain a 3-2 lead. And then we only had to wait 3 minutes more minutes until a break on the left hand side from Bugiel saw him slot another one past the keeper 4-2. We had 5 minutes to hold our victory. Three minutes later Woking's Tyrell Thomas received a header and slotted it past Sam Russell.

### Tuesday 28.02.17
### Tranmere Rovers v FGR Postponed
### DESTINATION TRANMERE
*Rambling Man*

The haphazard schedule of Rovers away games continued unabated. Disruptions aplenty by progress in FA Cup & Trophy – sadly by other teams not FGR – and for me, absences by illness and family stuff.

**F
E
B
R
U
A
R
Y**

So, there was a collective determination to enjoy the important fixture at Prenton Park, which might help to decide which Rovers would mount a challenge to IMPerious Lincoln City, and/or claim bragging rights ahead of a meeting in the end of season Play-Offs.

At any rate, Foggy, Compo and I decided that the Tranmere Rovers clash merited our fullest attention. Foggy duly booked accommodation in Birkenhead and a full calendar of visits was penned. We met at 9.30 at the Stonehouse Court Hotel, my filthy diesel being the weapon of choice. Slate grey skies, charcoal grey car, silver-grey heads – we should have noted the portents.

All went well enough as we lurched between the roadworks on the M5 and M6. Then back passenger Foggy came to life: "There's a pitch inspection at noon because of heavy overnight rain". (The expletives have been deleted to preserve the quality of prose). Suffices to say that we took a high powered executive decision to stop at the next watering hole to await word from the Wirral. You'd have to be desperate to stop at Sandbach Services.

Hot brown coloured drinks and tea cakes were consumed yet still no word. So we pressed on, secure in the knowledge that the clouds were higher and lighter in the west were they not? Wrong. As Birkenhead loomed, Foggy grunted, "Its off!" What to do?

If we turned back, the hotel booking fees would be lost. *Merde!* Besides, we'd targeted the attractions of Port Sunlight and the Albert Dock, so maybe a short break would be good anyway? And being in the North West, there were loads of fixtures scheduled that could fill our void: Blackpool v Barnet – we could cheer on Charlie Clough; or, Bury v Coventry City – might Chris Stokes be on show? We'd decide later, but the show would go on.

We arrived at Port Sunlight, bent on culture. The more so, as the excellent little museum had a decent cafe and we were starving. After, we walked a couple of vistas and admired the war memorial before this side of England did what it's best at – delivered a cold monsoon.

Everything around us was gloomy and monochrome and the rain did its best to remove the paint from my Passat. The street scene resembled a 'Lowry painting and I was already getting symptoms of vitamin D deficiency. We sought out Birkenhead Priory but it was closed and unattractively land locked by ugly industrial buildings. Unanimous choice was our Premier Inn.

In the comfort of our warm, dry rooms we set the free WiFi to work with Facebook messages. Stokesy admitted being fit again but not in the

Coventry squad. Blackpool was tempting but Bolton v Bristol Rovers at the Macron stood out, the more so as Senior Concession tickets were just £7! Thus, Bolton (Horwich that is) was our revised destination and was reached by 6.00pm despite stair-rod downpours. Italian pasta in the retail park adjoining the stadium restored our spirits.

Formerly known as the Reebok, the Macron is impressive and elegant from all angles. 20 years old, it looks bang spanking new. 14,000 or half full was respectable for a wet Tuesday night in Division 1. The Trotters started well and took the lead early on. Thereafter, the Gas dominated with Rob Sinclair's brother Stuart the best player on the pitch by his pony tailed head and shoulders. The equaliser came early in the second period but Rovers missed more open goals than you could shake a stick at and should have won comfortably. 1-1 it stayed.

As Lenny Henry keeps telling us, Premier Inn beds are very comfortable. We thought so anyway and the brekkie wasn't bad either. That set us up for a jaunt through the Queensway Tunnel under the Mersey the next morning to do a whistle stop tour of the Albert Docks, the Mersey Waterfront and of course the Liver Building. Close up, the latter is pure Gotham City.

All in all, a memorable couple of days even if the main act was cancelled.

More than any other, this month summed up Rovers regular season progress since autumn 2016. They flattered to deceive. 4 convincing wins out of 5 had enabled top spot to be recaptured from Lincoln, on the eve of the season deciding away fixture at that beautiful city. BT Sport covered the match live with 7,000 bathed in the sunshine at Sincil Bank. Doidge gave Rovers an early League but by the end City were convincing 3-1 victors. There should be a counselling service for distressed football supporters.

*"If you can keep your head when all about you are losing theirs – you have clearly misread the situation"*

(The Farmcotian quoting advice from his son)

### Saturday 04.03.16
### FGR 3 Macclesfield Town 0
### ROVERS CONFIDENTLY DISPOSE OF THE SILKMEN
*Richard Joyce*

Confident Forest Green strolled to a pleasing three points against Macclesfield Town at The New Lawn.

Rovers moved up to second in the National League table thanks to a clean sheet and goals from three different scorers.

Mark Ellis scored his first for the club since joining on loan from Carlisle United, while leading marksman Doidge extended his goal scoring total for the campaign before Noble's early second half finish.

Doidge's header after 12 minutes broke the deadlock early on. He notched his 18th of the season with a bullet header after he met Rob Sinclair's speared corner delivery from the right hand side perfectly at the near post.

The early goal gave FGR the control that allowed Mark Cooper's side to dominate, and another Doidge header from a teasing Darren Carter free kick almost went in, while the speedy Kaiyne Woolery was inches away from doubling the lead when his right footed hit flew just past the post.

Macclesfield would rue a huge opportunity to draw level on the half hour mark. Luke Summerfield's corner was touched onto the post by Niall Byrne and Connor Jennings saw his follow up effort deflected over.

Rovers had the ball in the back of the net minutes later as they looked to double their advantage before half time, only for Ellis to see his reaction to Ethan Pinnock's saved attempt ruled out by the linesman's flag.

The home side wouldn't have to wait long to extend their lead though after the interval as Noble finished off a forward move from close range.

Former FGR loanee George Pilkington's weak pass was seized upon by Woolery, whose fantastic dash down the right saw him produce a fine low cross that Noble smashed in.

Mitch Hancox tried to lead the Macclesfield response to going two down but he saw his powerful hit from a short corner stopped by Sam Russell.

The visitors struggled to create opportunities, and after Woolery almost saw a long run rewarded with a goal, the subsequent corner saw Forest Green net a third and final goal.

Ellis made up for his first half disallowed goal as he cleverly nodded in Pinnock's header back into the box after the Silkmen had struggled to initially clear the ball into the box.

It could have been four had the woodwork not denied Doidge his second as the game entered the last ten minutes.

Another thumping header from the Welshman slammed onto the crossbar in the final act of a controlled home showing at The New Lawn as Rovers made it back-to-back wins.

## ROVERS' TITLE ODDS SHORTEN
*Jokerman*

Whether today's opponents, Macclesfield Town's FA Trophy victory over Forest Green proves to be a blessing in disguise remains to be seen, as the annual fixture congestion farce approaches for successful cup teams. Rovers could have done without Tuesday's postponement at Tranmere, but a victory this afternoon against the silkworms would keep them in contention for the title.

On a cold but bright blustery day many headed for the ale house for some attitude adjuster and await team news. Manager Mark Cooper has given Keanu the day off and starts Woolery up front with Doidge. Wedgbury drops to the bench as Bennett regains his place in the starting line-up. New star Bugiel is again on the bench.

A stiff breeze is blowing into the Nympsfield Road end and this week Rovers have it at their backs as the game begins. Woolery is quickly off the mark in the fourth minute beating Macclesfield keeper Flinders to the ball. The angle however is acute and he fails to find the target.

Macclesfield reply when Halls forces Russell to save a useful shot at his near post, as a brief heavy downpour sweeps across the pitch.

Woolery is catching the eye with some good runs and wins a corner on the right that Sinclair takes on 12mins. His cross to the near post is met

**M**
**A**
**R**
**C**
**H**

by Doidge whose header squeezes inside the right hand post as Flinders allows the ball to slip under his body on the goal line.

It's a great start for Rovers and they proceed to take control of the game. Macclesfield are a physical side and when Bennett is unceremoniously chopped down near the right touchline, Carter picks out Doidge from the free kick. His header is cleared but allows Ellis to hurl a long throw into the box that causes panic, and a blocked Sinclair shot triggers penalty appeals. Despite their domination Rovers are given a scare on thirty one minutes from Macclesfields first corner. Crossed from the left to the near post, central defender Pilkington rises to head the ball across Russell, where it strikes the right hand post. Bennett under pressure is injured clearing the ball over the cross bar. Yet another free kick for Rovers is lifted into the area by Noble, where more slack defending allows Doidge to stab the ball goalwards. Ellis is on hand to poke it into the net but is ruled offside.

The half ends with Forest Green looking much the better side. The only downer is the cake has gone missing this week. The crowd of over fifteen hundred are in buoyant mood and the Green Army in good voice.

Macclesfield started the second half the brighter as one may have expected, chasing the game. It was short lived when, on 52mins, Pilkington let the ball slip under his foot on half way when his side were on the offensive, allowing Woolery to pounce and race clear. He charged down the right as Noble sprinted into the deserted penalty area, and as Flinders tried to narrow the angle for Woolery, the Rovers winger squared the ball for his skipper to rifle into the net. He celebrated with the fans behind the goal in style.

With the goal cushion Rovers appeared to take their foot off the gas and rather invited Macclesfield to attack. From a soft corner given away by Russell, Hancock took a pass and fired in a shot that the Rovers keeper unconvincingly punched up in the air, forcing Ellis and Carter to clear away the threat.

Both sides made substitutions. For Rovers Bugiel replaced Noble around the seventy minute mark. He was quickly involved putting Woolery through on Flinders, who did well to scramble the ball away for a corner on the right. Cooper took the kick crossing for Pilkington to head clear to the edge of the area, where the majestic Pinnock looped a header back into the packed goalmouth. Ellis, up in attack lurking on the six yard line, nodded the ball inside the left hand post wide of Flinders. It killed the game, although Forest Green had already proved superior in every department.

Wedgbury replaced Sinclair with fifteen minutes remaining. Another fine run by Woolery saw his shot blocked away for a corner, which was taken by Cooper on the right. Doidge met the ball with a typical leap and thundered a header against the crossbar. He really deserved a second goal to reward another fine performance.

For the final minutes Kelly replaced Wishart, who had also performed with distinction today. As the game ended one could reflect on a fine all round display. Every player was on his game and hopefully the Gateshead defeat has been well and truly buried. Two away fixtures are on the horizon at Dagenham and Sutton, but there is no reason to doubt that Forest Green Rovers are realistic contenders for the league title, with twelve matches remaining.

## FGR AMBASSADOR REPORT
*Floss Ellen, Deer Park School, Cirencester*
HI, my name is Floss, I'm 12 years old and this is my first season as an FGR ambassador for Deer Park School in Cirencester. It is my job to promote the club in ways such as: putting up posters, handing out vouchers and fixture cards and talking to people about the club. I'm really enjoying the experience. Here is my match report for FGR vs Macclesfield Town on the 4th of March at the New Lawn.

The atmosphere was buzzing as both teams walked out to much applause – everyone was eager to start! In the first few minutes there were some great crosses into the box, attempted shots, intense pace and smart passing. The Rovers were dominating with lots of possession. Then, in the 11th minute a corner came in from Rob Sinclair and deflected off Macclesfield's goalie, only for Doidge to rush in and header it into the back of the net.

With some hard work at the back putting off their strikers Macclesfield's few shots were saved with ease by Russell. With some handy free kicks and two of the opposition's players booked Doidge and Woolery unluckily missed possible goals. In the 34th minute Mark Ellis scored an off-side goal which was disappointingly disallowed.

In the second half Woolery made a spectacular sprint down the right wing and crossed the ball to Captain Noble, who smashed it into the top left-hand corner. Bugiel and Wedgebury came on and almost immediately made an impact; in the 70th minute Bugiel headed the ball to Ellis who headed it past the goaly's outstretched arms to make the score 3-0 to FGR. Ellis was named man of the match shortly afterwards.

With another 3 points bagged we were all pleased with the result of becoming second in the league. Great work Rovers!

**M**
**A**
**R**
**C**
**H**

**Saturday 11.03.17**
**Dagenham & Redbridge 2 FGR 1**
**LATE GOAL COSTS ROVERS AT DAGENHAM**
*Richard Joyce*

A last minute winner from Scott Doe condemned Forest Green to defeat against promotion rivals Dagenham & Redbridge at Victoria Road.

The Daggers skipper rose highest at the death to steal a point away from Forest Green in a second against fourth tussle in east London.

In what was a competitive 90 minutes of football Jordan Maguire-Drew's early second half finish put the hosts in front. But Christian Doidge levelled with a fine header against his old side towards the end, only to see his former teammate Doe claim victory in a cruel way to lose the game.

A frantic first half saw Sam Russell tested early on when he kept out Maguire-Drew's effort after Dan Wishart had been dispossessed, while Fejiri Okenabirhie dragged wide when he broke through minutes after.

FGR's first real opportunity was a massive one. Doidge's great work offered Kaiyne Woolery the chance to fire at an open goal with goalkeeper Elliot Justham stranded, however the on loan Wigan Athletic attacker couldn't find the net with Doe back on the line to make a heroic block.

Woolery did have the ball in the back of the net midway through the half, but it didn't count, as the linesman's flag denied his good finish when he latched onto a forward ball.

Daggers target man Oliver Hawkins saw a great chance go begging on 26 minutes as the end-to-end action continued. He couldn't find the net with a header from a deep diagonal ball into the FGR area.

Maguire-Drew offered a threat on his left foot for the home side and forced Russell into a good save when he got clear. And the Brighton & Hove Albion loanee came even closer to scoring the game's first goal when his rocket was tipped emphatically by Russell onto the crossbar shortly before half time.

The final chance of the half fell to Dagenham's Trinidad & Tobago international Andre Boucaud, although his dipping long distance strike flew just over the frame of the goal.

Woolery's volley wide ensured there was an early opening for FGR in the second half, but the hosts would go ahead when Maguire-Drew put them in front.

A fierce low cross from the left was slammed across the face of goal and Maguire-Drew was on hand to slide in.

The home side would have been disappointed not to have added to their lead on the hour mark. Boucaud's break forward after the ball had been stolen from Wishart in a vulnerable position saw FGR recover in time before Maguire-Drew pulled the trigger.

A string of Forest Green substitutions saw German forward Omar Bugiel attempt to make an immediate impact, but the goal Mark Cooper's men savoured finally came when Doidge silenced the supporters at his former club with a fine header.

Noble's lifted delivery into the box was nodded into the back of the net with a powerful header by Doidge for his 19th goal of the season.

Rovers were back on level terms and were now keen to seek the winner. Noble's free kick from 25 yards though with the clock ticking was gratefully held onto by Justham.

And within a minute it would be Dagenham who would make a free kick count. A fantastic delivery from substitute Frankie Raymond was perfect for Doe, who leapt highest to score the hosts winner.

Another Noble free kick that ended up in the side netting on the wrong side of the post was all FGR could muster in stoppage time, as Dagenham held on to condemn Rovers to defeat for their first of two trips to the capital in four days.

## DESTINATION DAGENHAM

*Rambling Man*

Urgent family stuff meant I missed the Daggers clash. Second born insisted I attend a gathering in Salisbury to sort out aspects of his nuptials in August. That left Compo playing chauffeur to Foggy in the silver 'beamer' and me scripting a second hand report.

So, as I headed over Salisbury Plain past Druid central, Compo set course with Foggy in the jump seat. The National Trust's Cliveden, was their intermediate stop. Not too shabby, they told me. Cliveden is a dazzling Italianate mansion in countless acres of landscaped gardens and woodland, about 2 miles from Maidenhead. The Duke of Buckingham commissioned the pile in 1660. With commendable foresight, he plonked it midway between junction 3 of the M40 and junction 9 of the M4, on a tump with views over the Thames. Our pair enjoyed the fleeting visit and prepared for the less scenic delights of Dagenham.

Sadly, Cliveden proved the highlight of their day as a disappointing Rovers frittered away good chances before succumbing to an 89th minute winner by the hosts. A 2-1 loss that all but rules out a chance of automatic promotion?

**M**
**A**
**R**
**C**
**H**

## ROVERS GUTTED AS DAGGERS TWIST THE BLADE
*Jokerman*

Forest Green Rovers bid for league status reaches a benchmark today with a visit to Dagenham & Redbridge, also well in contention. As the fixture list becomes compressed in the final weeks it will be a severe test of stamina and nerves for players and supporters alike. There should be no lack of confidence on the back of two convincing home wins.

This is reflected in the number of fans travelling; two coaches and many using the train. The Kendo Flyer surges through the M4 corridor under a steel sky, impervious to the rising sun. A pit stop at South Mimms is soon followed by a run through the east side of Greater London, a less than enchanting experience.

On arrival at Victoria Road away fans are made welcome in the club bar, providing a fair selection of ales. Those empowered with eye-phones were notified the team remained unchanged from the Macclesfield game last week. Keanu still injured, Doidge and Woolery lead the attack. The sun finally breaks through and spring like temperatures greet the teams. Rovers have well over one hundred and fifty fans behind the goal and the Green Army are in vociferous mood. The drum is disallowed and stewards do not seem enamoured by some members of the choir.

The game begins with early pressure from Dagenham, M-Drew testing Russell from outside the area, who gathers the ball at the second attempt. Whitely makes inroads down the right and forces two quick corners that are dealt with by the defence.

It was the visitors who should have taken the lead on thirteen minutes, when Doidge took advantage of Dagenham keeper Justham's misjudgement, squaring the ball to Woolery who failed to beat the defender Doe covering on the goal line. Dagenham began to press Rovers onto the back foot and were showing more purpose and aggression.

From a long clearance Rovers did have the ball in the net but Woolery was offside from Noble's pass. In reply M-Drew crossed from the right and Hawkins put a free header over the bar from six yards, when he really should have scored. Sheppard was getting plenty of room on the right and was shooting on sight. One effort had Russell stretching to tip the ball over the bar. He was also on hand to gather a curled shot from Boucaud, but could only watch on thirty six minutes when M-Drew cut in from the right and hit a left foot shot across him, only to see it strike the crossbar. The half ended with Boucaud firing the ball narrowly over. Rovers' supporters were ruing the missed chance but were thankful that the scores were still even.

Forest Green started the second half with more promise when Woolery made a good run down the right, but his low cross eluded Doidge who was crowded out. Attempting to press, Rovers were caught on 54mins when Okenabirhie went clear on the left and squared a powerful low cross into the area, woefully bereft of cover, and M-Drew crashed the ball past a hopelessly exposed Russell to leave Rovers chasing the game.

As the hour approached Rovers were getting little change from a stubborn Dagenham defence. Woolery was battling well and had a penalty shout waved away. It needed changing and Cooper did so on the hour with Kelly and Bugiel replacing Wishart and Carter. Things improved as Rovers endeavoured to break down the home defence but important blocks were made from Woolery and again from Cooper following up.

Robert replaced Sinclair on sixty five minutes. The Green Army were giving it some to lift their side, though the television language and Bugiel song in particular was beyond the pale. But on 81mins they were rewarded. An attack down the left moved the ball inside to Noble who lofted a cross to the right edge of the six yard box, where Doidge, spring heeled, headed the ball back across Justham inside the right hand post.

Green Army became Barmy and on eighty eight minutes Rovers won a free kick on the D and Noble kissed the ball before placing it. He hit it over the wall but it was saved low down by Justham, who quickly cleared it down the right, which had Rovers in retreat and Kelly conceded a free kick out wide, which found Rovers defence sadly lacking. Raymond hit the ball into the area with pace and Doe, from defence to attack, promptly thumped a header past a despairing Russell.

It left Rovers fans throwing up like there was money in the pastime. Five minutes added time gave them one chance of redemption but Noble's twenty yard free kick shaved the left hand post and found the side netting, with Justham beaten, but the game was up.

It was a bitter pill to swallow for Forest Green, conceding the points to a near rival. They were out of touch but had battled back gamely for a point, only to throw it away at the end. Manager Mark Cooper will have to come up with a good recipe to cook Sutton's goose at Gander Green Lane on Tuesday night.

**Tuesday 14.03.17**
**Sutton United 1 FGR 2**
**ROVERS BOUNCE BACK WITH FINE SUTTON WIN**
*Richard Joyce*
Two first half goals helped Forest Green get back to winning ways at Sutton United's Gander Green Lane.

**M**
**A**
**R**
**C**
**H**

Mark Cooper's charges bounced back from defeat at Dagenham & Redbridge a few days before with an easy win on the 3G surface against one of the National League's stand out FA Cup giant killers this season.

Centre back Mark Ellis notched his second goal for the club to set FGR on their way, and Christian Doidge ensured the points would be returning to Gloucestershire with a second following a disastrous moment for Sutton goalkeeper Will Puddy.

One blot on the night though saw Ellis given his marching orders late on for a late tackle – becoming the first FGR player to be sent off in the division this season.

Earlier, German forward Omar Bugiel saw his sixth minute chance saved after excellent work by Drissa Traore and Dan Wishart had played him in.

Although opportunities were limited for both sides until a crazy attacking sequence just after the half hour mark that should have seen FGR break the deadlock.

Dale Bennett's cross for Doidge saw Rovers leading marksman crash a header against the bar, his follow up was then blocked by Puddy, while Dan Wishart's attempt to stick the ball in the net was also blocked, before a final shot was cleared before it crossed the line.

But from the subsequent corner Forest Green did take the lead. Liam Noble's delivery to the back post was met by Ellis, and the Carlisle United loanee saw his header creep in.

And it was 2-0 minutes later. A long ball over the top was dealt with awfully by Sutton's on loan Bristol Rovers stopper Puddy, and Doidge reached 20 goals for the season with the easiest goal he'll score all year, rolling into an empty net.

Noble's audacious 45-yard volley immediately after half time almost caught Puddy off his line as Rovers looked to extend their lead, while the hosts almost drew a goal back themselves when former Arsenal man Craig Eastmond saw his powerful hit go the wrong side of the post.

The home side were struggling to find a way back from their negative position, although Maxime Biamou's overhead kick on 66 minutes did see them develop a rare chance in a fairly quiet second period.

Former FGR man Jamie Collins' powerful shot from distance would fly over ten minutes later, and the quiet Roarie Deacon saw his hit zip off target.

But there would still be a late glimmer of hope for the home side. Ellis saw his night end early when his tackle on Biamou saw him win the ball, but not in the eyes of referee Carl Brook, and he headed for an early shower. However the resultant free kick from Adam Coombes couldn't see him take advantage as he powered wide.

Sutton did however draw a goal back six minutes into the five minutes allotted stoppage time. Substitute Kieron Cadogan finished inside the area to add some unneeded late nerves, but it didn't matter, as the three points belonged to the strong characters of FGR, who held on for the win.

## DESTINATION SUTTON
*Rambling Man*

A Tuesday night re-acquaintance with the plastic turf of Sutton United did not have us bubbling with enthusiasm. Rovers had already tasted defeat there in the FA Cup, dumped 2-1 by another last minute effort. County rivals Cheltenham received identical treatment in the next round. Nonetheless, Compo, Foggy and I were all committed to go, though travelling independently as we had conflicting appointments during the day. Deep-Throat was due to share my ride, but had to back out as his Editor gave him detention, insisting that putting the SNJ to bed held greater priority.

Jonny-no-mates I may have been, but I was still up for some pre-match entertainment. For that I chose good, old fashioned boys toys. Brooklands Museum and the adjacent Mercedes World. Anyone who has watched scratchy Pathe Newsreel films of enormous 'Blower-Bentleys' tearing up rudimentary Grand Prix circuits early in the twentieth century, will love Brooklands. Sections of the famous concrete, banked track remain to marvel over, whilst the collections of vintage racers – cars, motorbikes and even Tour de France cycles will have you salivating. Add loads of aircraft, including icons such as the Sopwith Camel, a Bus museum and more motor epoch memorabilia than the most hyper-active boy could wish for, and you have a compelling location for a great day out.

Still want more? Pop next door to the free-to-enter Mercedes World for more of the same plus grand prix racer simulators, test track & skid pans ... A petrol heads cup runneth over.

Thus inspired, my un-supercharged Passat chugged to Sutton, me and it in very good fettle. Gander Green Lane is a chummy place and a decent gate of 1,400+ (with 100 or so from the 5 Valleys) was in good voice. Personally, I'm not a great fan of the stadium as, unless you stand at the pitch rails, it's hard to be high and near enough to get a great view of the game. And the 3G pitch is harder, bouncier and more slippery than its excellent counterpart at Maidstone.

**M**
**A**
**R**
**C**
**H**

Rovers' 2-1 victory was well deserved, the 'one' only coming deep into time added on, after what proved to be the wrongful dismissal of Mark Ellis. His 'red' was rescinded days later. Mark himself, and inevitably Mr Reliability (Christian Doidge) had fired a quick brace in the first half. It pleased many that Driss Traore made an appearance for the first time in months, and that Rovers dealt capably with the physical approach of their opponents. As usual Ethan Pinnock was his cool, outstanding self drawing admiration from all sides.

Thus, the pained existence of a FGR supporter switches once more to optimism. Two home games now, in quick succession. If, with the help of the Gods, we can manage 6 points, then the titanic match with awesome Lincoln City on 24th March may yet be a true test for the automatic promotion place.

**Saturday 18.03.17**
**FGR 3 Wrexham 0**
**FLYING FOREST GREEN EASE PAST WREXHAM**
*Richard Joyce*

A resounding home performance saw Forest Green romp to victory against Wrexham.

Goals from Dale Bennett, Liam Noble and Christian Doidge gave Rovers the win they deserved on a dominant afternoon at The New Lawn.

Bennett's goal just before half time was followed up by Noble's penalty after the break. Meanwhile leading marksman Doidge added to his tally for the season with a fantastic third.

Keen to gain revenge on a frustrating defeat at the Racecourse back in November, from the start Mark Cooper's side were at it, and Chris Dunn was forced into action to keep a Noble shot out after just four minutes.

Darren Carter's header from a Noble free kick later in the half slipped wide, and another chance from former Birmingham man Carter saw his free kick fly just off target before the half hour mark.

FGR kept up the pressure, and kept Dunn busy, when Noble again saw another hit saved following good work by Kaiyne Woolery.

A number of niggly fouls contributed to Rovers frustration for having not earned a first half lead, but the goal they were after would come just before half time.

Both teams scrapped for the ball in the Wrexham six-yard box following a set piece delivery that saw Woolery ease the ball into the path of Bennett, who kept his head to slot in the first.

Forest Green wouldn't have to wait long to find themselves in the driving seat after half time.

Woolery was upended in the box, and Noble stepped up to confidently smash in from 12 yards, to double the score line.

Wrexham were indebted to their goalkeeper for a string of important saves that would keep the score line down as FGR eagerly fought to add to their lead.

The former Cambridge United goalkeeper saved from Doidge, and then produced a strong right hand to keep out a strike from Carter.

He couldn't stop Doidge from netting Rovers third just after the hour mark. The FGR number nine scored with a wonderfully taken looping effort after he had raced to latch onto Noble's forward ball.

In the hunt for more goals Cooper's side piled on the pressure towards the end. Dunn again had to be at his best to keep out Carter's left footed effort, while he stood up tall to save from Omar Bugiel after the German substitute had been put in down the left hand side.

Woolery was the next to try and add a fourth. His powerful run saw him have options to his right, but he elected to go alone, and saw his shot deflected behind for a corner in what would prove to be the final action of an afternoon full of positives at The New Lawn.

## FOREST GREEN STEP IT UP AND GO
*Jokerman*

Ten to go. The gloves are off. For Forest Green Rovers the time has arrived for the team to get serious about the title and exert pressure on the City of Lincoln, with a victory against Wrexham this afternoon. This would set up the possibility of overhauling their rivals on Tuesday night prior to seeking a result at Sincil Bank.

A vital three points were won at Sutton on Tuesday and equally important, Mark Ellis is available today following an appeal to rescind his red card during that game. Traore and Pinnock support him today with Bennett while Woolery and Doidge continue in attack. Air temperature is on the mild side but a bitter wind adds a vicious chill factor.

A crowd of over two thousand, including nearly three hundred from Wrexham, greet the teams. Rovers kick off with the wind at their backs and go on the offensive immediately. Carter finds Noble who forces Dunn the Wrexham keeper to palm his shot away for a corner resulting in a Doidge header over the bar. Noble returns the favour picking out Carter from a second corner, but his shot sends the ball into the mist down the valley.

On eighteen minutes Pinnock falls awkwardly in a challenge and damages a knee and has to be replaced by Wedgbury, after failing to recover. Bennett drops into the centre. The visitors appear to be on a mission to break up the play with every challenge and give away free kicks for fun.

The Rovers players are having to keep a grip on discipline as the game progresses. On twenty seven minutes Carter bends one such free kick just wide of the angle. Soon after Woolery makes a run down the left and cuts the ball back into the path of Noble, who brings a fine save from Dunn to win another corner. Forest Green are well in control of the game despite the card count increasing to seven, Wrexham in front by one.

Wrexham win a first corner on thirty five minutes but are causing little disturbance to Rovers back line. They get their comeuppance on 45mins, conceding a free kick wide on the right. Kelly drops the ball into a crowded penalty area where the mother of all goalmouth scrambles ensues. Both attackers and defenders take turns to shoot and block, before the ball finally rolls out to Bennett waiting patiently in the queue on the edge of the area. He promptly drills the ball low into the back of the net, plumb centre through a litter of bodies.

The half time cake goes down a treat while the talk is mainly around red card certainties. Whether the referee had a word in the respective dressing rooms is unknown but the second half was a completely different game.

A big factor may have been a penalty awarded to Rovers two minutes into the half when Woolery was brought down. Noble stepped up and struck the ball hard inside the left hand post. He was mobbed by team mates and acclaimed by the Green Army behind the goal. Thereafter Forest Green went through the gears and Wrexham hardly had a look in.

Fifty two minutes a bouncing ball in the box and Doidge tried the overhead, easy for Dunn to gather. Sixty one, Noble put Woolery through, his effort was saved only to Doidge who was blocked and finally Carter tried to curl a shot, but Dunn, still grounded made a fine one handed save. 64mins Noble put a ball over the defence on the left and as Dunn advanced Doidge stepped in and hooked it high over him into the net from twenty five yards.

It was all over bar the shouting and there was plenty of that from the Rovers fans. Doidge was replaced by Bugiel on sixty eight minutes and soon after Traore gave way to Sinclair. Both players left to standing ovations. On eighty four minutes Dunn foiled the 'goal' of the day, when he was at full stretch to beat away Carters shot following a prolonged spell of possession. The Wrexham keeper was again on hand to prevent Bugiel adding to the scoreline blocking his acute angled shot at his near post.

The game ended with Russell, deprived of action by his defenders, probably frozen to the marrow. Wrexham were not good but take nothing away from Forest Green. They handled a frustrating start well and can build on this performance. Solihull on Tuesday night is the next step to keep the pressure on.

Then the underdogs of war can head north.

### FGR AMBASSADOR REPORT

*Eddy Turner, Avening Primary School*

Hello, my name is Eddy Turner, FGR ambassador for Avening Primary School, and I am 10 years old. This is my first year as an ambassador and I am really enjoying my role.

On the 18th of March FGR hosted Wrexham at the New Lawn. During the first half of the match, Wrexham's goalkeeper was continuously tested by some cracking shots from FGR, which he either saved or let fly wide. But Rovers kept on pressurizing, and just before half time Dale Bennett put us ahead following a goalmouth scramble.

Two minutes into the second half and Wrexham conceded a penalty. Liam Noble sent the keeper the wrong way, giving us a 2 goal lead; unfortunately, most of our fans missed it as they were either still in the bar or queuing for their chips! It wasn't over yet though. In the 64th minute, under pressure, Doidge chipped the onrushing goalie from outside the box, putting Forest Green 3-0 up. They held onto this scoreline and were worthy winners of the match.

It was quite a physical, feisty game and there were several bookings during the match. However, the 2,146 large crowd, 295 of whom had travelled from North Wales, really enjoyed the game and we FGR fans all went home happy, dreaming of promotion. Come on FGR!

### Tuesday 21.03.17
### FGR 2 Solihull Moors 1
### DOIDGE STRIKES LATE TO EARN SOLIHULL WIN

*Richard Joyce*

In the depths of stoppage time Christian Doidge notched his 22nd goal of the season to help Forest Green to three points over Solihull Moors.

With just seconds left on the clock Rovers leading marksman struck to help his side back to the top of the National League, after Fabien Robert's first half finish had broken the deadlock at The New Lawn.

**M**
**A**
**R**
**C**
**H**

Oladapo Afolayan had looked like he had earned a spirited Moors side a point with his goal after half time.

However attacking persistence would tell for Mark Cooper's men who were rewarded at the death with a winner.

The night had started well for Forest Green with Solihull's on loan Chelsea goalkeeper Nathan Baxter saving well from an early effort.

Meanwhile the 18-year-old keeper also kept out a Mark Ellis header on seven minutes after Sam Wedgbury had teed up his fellow defender.

Dan Wishart would smash wide minutes later, as Solihull's influence on the game grew throughout the half, and both Ashley Sammons and Afolayan saw efforts go close.

Excellent build up play would lead to the night's opener five minutes before half time as Robert found the net.

He picked up on Wishart's outstanding through ball and kept his cool to roll the ball past Baxter.

Frenchman Robert almost doubled the tally shortly after, but his stinging drive was this time kept out by Baxter, with another strong hit also saved.

After half time the lively visitors attack would cause FGR problems. Afolayan went close and substitute Nortei Nortey also had an attempt on goal, but they would eventually find a way past Sam Russell.

A direct ball over the top wasn't dealt with and Afolayan coolly slotted to level for the visitors on their first ever visit to The New Lawn.

The game was there to be won for both sides from that point onwards. Charlie Cooper tried to restore FGR's advantage with a long distance strike that whistled just over, and down the other end the hard working Afolayan's shot skimmed the post.

With quarter of an hour to go Forest Green would see a major chance go begging as Kaiyne Woolery came off the bench to hit the bar.

He headed onto the woodwork after meeting Robert's fantastic cross after the former Lorient man had seized upon Liam Noble's excellent forward pass.

The away side too would miss a big opening when Afolayan couldn't convert with a chance inside the FGR six-yard box on 81 minutes.

Loan duo Woolery and Jake Gosling tried to find the goal the home crowd were desperate for with late chances, but as is so often the case with this Forest Green side they battled to the end to claim all three points.

Ellis' clever chipped ball into the area found Doidge who swivelled and finished perfectly to record a significant win.

## CHRISTIAN ACT CAUSES A STIR

*Jokerman*

Solihull Moors, a band of hostiles from the Barbary Coast? Maybe not but they cut Ferriby recently. Rovers will have to be on their guard. On a very cold evening refuge is sought in The Green Man to await the team news. Manager Mark Cooper shuffles his team again which has become the norm for his style of management.

Pinnock sustained a long term injury against Wrexham, a major blow. Robert starts in attack alongside Doidge, Woolery and Carter drop to the bench while Bugiel, Sinclair and Wishart all start. A crowd of fourteen hundred are in place to witness the start of a crucial evening as the season counts down.

Forest Green start brightly, Noble finding Robert who powered a shot on target that Solihull keeper Baxter did well to parry away for a corner. Five corners in the first six minutes told the story and on eighteen Bugiel was put clean through inside the area, only for his first touch to desert him.

Solihull were by no means overawed and hustled Rovers, disrupting their possession game. Around the thirty minute mark they enjoyed a spell during which Afolayan saw his shot deflect off Bennett, leaving Russell just a spectator as the ball went inches wide. Sammons was shooting on sight and twice forced saves from Russell.

On 40mins it was the home side that gained the advantage following a long build up, when Wishart down the left, threaded a pass into Robert inside the box. He deftly beat his marker and struck a fine low shot past Baxter into the right side of the goal. It brought some relief to Rovers who were not having it all their own way.

Robert was certainly taking his opportunity. He tested Baxter from distance and then showed good skill inside the area, to unleash a scorcher that brought out the best from the keeper, who deflected the ball over the bar. The half time break left the game wide open and home fans were agreed one goal was looking a very slender lead.

The temperatures dropped further as the second half got under way and heavy showers persisted. Solihull came out to some purpose from the start and Rovers passing game looked fragile. Quick challenges forced most of the build ups to end up back with Russell and were causing concern not least among home supporters. On fifty five minutes a mistake by Ellis forced Wedgbury to make a goal saving block, and soon after Charles-Cook was through on goal but blazed the ball wastefully over the bar. 59mins and Solihull made Rovers pay the price. A ball over the

**M
A
R
C
H**

top caught the defence in several minds. Russell came out and was left on the floor, as Sammons kept a cool head to cut in behind and slot the ball into the unguarded net. The Solihull fans behind the goal charged the barrier to celebrate with their players. They didn't sit back and Carline strode forward unopposed and hit a fierce shot over the bar.

Cooper replied for Rovers skimming the bar at the other end. Woolery replaced Bugiel on sixty seven minutes. The game was getting stretched end to end. Afolayan free on the right blasted a shot from the edge of the area that beat Russell, but deflected wide off the foot of the left hand post.

Robert then reached the byline on the right and crossed brilliantly to find Woolery six yards out, but his header crashed against the cross bar and Noble following up could not force the ball home.

Inside the last ten minutes and Solihull should have taken the lead. Attacking down the centre the defence was breached, but for a goal saving block by Bennett that left him rolling on the floor. The ball found its way out wide to substitute Nortey, who cut in and hit a brutal shot from the angle that Russell could only block straight to Afolayan who seemingly did the impossible, and put the ball high and wide from under the crossbar.

The bitter night just got colder, fans beginning to think a point would be good. Kelly and Gosling replaced Wishart and Cooper as the clock ran down. In the ninetieth minute Gosling jinked his way into the area, created room and then fired the ball wildly over the bar. Some fans had seen enough and as the board indicated four added minutes were on their way. Rovers again gave the ball away and Afolayan raced through but his shot on target was collected by Russell.

The final minute. Rovers in possession. Noble on the edge of the 'D' seemed to take an age on the ball. Players were up for a final push, the defence standing firm. He dinked the ball left, it came to Ellis who knocked it inside. Doidge hooked on to it, man on and back to goal he swivelled round him to the left and struck a right foot shot, all in a split second. The ball fizzed low and true past the despairing Baxter and arrowed into the bottom left hand corner of the net. Celebrations? Just a few. As the players crowded in front of The Green Army, some of whom trespassed to join the party, Noble lay flat on his back some distance away.

It's been emotional. Whatever happens, for now Forest Green Rovers are sitting on top of the league. Lincoln City? They are sitting on the big white telephone with their foot against the door. We're on our way.

**Saturday 25.03.17**
**Lincoln City 3 FGR 1**
**DISAPPOINTMENT FOR ROVERS AT LINCOLN**
*Richard Joyce*

Forest Green threw away a first half lead and their spot at the top of the table against nearest title challengers Lincoln City at Sincil Bank.

The BT Sport cameras were at the home of the Imps for a first against second clash that saw FGR never get going, and falter to their most disappointing performance of the season.

Christian Doidge found the net yet again to open the scoring for Rovers. But Lincoln hit back with three goals after half time to seal a comfortable win.

A jumpy start saw neither side gain control early on, however after Terry Hawkridge had fired wide for the hosts in the opening ten minutes, Doidge broke the deadlock in FGR's first attack.

He did well to steal the ball on the edge of the Lincoln box, and after a one-two with Liam Noble, finished confidently to put Rovers ahead.

It would be the only joy of the afternoon for Forest Green, who saw Lincoln begin to dominate, with Luke Waterfall wasting two good chances from set pieces in response.

At the end of the half Noble saw hit shot from 25 yards go over the bar, while Marcus Kelly's effort on his weaker foot dragged wide.

Behind at the break, Lincoln were threatening for the entire second half, and on 48 minutes Sam Wedgbury was in the right place at the right time to keep out an Alan Power shot from outside the area by clearing off the line.

But minutes later the Imps had their equaliser. Paul Farman's long kick forward wasn't dealt with at the back, and Peterborough United loanee Lee Angol kept his cool to finish across the face of Sam Russell's goal.

The turnaround was complete after the hour mark. Sam Habergham's run down the left saw the full back level a ball into the danger zone, where Kelly was the unfortunate party to unintentionally touch the ball into this own net off the post.

After Charlie Cooper had fired wide following a rare FGR opportunity down the other end, Habergham added to his assist by scoring the afternoon's final goal.

His terrific free kick confirmed the win for the former Football League side as it found a way into the back of the net.

There were half chances as Rovers chased an unlikely comeback in the final ten minutes. Darren Carter and Noble both saw shots fail to test Farman.

**M**
**A**
**R**
**C**
**H**

A stoppage time free kick from Kelly did force the Imps keeper into action, while the home side should have had a fourth at the death, only to see Matt Rhead miss a glorious opportunity in front of goal after Nathan Arnold had teed up the large strike perfectly.

## DESTINATION LINCOLN
*Rambling Man*

On 19th November, Rovers final quarter collapse against Lincoln City made the return fixture an important event. Even then it was seen as a possible title decider. Since, the Imps advance in all competitions has seen them concede top position only once since November – to Rovers last Tuesday night.

A win for Rovers would see a six point advantage open up as well as goal difference superiority. Pressure would then mount on today's home team and give Rovers a realistic chance of wresting the automatic promotion spot. Defeat though would surely condemn Rovers to the play-off lottery. Hence, for both teams this is undoubtedly the most important League match of the season, watched with close interest by near contenders Tranmere Rovers.

With Compo exploring his revolutionary roots in Cuba, Foggy meeting near family elsewhere and my other usual companions absent or taking different roots, I elected for Tomcat's coach. Or rather coaches, 2 number in response to the high demand. BT Sports' live coverage meant a 12.15 kick off and a very early start, with the coaches departing New Lawn Central at 6.30 am.

Whenever faced with coach travel, my mind lies not in the destination but travel sickness endured since childhood. So, I rattled with all the tablets I'd consumed and chewed furiously through countless flavours of Wrigley's finest. Everyone aboard was in good heart and sunshine lit the countryside as we sped East.

First stop was Leicester Forest East services on the M1, incongruously entered from the West side of said autoroute. I have passed this 1966 monument plenty of times but never entered its portals. Its name brings to mind arch rivals of Roy Race's Melchester Rovers or maybe a mid-term by-election reverse for an unpopular government? "As Returning Officer for the said constituency of Leicester Forest East … " You get my drift. Anyhow, both coaches parked up enabling old friends to share tall tales over smaller coffees, whilst the younger element sought out fast food and cans. Back in the coach, the volume increased as we neared Sincil Bank.

I've travelled to this fixture most years since Lincoln was relegated from the Football League. The supporters and Directors had become gloomy, gates dwindled to 1800 odd and the club seemed to be going nowhere in a hurry. Last season we beat them with 10 men and bullied their muscular front man Rhead to his distraction. How things have changed. The stadium was filled with 7,000 locals - colourful, noisy and rocking all gris to BT Sports' Mill. And our contingent of 200 was doing a convincing impression of 1,000. I doubt that many grounds in the EFL boasted as good an atmosphere on the day.

On 10 minutes, things got better still for the Nailsworth hordes. After a fast start, inevitably Christian Doidge notched the game's first goal, a lead held for a tightly contested first half. But the Imps roared back in the second period and ran out convincing 3-1 winners. That said, their equaliser and third goals owed much to the officials ignoring clear fouls on Ellis and Cooper in the build up. And Rhead and Angol did themselves and their club no credit by taunting the incensed away fans, which shamed an otherwise fine occasion and should have been prevented by referee and stewards.

All of which leaves FGR fighting over positions 2-5, and hoping for play off glory at the third straight attempt. The Imps however are in pole position for a return to the English Football League, though Tranmere Rovers may push them closest. Oh bother – I'd been hoping for a break from the intensity of football, starting in May.

## SINCIL BANK TOO STEEP FOR ROVERS
*Jokerman*

Forest Green Rovers fans rise with the sleep still in their eyes to travel north. BT Sports TV dictate an early kick-off at Lincoln City, on what is the nation's top game as far as both sets of supporters are concerned.

The outcome is very important but not decisive, though many would argue otherwise. Rovers' victory over Solihull on Tuesday placed them at the top of the league table and encouraged fans to fill two coaches. The ageless Kendo hits the cruise control and the sunlit landscape unfolds. The sky was hugely blue, the clear, cool blue of tropical water with thin drifts of herring bone clouds sketched in to give it greater depth. Just saying.

Following a pit stop and side-stepping a couple of RTA incidents, the Flyer crawls into Sincil Bank. Lincoln fans have re-emerged following recent success, and the twenty minute queue for an ale makes it a futile exercise thirty minutes prior to kick-off. One hundred and sixty Forest

**M**
**A**
**R**
**C**
**H**

Green Rovers fans occupy the away corner as opposed to over six and a half thousand Imps supporters.

Manager Mark Cooper goes for experience, Traore and Carter alongside Ellis and Bennett at the back, with Woolery preferred to partner Doidge in attack. A minute's silence was immaculately observed to remember those murdered in London.

From the kick-off Lincoln attacked Rovers but it was the visitors who struck in 11mins, with their first serious threat on the home defence. A ball through the centre was contested by Doidge, who exchanged passes with Noble, and ran clear to strike a low shot past keeper Farman into the bottom right hand corner of the goal. The Green Army who had been in good voice rushed the barrier and upped the volume.

The Lincoln thousands were hushed. Their side had been on top and stung by the goal continued on the offensive. A corner from the right was met by Waterfall who sent a powerful header wide of the post. Forest Green were fighting a rearguard battle and survived a series of Lincoln free-kicks. Ellis, Traore and Bennett were stoic in defence and Wedgbury was blocking well.

Rovers' first corner was won in the forty third minute. Cooper hitting a planned low pass to Noble running on to the ball, but Rovers skipper blasted it over the bar from eighteen yards. In added time Lincoln went closer from a corner when Raggett sent a header only inches wide.

At the break Rovers fans were happy to be in front but by no means over confident given the pattern of play to date. Looking north over the roof of the stadium the sun illuminated the magnificent cathedral at the top of Steep Hill. Maybe a moment to pray Russell keeps a clean sheet.

Lincoln took up where they left off at the start of the second half. Angol fired in a shot from the edge of the area and Russell needed assistance from Wedgbury to clear the danger. On fifty two minutes there was some histrionics from Rhead when he fell to earth on top of Ellis under a challenge pinning the Rovers player to the turf. Ellis withdrew a leg and the beached whale embarrassed himself by holding a flipper and screamed in agony, breaching about on the floor. The referee was unimpressed.

Soon after on 56mins the scores were level. A high ball down the centre was contested by Ellis and Angol who appeared to foul the Rovers defender. The ball dropped into the box and Angol raced through and fired a low shot across Russell, into the right hand side of the goal. Six thousand were on their feet. Angol stood in front of the Forest Green fans behind the goal and should have been 'shot' for incitement.

The crowd were up and it was time for cool heads in Rovers defence. It was not to be and the gods on the hill were not smiling on Forest Green. 61mins and Habergham got the better of Wedgbury near the left hand corner flag, raced along the goal line and hit a fierce cross that struck Kelly on the hip, and deflected the ball inside the near post. It was a desperate blow for Rovers.

New signing Curtis Tilt replaced Traore before play restarted. Rovers could not hold the ball up front and were short of ideas, while Lincoln full of confidence kept up the pressure. 76mins Lincoln won a free-kick twenty yards out in a central position. Habergham struck a firm low shot around the wall and into the left hand corner of the net.

There would be no reply from Rovers. Bugiel and Robert replaced Woolery and Wedgbury. Apart from a Kelly free-kick in added time that Farman gathered at the second attempt Rovers battled to little effect. The final cheers from Rovers fans were ironic ones for Rhead who missed a sitter as the game ended. After taking the lead, it was disappointing for the travelling fans, but they can have few complaints on the balance of play. Failure against their closest competitors continues to haunt Forest Green Rovers.

However, heading home they are still equal on points with Lincoln City. That old sun is still shining in a sky of blue. The title race still ain't over.

# A P R I L

April brought yet more extravagant highs and depressing lows. A wonderful win at Tranmere Rovers (that virtually handed the championship to Lincoln City) and impressive wins at Guiseley and at home to Boreham Wood. But still time to lose at home to North Ferriby United and at Southport, both bottom of the table when the games were played. The regular season was completed with two 2-2 draws, the last at York City which saw the home team relegated to National League North despite 2 goals and a vintage showing from former New Lawn favourite, 'The Beast' John Parkin. Which Rovers would turn up in the play-off legs with Dagenham & Redbridge? And if that hurdle was negotiated, a probable meeting with in form Tranmere Rovers? Simply, anyone's guess, and the Fans Forum was in turmoil as a phoney war played out ahead of the 2 or hopefully 3 games in May.

*Our true fans, we don't wanna know you,*
*You are a disgrace to the human race we say,*
*How can you show your face,*
*When you're a disgrace to the human race?*

(Excerpt from Voodoobluesman's rendition of a Madness song, taking aim at some *sad* fans who abused Charlie Cooper)

**Saturday 01.04.17**
**FGR 0 North Ferriby United 1**
**FOREST GREEN FALL TO RARE HOME DEFEAT**
*Richard Joyce*
Bottom of the table North Ferriby United became only the second team this season to win at The New Lawn as they aided their slim survival hopes with all three points.

Reece Thompson's second half header was enough to help the strugglers to maximum points as a Ferriby side who had conceded 16 times in their last four games held on to what may be a vital win.

Fabien Robert had hit the post in the first half for FGR, but Mark Cooper's side struggled to break their compact opponents down and are now going to need something special if they are to still try and win this year's National League.

There were big chances early on for a Rovers side playing a new system. North Ferriby had been given special permission to bring in goalkeeper Owen Evans on an emergency loan from Wigan, and the youngster had to be at his best to deny Jake Gosling from close range when the Bristol Rovers loanee looked all but set to score.

Mark Ellis then almost got on the end of a fine Marcus Kelly delivery minutes after Ryan Fallowfield had tried his luck with a long distance volley for the visitors.

Leading goal scorer Christian Doidge was the next to try his luck, but he saw his hit deflected just wide after right wing back Charlie Cooper had done well to supply him with the ball.

North Ferriby would have been encouraged by the open nature of the first half. They almost went ahead were it not for Sam Russell's key stop and Drissa Traore's much needed headed clearance off the line when Middlesbrough loan man Robbie Tinkler looked to fire in.

Thompson's deft header kept Russell on his toes, while Forest Green's latest opportunity to break the deadlock saw Gosling fire wide on his weaker foot after a brilliant exchange of passes outside the North Ferriby area.

The goal Rovers desperately sought came ever closer a few minutes before half time when Robert tried his luck from distance and saw his strike slam onto the post.

A number of good chances had fallen FGR's way in the first half, but they were limited in the second 45 minutes, and it was in fact North Ferriby who would score the afternoon's only goal.

Danny Emerton picked up the ball on the right and drilled a low ball into the six-yard area where Thompson continued his decent goal scoring form this season with a near post finish.

The pressure was immediately on Rovers who now needed to score twice in the remaining 20 minutes.

However opportunities were limited as substitutes Omar Bugiel and Kaiyne Woolery saw hopeful shots fail to find the net, and Doidge drove over the target after Cooper had slipped a ball into his path.

A difficult late-headed opportunity from Doidge couldn't provide a dramatic stoppage time leveller, as the away side held on to the win and to leave FGR without a share of the points for a second consecutive weekend.

### ALL FOOLS DAY AS FERRIBY TAKE THE SAP OUT OF FOREST
*Jokerman*

From top to bottom in seven days in opponent terms, as Forest Green entertain North Ferriby this afternoon. Seven games remain and seven wins are the pundits' requirements if Rovers are to have any chance of taking the title, following their second half capitulation at Lincoln last week.

North Ferriby, although in dire straits at the foot of the table, remain the quintessential non-league club at this level. Basic infrastructure surrounding a field behind the allotments alongside the railway embankment. The rapidity of their over achievements has left them struggling for finance.

A familiar story but remarkable nonetheless.

Forest Green from a similar background have overcome the financial issues but manager Mark Cooper has spelt out succinctly this week the difficulties a club of this ilk faces to make the transition to the Football league. There are no easy games, to roll out the cliché but odds of 14-1 against the visitors were seen on Thursday. When the team news came through there were a few eyebrows raised at the absence of skipper Noble and still no sign of Keanu. Robert and Gosling were given starts and Tilt made his debut. For whatever reason manager Mark Cooper was rolling the dice.

A crowd of seventeen hundred, including a score from Ferriby, were present to see the game kick off in bright sunshine. Forest Green started not unexpectedly with the lion's share of possession. Eight minutes in and a great cross from Kelly found Gosling who appeared to beat Evans the Ferriby keeper but the ball was deflected wide for a corner. Ellis, up in support, headed Kelly's cross wide. Doidge also headed wide from another Kelly free kick and went closer having a shot blocked away following good work by Traore and Cooper on the right flank.

Despite their dominance it was Ferriby who came closest to open the scoring on fifteen minutes. The Rovers defence were hesitant inside the box allowing, the ball to run for Fallowfield, who was only denied by a brilliant block by the diving Russell. The ball rebounded to the edge of the area and was leathered goalwards where Traore, standing on the goal line, headed the ball clear. It was a let-off for Rovers who resumed on the offensive.

Half hour in and Robert and Doidge worked an opening for Gosling, but he was wasteful, blasting the ball over the bar from a good position. Robert went closest to scoring for Rovers when his shot from the edge of the area came back off the right hand post, struck Evans and went wide for a corner.

The half ended and left the home fans with little to cheer after a very lack lustre and uninspiring forty five minutes. The half time cake was nice though.

Attack was the main theme for Rovers from the re-start but Ferriby were frustrating them and they were struggling to break through. Gray at the heart of the Ferriby defence was having a fine game.

Around the hour manager Cooper made changes. Wishart replaced Kelly. He was immediately in action down the left and cutting inside, forced the ball through to Doidge who stabbed it goalwards, but Evans gathered low down.

Bugiel then came on in place of Robert. Sixty six minutes and Bugiel reached the byline down the right and hit a terrific low cross into the six yard box, but Doidge failed to make contact. The atmosphere in the stadium had been fairly subdued throughout as Rovers lacked all semblance of a cutting edge against such modest opposition.

Then came the gut-wrencher. 68mins Ferriby in the shape of Emerton broke down the left, hit a cross to the near post to the unmarked Thompson, who glanced a header past Russell inside the left hand post. Simple. The twenty Ferriby fans behind the goal were possibly more shocked than their counterparts. It gave them a boost and left Rovers bereft.

Woolery replaced Traore as a last throw of the dice but Ferriby began to believe big time and manned the barricades. Woolery and Doidge put efforts over the bar while Ferriby's Evans and his defenders dealt well with an attack that lacked the invention to deny them a deserved victory.

The referee's final whistle left Rovers, players and fans alike, with a nauseous sinking feeling. Manager Mark Cooper will no doubt receive brick-bats from all and sundry after this display. He must also lift his players to ensure Forest Green Rovers stay in contention for the two promotion places.

It's a hard road and following twelve pages on the Forum web-site after the demise at Lincoln, the obituary after this one will probably take even longer to bleed out. Best sign out for a while.

### FGR AMBASSADOR REPORT
Wilf Doble, Woodchester Primary School
Hi I am Wilf Doble. I am FGR ambassador for Woodchester Endowed C of E primary school. As an ambassador I put up posters, hand out half price vouchers and try and get as many people coming to matches as possible. I have been supporting Forest Green for as long as I can remember and I really enjoy my ambassador role.

**A**
**P**
**R**
**I**
**L**

My match report is on the game with North Ferriby. Jilly Cooper gave me some advice before the game. Jilly told me to concentrate on detail and to make sure I tell a story. So, here goes!

North Ferriby is a village that is 8 miles from Hull near to the northern end of the Humber Bridge. The village is even smaller than Nailsworth (less than 4,000 people). The football club is known as 'The Villagers', they are semi-professional, and their squad is all English. They were promoted to the National League this year so this is the first time they have played at the New Lawn. They won promotion in the play-offs from the National League North, finishing behind Solihull Moors. A fantastic achievement for a side that have a home gate of about 600 and are probably the smallest club in the National League.

FGR have scored more goals at home than any other National League side (42), and more goals away from home than any other National League side (38). A total of 80 goals puts FGR top of the National League goal chart so far this season (ahead of Dover then Lincoln). North Ferriby had only managed 26 goals in their 40 games and were at the bottom of the League coming into the game.

Early in the game Fabien Robert had a shot that smacked the post which made me think we had the game in the bag but I was wrong. North Ferriby's goal in the 68th minute seemed to come as a surprise to the 20 travelling fans. FGR continued to have most of the possession without making too many clear scoring chances and it finished 0-1. I'm hoping Jilly won't mind that there's not more detail about the match.

### Saturday 08.04.17
### Guiseley 0 FGR 1
### DOIDGE HEADER HELPS FGR TO GUISELEY WIN
*Richard Joyce*

A first half header from Christian Doidge helped Forest Green return to winning ways on a tough outing at Guiseley.

The forward notched with a well taken header to help Rovers return to winning ways after their first back-to-back defeats of the season in the past fortnight.

Guiseley were reduced to ten men early in the second half after Jake Cassidy was given his marching orders, but Mark Cooper's men still had to produce a robust showing to keep out the in-form Lions.

It was a lively opening 20 minutes with both sides doing well to create opportunities. Shamir Mullings saw a shot deflected wide and

Omar Bugiel powered over, while Kevan Hurst forced Sam Russell into action with a save from the Mansfield loan man's header.

Doidge almost came close to breaking the deadlock as he attempted to latch onto Mullings' cross-come-shot, and Jonny Maxted did well to block Bugiel's powerful hit.

Russell was kept on his toes at the midpoint of the half to deny Will Hatfield. The Guiseley central midfielder produced a good shot after Derek Asamoah had done well to square the ball.

Another pull back from the left hand side from the hosts saw Cassidy blast over after making a good connection with the ball shortly before FGR scored the goal that would see them go ahead.

Charlie Cooper shipped an excellent ball to Dan Wishart whose header across goal at the back post was met expertly by Doidge to glance the ball into the back of the net.

It was advantage Forest Green and following a quiet period after the goal near the end of the half Cooper's free kick and Mullings shot over the bar were minor opportunities in a pleasing opening 45 minutes.

After half time Guiseley's task was made even harder when they were reduced to ten men. Cassidy was adjudged to have elbowed Mark Ellis shortly after the break, and he was ordered off by referee Joseph Johnson.

FGR chased the cushion of a second goal and Bugiel went close with good openings shortly after the hour mark, while Hatfield's strong shot that flew just wide proved the threat Guiseley still possessed despite their one man disadvantage.

It was a good battle in the second half but chances were limited. Substitute Fabien Robert's long distance effort went over after the ball dropped to the former Lorient man, and Doidge saw a difficult headed chance saved by Maxted.

Michael Rankine's late free kick failed to threaten the equaliser Guiseley were looking for as the hosts looked to run out of opportunities.

There was one big late chance for FGR at the death in stoppage time that Cooper couldn't take advantage of.

The Birmingham City loanee was slipped in on the right by Robert, but could only power off target with the goal gaping.

## DESTINATION GUISELEY

*Rambling Man*

The sun was out, the birds had cleared their throats and a trip to West Yorkshire beckoned. A proper 'Last of the Summer Wine' outing for Foggy, Compo and me. Recent away games had seen absences of one or

**A**
**P**
**R**
**I**
**L**

other of us but the Guiseley date would see the band re-united like so many ageing rock stars. Foggy had offered to drive, the chariot being the new scarlet Astra generously released from Mrs Foggy's grasp. As usual, we met outside Stonehouse's version of Tudor England, Compo installed his cushion and we were away.

Tired of the continual delays on the M1, we gave the M5/M6/M62 route a try. Garmin and RAC reckoned it was faster. Wrong. We reckoned more of the 200 & odd miles were completed on workman-free 50 mph restricted sections, than on those technically capable of 70. Once free of the M62 we headed towards the Northern Powerhouse, so called. I had not previously understood the title, but as we ground through Bradford and the World Heritage Site of Saltaire, the meaning became clear. Sets of traffic lights stretching as far as the eye can see, draining power from the grid.

As the sun baked the traffic, we droned to our intermediate cultural destination, East Riddlesden Hall. Mind you, the journey had taken so long, we barely had half an hour to scoot around the place and get some liquid down us.

The hall was built in 1642 by James Murgatroyd, a wealthy local cloth baron. It is a picturesque Grade 1 Listed Building fashioned from the attractive blackened buff millstone grit you see across the region. The Hall perches on a small plateau overlooking a bend in the River Aire just downstream from Keighley. It's a cosily proportioned place, painstakingly restored by the National Trust and drips with period furnishings, notably 4 poster beds. Oh and there are purported to be a couple of ghosts.

East Riddlesden Hall, its lovely gardens and lake merited several hours more than we could spare. But it banished memories of traffic controls and gave way to a scenic 8 mile leg across t'Dales into Guiseley itself.

This was my third visit to Nethermoor Park in a year, albeit the first with Foggy last January was an abortive one, arriving as we did 30 minutes after the referee has deemed the pitch unplayable. In the second, Rovers rode their luck to record 1-0 victory though the goal posts had to be replaced afterwards, having taken a year's punishment in 90 minutes.

It's a cute, uncomplicated stadium, the centre of a town sporting complex. Throw in a few more Portakabins and you'd have something similar to the Meadow at Brimscombe or Meadowbank at Shortwood – without the steep bits. The locals are also a cheery lot, the complete opposite of angry types found at nearby Halifax.

As last year, the hosts have overcome a sticky start to the season and are happily aspiring to mid table. The Forest Green connection is also alive and well, old boy Adam Lockwood being manager with goal custodian being the popular Jonny Maxted, who has captured the admiration of the town.

After consecutive defeats to Lincoln and North Ferriby United, an injury hit Rovers line-up, shorn of Liam Noble, Rob Sinclair & Sam Wedgbury, might have anticipated a difficult afternoon. In their place, Curtis Tilt, Manny Monthe, Omar Bugiel and Shamir Mullins all took their place in the starting line-up, with 23 goal Christian Doidge taking the skipper's armband.

The pitch was as bouncy as a trampoline, but then so were Rovers. Inevitably, Christian scored the winner midway through the first half, courtesy of a peach of a cross by Charlie Cooper, nodded on by Dan Wishart. More might have followed, but importantly the relative 'newbies' stepped up to the plate impressively.

Another big game awaits at Prenton Park on Tuesday night. Fresh from a 9-0 romp, James Norwood and his friends will be chomping at the bit to spoil Lincoln City's title hopes. Just as our Rovers will be looking to take some form into the play-offs. A mouthwatering prospect!

## Tuesday 11.04.17
## Tranmere Rovers 0 FGR 1
### WOOLERY STRIKES LATE TO BAG TRANMERE WIN
*Richard Joyce*

Kaiyne Woolery came off the bench to earn Forest Green Rovers a superb away win against title chasing Tranmere Rovers at Prenton Park.

The Wigan Athletic loan man stunned a crowd of nearly 7,000 roaring on the former Football League side with a late finish as Mark Cooper's men held off immense pressure to secure all three points.

FGR were at their defensive best to keep out a Tranmere side looking to move ahead of Lincoln at the top of the table, and Sam Russell made some fine stops alongside a brave away showing which contributed to the win.

The noisy Tranmere crowd roared the home side forward early on. Ex-Forest Green man James Norwood tested former housemate Russell with a good shot the stopper was equal to after five minutes, while a breakdown in communication at the back almost saw the hosts find the net shortly after.

Resolute defending was required and Curtis Tilt was up to the task when on 17 minutes he bravely blocked Norwood's goal bound effort. Russell followed up Tranmere's next chance with a fine save with his feet after Norwood had set Connor Jennings, brother of former FGR defender James, with an attempt in the box.

The host's closest chance yet came on the half hour mark. Adam Buxton's free kick was brilliantly struck and smashed against the woodwork with Russell left stranded.

Russell was at his best though five minutes later to deny Jennings' low header after the former Macclesfield attacker had stooped to meet Liam Ridehalgh's cross.

By half time it had been all Tranmere. But the first chance of the second half fell the way of Forest Green, as Scott Davies was forced into making a fine save from Marcus Kelly's fine left footed curler from outside the box.

Russell had been a busy man in the first half, and the FGR keeper was kept on his toes again ten minutes into the second 45 minutes when he kept out Jennings effort after good build up play.

And he was again called upon to deny another dangerous Buxton free kick after referee Craig Hicks had awarded them a good opening from a central position.

Tranmere's frustration continued to grow. Norwood spurned a couple of good opportunities, while as the half progressed FGR showed they could provide a late sting to the night's tale.

Charlie Cooper's pass into the feet of substitute Woolery allowed the forward to burst forward, he slotted Omar Bugiel in at the last second but Tranmere were saved by a heroic last gasp stop from Davies.

The question was whether Forest Green would get another chance? The answer was yes, and just minutes later they took the lead as Woolery kept his cool, and his feet, to jolt his way through the Tranmere box and finish low into the back of the net.

It was the goal FGR's patience in the second half deserved, although Tranmere nearly levelled in the final minute of normal time, only to see Michael Ihiekwe head over from a good corner delivery.

Forest Green's magnificent defensive showing was complete as they held on for three points to record a memorable away win.

## DESTINATION TRANMERE (AGAIN!)
*Rambling Man*

Rovers' final 4 away games in 2016/17, (including Saturday's win at Guiseley) comprise a northern tour. Six weeks on from the rain-cancelled Tranmere fixture, the match had been re-set for Tuesday 11th April. Easter Monday would see a trip to Southport and the regular season would end at York. My team of companions was scattered over the country yet again. Foggy was staying up country, *en famille*. Compo was in London, making his way by iron horse. Deep-Throat was throwing a sickie and by the time the Rovers return to Birkenhead had played out, would be as sick as a parrot for his absenteeism. Still, Rochdale convert Woody was available for selection, and I picked him up at Tewkesbury early doors.

We had a plan to make the most of a bright sunny day. First stop, the gorgeously wonky Tudor black and white masterpiece, Little Moreton Hall, just off M6 Junction 16. Reported several times in the Rambling Man journals, only brief notes follow this time. The plan was for elevenses at its splendid tea shop and a quick stretch of the legs around the house. New since last year was the revealing of beautiful wall paintings in the rear reception room, previously hidden behind panelling. They resembled giant pages of an illuminated manuscript and alone were worth the visit.

Moreton's caffeine and culture shots worked wonders. We dodged the saturated M6 to find ourselves in Sandbach. More 17th century black and white jobs, some intriguing Saxon obelisks and a delicious plate of liver, bacon, onion, mash and gravy. The day was going well.

Next came Northwich. I always think well of this town since Victoria's insufficiently completed new stadium staved off FGR's relegation in the noughties. However this jaunt was about the Victorian scaffolding otherwise known as the Northwich Boat lift. A way of conveying narrow boats from the Northwich basin to the canal that towered above, and vice versa. Given time, I reckon I could have replicated this wonder in Meccano or Lego, but it was fun to see the ironwork doing its job.

By early evening, we had reached Birkenhead and decided to suss out parking near Prenton Park. Who should cross the road to an iffy looking pizza place than James Norwood, formerly a favourite of our parish. He was as chatty as ever, but Woody and I decided on mind games, chiding him for missing out on the score sheet in Tranmere's 9-0 demolition of Solihull. Chuffed with our psychology, we parked up at the green lung of impressive Birkenhead Park and walked to the nearby docks. The day had turned into a marathon. Sorry, snickers.

We could put it off no longer. Into the lion's den to pick up our tickets and watch the slaughter of FGR that the vast majority of the 7,000 gathered souls was expecting. Not sure that it helped that Tranny fans, stewards and officials were so naturally hospitable, friendly and *'bloody nice blokes'*. All I could think was "please do not let my team be humiliated".

**A**
**P**
**R**
**I**
**L**

What ensued was as near a miracle as I've witnessed in a football stadium. Brimming with confidence, Tranmere sliced into our boys in green and black. They murdered us 0-0 by the break, kept out only by Sam Russell's heroics, dogged and last ditch defence, the stout local woodwork and a chunk of good fortune. Yet there was an increasing edginess in Tranny's play, given that their championship hopes depended on a win. Half 2 was oh so different. Our Rovers had not mustered a shot in the first period, yet in the opening seconds of the new half, only a fingertip save repelled Marcus Kelly's curler. Tranny retaliated yet increasingly it was their guests who carried the greater threat. Cooper found Woolery whose run set up Bugiel whose shot was smothered. Chances came and went at both ends yet it was dawning on FGR's noisy support that an upset was possible. Then delirium as Woolery won it with 5 minutes to go. A seminal result in the context or the season's promotion race and a coming of age for the class of 2017.

The venerable Passat chuckled away as it bore its happy crew homeward. Compo had come along for the return trip. Even the Highway Agency's latest sabotage – closure on M6 Junctions 17 to 16 and M5 Junctions 4A to 6 – could not repress the glow. Passengers delivered, I crawled into bed at 2.30 am, smile plastered over my *boat race*.

## KAIYNE PULLS THE WOOL OVER THE WIRRAL
*Jokerman*

As the season moves into the closing stages it has become increasingly difficult to predict Mark Cooper's line-up for Forest Green Rovers. Equally so the quality of performance. Having been beaten by top and bottom clubs recently they head to Tranmere on the back of a workman like win away at Guiseley on Saturday.

On current form the league title is still possible but unlikely, whereas tonight's opponents could yet take the title away from favourites Lincoln City. As the FGR special headed north, for those on board an air of apprehension prevailed and most would take a draw result in a heartbeat. A victory would go some way to burying the 'top club' hoodoo.

The journey to The Wirral was reasonably trouble free despite the endless speed restrictions. On arrival at Prenton Park there was time for an ale under the chandeliers, inside the giant marquee serving as a bar for both home and away supporters. The team news was wired through to disclose the same team that played at Guiseley, except Kelly and Wedgbury replaced Traore and Buguiel. Cooper keeping faith with his defence and giving Mullings another chance to partner Doidge in attack.

Fans remain apprehensive. A crowd of nearly seven thousand greeted the teams under the lights on a fine spring evening. Over a hundred Rovers supporters were situated in the 'cowshed' of this magnificent stadium. The Green Army were in fine voice throughout the night and security had no issues, unlike Dagenham, with the huge drum that added to the dulcet tones of the choir.

The game kicked off and Tranmere attacking the cowshed end treated the Rovers fans to forty five minutes of sustained pressure. Russell palmed away an early shot on target which set the tone. On twelve minutes the pressure intensified following a mix-up in Rovers defence between Monthe, Russell and Ellis, that ended with Ellis making a goal saving block to concede a corner. From the kick Monthe blocked a shot from Vaughan inside the box, the ball falling for Norwood who seemed sure to score, only for Tilt to throw himself to block heroically.

There was some respite when Hughes was booked for a foul on Wedgbury and Mullings was felled by two Tranmere players, as he tried to hold the ball up. As the giant fell to earth, his opponent Harris had the disagreeable experience of cushioning the fall. His legs refused to work properly afterwards as he tried to continue and was soon replaced by Wallace on twenty six minutes.

Around thirty minutes a mistake by Wedgbury forced Cooper to concede a free kick twenty five yards out in a central position. Buxton stepped up and struck it sweetly over the wall past Russell, who watched the ball cannon back off the crossbar. It was unrelenting as the corner count mounted. A short corner on the left by Hughes to Ridehalgh was crossed to Jennings, whose downward header was saved on the goal line by Russell.

More relief for Rovers as Jennings fouled Cooper on the half way line and bent over his prostrate form to wish him a pleasant evening. This all escalated into a hand luggage convention that the referee handled brilliantly by just walking away and letting twenty players get on with it. The game resumed to half time enabling Tranmere keeper Davies to finish his library book.

The onslaught had produced no goals for Tranmere the Forest Green defence having been strong and defiant, deserved their luck. The meat and potato pies went down well at half time.

The second half produced a shock on forty eight minutes when the visitors attacked down the right and Kelly, from the corner of the box curled a shot heading inside the left hand post, forcing Davies to dive full length to palm away for a corner. Cooper crossed and only Mullings will know why he failed to connect.

The Green Army sensed this was going to be a different game and stepped it up a notch. Tranmere replied working the ball well from the left, exchanging passes to create an opening for Jennings with a close range side foot goal. Russell's reflexes were quicker and he produced an awesome save diving low to his right. Another chance gone for Tranmere and Forest Green boss Cooper replaced Mullings with Woolery as the hour approached.

Woolery made an impact attacking down the left and winning another corner. Cooper crossed to the back post where Ellis headed the ball over the bar. Rovers were enjoying more possession and playing in the Tranmere half. One sensed a feeling of disquiet amongst the home contingent. Russell was still kept busy and did well to hang on to a dangerous corner kick gathering the ball at the second attempt under extreme pressure.

On sixty seven minutes it was hearts in mouth time for Rovers fans as Tranmere gained a free kick on the edge of the 'D'. Buxton kept his shot lower, this time around the wall, only to see Russell produce another breathtaking save diving to his right. Cook replaced Stockton for Tranmere on seventy two minutes and soon after Bugiel replaced Kelly for Rovers.

Both Forest Green substitutes raised the pulse inside the final ten minutes of the game. Woolery knocked the ball down for Bugiel who was through on Davies, but the Tranmere keeper was quickly off his goal-line, diving at his feet to concede a corner. Rovers were really pressing and the home defence was looking more than a little unsettled. From the corner a series of passes ended with Woolery being blocked out somewhat desperately.

85mins and the already nervous thousands experienced an uncontrollable motion, as Forest Green produced the laxative effect. Another run into the area by the Rovers subs saw Bugiel thwarted, but Woolery following up took the ball on and as Davies came off his goal-line to block, he prodded the ball past him and the ball gently rolled over the line into the back of the net. There was an avalanche of Green Army personnel behind the goal who appeared quite animated by this turn of events.

Tranmere were desperate and forced a couple of corners in search of an equaliser. From the second Cook's powerful header grazed the bar and their heads dropped. Four added minutes were played out to the Green

Army drum. Players and fans applauded each other it was quite a night. Not even the Prenton Prat could spoil the occasion, bouncing a brick off the window a foot above Hopoe's head, it nearly woke him up as we headed into the night.

In some ways reminiscent of a night in Doncaster with 'Gregans Boys' when 'Oggy' blasted the ball past Neil Southall. A catalyst for survival. Different times, but maybe the tenacity of this performance could lead to taking the next step.

**Friday 14.04.17**
**FGR 2 Chester 0**
**SECOND HALF STRIKES HELP FGR TO CHESTER WIN**
*Richard Joyce*
Christian Doidge and Liam Noble helped Forest Green claim a third victory, and a third clean sheet in as many games, as they beat Chester at The New Lawn.

In control throughout, Rovers brushed Chester aside for the third time this season, and made it nine straight wins in all nine of the two clubs clashes with one another.

The victory also confirmed Mark Cooper's sides place in the National League play-offs for a third consecutive season.

Rovers started in spectacular style as Doidge struck the upright in the opening minute, while Omar Bugiel's header from an excellent Charlie Cooper corner was hacked off the line when it looked close to going in.

FGR's lively start continued when Doidge turned and shot wide, Kaiyne Woolery saw his strike tipped over and another shot cannoned off the bar as Bugiel saw his hit take a deflection on its way through.

A dominant first half saw Manny Monthe advance forward to try his luck, and Dan Wishart's mazy run almost saw him find the net.

Chester would have been relieved to go into half time with both sides still level, although they were behind five minutes into the second half, when the deadly Doidge struck.

He latched onto a terrific Bugiel through ball and slotted confidently past the on rushing Lynch to gift his side the lead.

Chester's Welsh stopper had to be at his best to keep out a deflected cross minutes later and Woolery fired wide following good build up play.

Wigan Athletic loanee Woolery was a thorn in the visitor's side. He very nearly added to Doidge's goal midway through the second half when he burst through on the left and slammed against the post with his left foot.

Chester were offering little threat, however Rovers still pushed on in search of a comforting second, and it would eventually come when Noble's return from injury from off the bench saw him put FGR in the driving seat.

It was a wonderful finish from the midfielder who stroked in from distance for his ninth goal of the season.

Noble then laid off Doidge who looked to make it 3-0 with a great threaded pass but Lynch was quick off his line to make a fine block.

After his stand out performance in midweek at Tranmere, Sam Russell enjoyed a quiet afternoon, although he did have to watch Elliott Durrell's rare attempt go just over his bar, and watch youngster Matty Waters' strike get charged down, as Chester chased a late consolation that wouldn't come as FGR capped another terrific performance with a third consecutive clean sheet.

## MAJESTIC NOBLE RETURNS
*Jokerman*

Odds of 66-1 and upwards are available on Forest Green Rovers winning the title with four fixtures remaining. This makes it a forlorn hope, though following a home defeat against N. Ferriby and an away victory at Tranmere, it illustrates the unpredictability of this game. The extraordinary performance at Prenton Park on Tuesday night will go down in the memorable section in the history of the club.

Mohammed Ali would have appreciated the 'Rope a Dope' tactics employed by Mark Coopers team. The players will take confidence from this benchmark victory and fans will be hoping they will bury the Ferriby result at home against Chester this afternoon. The manager again makes changes to the starting line-up. Traore, Woolery and Bugiel all start while Mullings and Kelly return to the bench alongside Noble returning from injury.

The teams are given a warm reception though the weather is anything but. The clouds are keeping the sun at bay and a keen breeze adds to the chill factor as the game kicks off. Forest Green start on the front foot and Traore provides Doidge with an early chance. His shot beats Chester keeper Lynch but the ball strikes the foot of the left hand post and is cleared for a corner. Coopers kick is met by Tilt but his close range header is cleared off the line by Durrell with Rovers players appealing the ball had crossed the line. Still in possession Woolery beats two defenders and sets up Doidge, who hits the ball wide from ten yards.

Chester are struggling but Durrell breaks down the left and crosses from the byline, but Russell cuts out the danger. Woolery is looking up for the challenge and has a goal bound shot bravely blocked by Hughes. On thirteen minutes Russell uses a back pass to demonstrate his on the ball skills and presents Chester with a corner. He then reverts to his proper job and stretches to collect the resulting cross.

A piece of magic from Woolery nearly opens the scoring when, seemingly going nowhere, he unleashes a shot from the edge of the area that takes a flying save from Lynch to tip away for a corner. Twenty minutes in and Wishart squares the ball to Bugiel whose well struck shot loops off a defender and over Lynch, but bounces clear off the crossbar.

Chester are up against a determined Rovers defence that are improving with every game. On thirty minutes Bennett protects his keeper by blocking a powerful shot from Vassell. At the other end Wishart runs through the entire Chester defence only to be blocked by Lynch. Woolery has another shot on target blocked away as half time approaches. Just before the break Vassell collides with Bugiel and has to leave the field to staunch the flow of crimson to a facial injury.

No score at the break is frustrating for the home fans their team having outplayed their opponents. The cake gets a Michelin Star today. The second half started as the wind chill cut a little deeper.

Forest Green were at it from the off forcing an early corner and keeping the pressure on took a deserved lead on 50mins. Bugiel split the defensive line with a delightful pass to Doidge inside the box and he drove the ball low past Lynch, for his twenty fifth goal of the season. Three minutes later Bugiel almost created a second when his fierce cut-back from the byline was deflected goalwards by Chester defender George, but Lynch made an excellent save.

Rovers were now well in control of the game but fans wanted a game clincher. It almost came when Woolery drove into the area and smashed the ball past Lynch, only to see it strike the inside of the left hand post and stay out. Sixty eight minutes and Noble replaced Bugiel, both players getting a standing ovation. The Rovers skipper was soon into his stride spraying the passes and on 73mins his return to the side was complete.

The hard working Bennett collected the ball on the right squaring it to Woolery, who in turn laid it into the path of Noble, who stroked it into the top right hand corner of the net from twenty yards with Lynch spectating. Four minutes later he slipped a pass into Doidge but he was denied by Lynch, who made a goal saving block.

Woolery was replaced by Mullings on eighty minutes and was rightly given rapturous applause as he left the field. The game was up for Chester though they pressed for the final minutes as Rovers relaxed, but apart from a shot that skimmed the top-netting, Rovers defence never looked likely to be breached. The play-offs are assured with this result and the team look on course to be in good form as they head for this butt-clenching competition.

### FGR AMBASSADOR REPORT
*Elsie Heslop, Sir William Romney Secondary School, Tetbury*
Elsie's FGR Experience. On the 14th of April my dad and I went to watch Forest Green Rovers play against Chester in front of a crowd of 1936 people. The match started well as we were the dominant team; we managed to keep the ball up in the attacking end for the large majority of the first half, which meant we had many chances to score. However, we couldn't score one in the first half despite all the chances we had, but we did hit the post a couple of times which kept things tense. Although, when Chester did have the ball they used all their pace to get into the other half of the pitch to challenge Sam Russell (FGR's Goalkeeper.) Luckily their shots: missed, got saved or were blocked; in one case we managed to get the ball back from them but one of our defenders passed it back to the Goalkeeper, and he was taking his time to kick it up the pitch. As he was doing this, a Chester player ran towards Sam pressuring him to do a big circle with the ball, in attempt to get away from the attacker, and gave away a corner kick which isn't good. Thankfully, that was no threat to us as we got it straight back up in the other end.

During half time the FGR ladies team came onto the pitch to receive their awards and trophies. They did incredibly well this season winning their league which means they're getting promoted next season. Well done to the ladies and the people who supported them through their journey.

On to the second half now where there was a lot more action because in the 5th minute of playing Christian Doidge scored his 25th goal of the season! Putting Forest Green 1-0 up. After this both teams started to get a bit more physical with each other for one instance one of our defenders Emmanuel Monthe was dribbling with the ball and a Chester player came up to him, ran into him, and bounced off of him so hard that he fell over! This was so hilarious because Emmanuel Monthe just carried on not fazed by what had happened and the look on his face looked like he didn't know that anything had happened. Further on in the second half Liam Noble scored an amazing goal from quite a distance. It was like everything was still and no one moved, even when it had gone past the goalkeeper. My dad and I were so confused why people weren't cheering but there was nothing wrong with the shot and people started to realise that a couple seconds after it was scored, and then the whole stadium started cheering. It was really weird but a fantastic goal scored by Liam. Kaiyne Woolery had an outstanding game but was very unlucky; he had several chances to score but they either hit the post, hit the crossbar or missed the goal by a centimetre but the game finished 2-0 to Forest Green Rovers which means we are guaranteed to have a play-off place.

Overall it was a great win for Forest Green with Kaiyne Woolery getting man of the match. Let's hope they can keep it up. Come on you Rovers!

**Monday 17.04.17**
**Southport 2 FGR 0**
**NO EASTER MONDAY JOY FOR FGR AT SOUTHPORT**
*Richard Joyce*

An Easter Monday lacking any true football quality saw Forest Green go down to already relegated Southport at the Merseyrail Community Stadium.

A drab afternoon of football did little to capture the imagination, but a Southport side who had only won twice in 2017 before the game snatched three points thanks to goals from Robbie Cundy and Rory McKeown.

Cundy struck with a good finish and McKeown got on the end of a dangerous delivery into the box to end FGR's run of three consecutive wins.

It was a first half that wouldn't live long in the memory as neither side ever got going. Sam Wedgbury tried to get on the end of a deep Charlie Cooper cross early on, while it took until the 32nd minute for the one and only shot of the half.

Jamie Allen did well for the hosts down the left, pulled the ball onto his right foot, but couldn't find the target as his effort flashed across the face of Sam Russell's goal.

The second half was equally as drab in its opening exchanges, and finally the game had some life brought to it when just past the hour mark the home side went in front.

Oxford United loanee Robbie Cundy kept his head to hammer in from the edge of the box after the ball had fallen to him from a corner.

And remarkably Southport doubled their lead just minutes later. McKeown got on the end of a ball into the box and provided the touch necessary to beat Russell.

It should have been three were it not for an unbelievable miss from Allen. Another McKeown effort beat Russell, but not the post, and as it cannoned out into the path of the home side's forward Allen he blazed over with the goal gaping.

Any possibility of FGR getting back into it seemed unlikely given their lack of creativity in front of goal, and a rare chance fell Doidge's way in the last ten minutes, but he could only touch the ball wide from Liam Noble's cross.

Southport still offered a threat on the break - so much so that when Liam Nolan found a way past Monthe, Russell had to be called upon to make a good save diving low to his right.

Meanwhile down the other end another Doidge opening saw the front man glance a header wide from Wedgbury's driven ball into the area.

It would be the final opportunity of a forgettable afternoon for Rovers, who welcome Maidstone to The New Lawn next on Saturday.

## DESTINATION SOUTHPORT
*Rambling Man*

Easter Bank Holiday Monday beckoned. As did the inevitable chaos of the nation's laughing stock of a motorway network. Compo and Cleggy pleaded family functions, so it was left to Foggy and me to resolve how we might get to beleaguered Southport FC. Contrary to what our coach fearing stomachs told us, we went with Team Kendo organised by the most faithful of all Rovers supporters, Sir Tomcat.

All went swimmingly on the outward journey as the traffic parted ahead of us like the Red Sea. Until that is, we honed in on Manchester. Even that grind was offset by a pleasant enough stop at Knutsford Services which always brings Tina Turner to mind – *Knutsford City Limits* .... There I go showing my age and fragile mental state again.

I've made the Southport away fixture many times over the years. It is a properly welcoming club that is becoming ever smaller as FGR heads in the opposite direction. Rivalry with Fleetwood in years past now seems like a distant conflict indeed.

Significantly, the people you meet are the same too – lovely older guys in smart ties and blazers who are exhausting the energy and capital reserves needed for the current demands of the national game. Already relegated Southport and its supporters are down on their uppers and the Mersey Rail Stadium smelled of death. I was possessed by an overwhelming feeling of sadness, mirroring the fraternity of true football club supporters.

Avid readers will know that I do not delve too much into match reporting in these columns. Just as well. Playing at half pace, no doubt with the imminent play-offs in mind, Rovers were disposed of 2 nil by a bare bones home XI. At least the home supporters sampled a rare happy event in a troubled season.

The return trip matched the mood of Kendo's passengers. Tortoise pace jams along the M56, M6 and M5 seasoned with the usual unmanned 50 mph restrictions. And the late afternoon sun was cooking the right side of my face at gas mark 4. So, Foggy and I sought a distraction to help while away the time.

That was supplied by the pointy heads who decide what to post on the expensive white elephants, otherwise known as motorway signs. It's bad enough that we tax payers are extorted squillions to erect the damned things which also cost the lives of hordes of valiant cones, and result in yet more traffic halting lane restrictions. But the inane messages - "think bike", "don't drive tired" or my personal favourite, "sign not in use" simply underscore the impression of equipment with no sensible use or operators. As we ground south on the M6 in the best light of the day, two consecutive signs announced "Caution Fog". Then, "Beware pedestrians in road". "Presumably lost in the fog" growled the voice to my left.

But that got us thinking up our own messages, the top picks being as follows. "Caution darkness at night time. Scary". "Boredom Sucks". "Brrrr it's cold. Wrap up well". "Indigestion 3 miles". "Think tank". "Workforce in road. Check bumpers and set phasers to stun". Well it helped.

Have mercy upon us en route to York.

**Saturday 22.04.17**
**FGR 2 Maidstone United 2**
**THE STONES HIT BACK TO DENY FOREST GREEN**
*Richard Joyce*
In form Maidstone United struck twice in the second half at The New Lawn to limit Forest Green to just a point on their final home outing before the play-offs.

Two goals up thanks to a first half goal from Keanu Marsh-Brown and second half own goal, FGR were pegged back as the Stones returned to

**A**
**P**
**R**
**I**
**L**

Kent with a share of the spoils thanks to Harry Phipps and Joe Pigott's strikes.

A crowd of over 2,000 were in attendance for what will be next a home play-off match – with Rovers set to take on Dagenham & Redbridge.

From the start Forest Green were lively. Christian Doidge almost headed in Dale Bennett's first minute cross and Kaiyne Woolery shot wide after a mazy run saw him shift the ball onto his left foot.

Charlie Cooper and centre back Manny Monthe also tried their luck with long range openings, but it would be the class of Marsh-Brown who would break the deadlock after just ten minutes.

Starting his first game since January, the former Fulham youngster cut inside on his right foot after steady FGR build up play, and executed a terrific finish into the bottom corner – out of the reach of Stones goalkeeper Lee Worgan.

Maidstone responded with two long distance efforts via former FGR loanee Odubade and Pigott, but it should have been Rovers who scored the next goal, only to see Woolery fire over after Doidge had teed up the young attacker against his former side when Liam Noble's shot proved too hot to handle for Worgan.

The visitors former Wales under-21 international stopper had to be switched on to keep out a Doidge smash on 24 minutes though, while another Doidge opportunity past the half hour mark saw Rovers leading scorer blast wide when put through on the right.

Deservedly ahead at the break, Forest Green's advantage was doubled ten minutes into the second half when Kevin Lokko turned into his own net.

A fantastic low cross from the right hand side from the advancing Bennett saw Lokko unintentionally knock the ball past his own goalkeeper.

Maidstone are one of the National League's most in form sides though, and they proved their worth when they fought their way back into the contest in the last half hour.

Their comeback began when on the hour mark Phipps was in the right place to take advantage of a spilled ball to stroke in.

They showed plenty of promise in their search for an equaliser with Pigott shooting just wide shortly after.

At the other end though FGR continued in their attempts to restore their two goal advantage. Noble was denied with his 25-yard effort and Woolery's fantastic run down the right saw his final shot go wide.

Pigott went close again for the visitors. Bobby-Joe Taylor's good work set him on the edge of the box and he swivelled and then shot just wide of Sam Russell's right hand post.

The woodwork denied Noble from finding the score sheet after Woolery's blocked shot by Lokko had fallen to him, and it would prove to be a significant milestone, as Maidstone equalised as the game entered the last ten minutes.

Pigott sent their excellent travelling support into pandemonium as he finished inside the area after an error had presented him with an unmissable chance.

Taylor's shot after good work by Odubade was kept out by Russell as the away side looked for the ultimate turnaround, but it was FGR who should have won it late on were it not for some magnificent last ditch defending.

Woolery had found a way past Worgan in stoppage time, but he couldn't find a way past Seth Nana-Twumasi's splendid committed block, which ensured Maidstone would leave Gloucestershire with a point and with Forest Green now facing a final day trip to relegation threatened York.

## ROVERS LOOK DRAWN

*Jokerman*

The league fixtures are all but done and Forest Green Rovers, for the third season in succession, will contest the play-offs. What might have been could arguably be pointed at the team's home performances where, like Mourinho's outfit, there have been too many drawn matches.

Today's final home league game against Maidstone United comes on the back of a performance at Southport that showed a distinct lack of ambition. The play-off objective had been achieved against Chester but this 'already on the beach' attitude was not appreciated by the travelling supporters.

The 'run-in' is heavily overshadowed by the imminent promotion battle, but hopefully this afternoon's game will give the players an opportunity to demonstrate the fundamental necessity of propelling the football in a goal scoring direction.

Bright sunshine with a cooling breeze greeted a crowd of two thousand to TNL, boosted by nearly three hundred supporters of Maidstone United. The Green Man bar was busy and fans watched Lincoln City defeat Macclesfield Town to win the National League title, in the early kick-off. Few would argue they were not worthy winners.

**A**
**P**
**R**
**I**
**L**

Forest Green manager Mark Cooper named Keanu in the starting line-up and Traore came in for the injured Tilt. Rovers started the game in confident mood and in only the second minute Bennett's cross from the right was headed just over the angle by Doidge. It set the pattern and a mazy run by Woolery ended with a shot inches wide of the right hand post. Even Monthe was in the action running sixty yards with the ball before hitting it halfway down Spring Hill.

On 11mins the pressure paid off when Woolery linked with Noble, who in turn slipped a pass to Keanu on the left corner of the area, and he promptly struck a low shot across Worgan the Maidstone keeper and inside the right hand post.

It was all Rovers and on twenty minutes they should have doubled the lead, when Nobles shot was fumbled by Worgan and Doidge nipped in and laid the ball back to Woolery, who struck it over the empty goal. There was little reply from the visitors and Worgan was forced to make further saves from Noble and Doidge. As half time approached ex-Rover Odubade struck a free kick over the bar for Maidstone and Flisher robbed Cooper and blasted a shot wide with Russell untroubled.

Over the double helping of half time cake were mutterings of one goal not being enough despite the superiority.

Forest Green took up where they left off and took the game to Maidstone and on 55mins went into a two goal lead. Bennett from the right hit a low cross to the near post and Worgan dived to collect. Unfortunately his central defender Lokko stretched a leg and deflected the ball over him into the net for an own goal. Worgan punched a hole in the floor in frustration.

Whether Rovers switched off is a moot point, but five minutes later they were pegged back when Odubade attacked down the right and hit a low cross into the area, which Russell failed to gather cleanly. It spilled to Phipps who struck the ball past him into the net. Cooper replaced Traore with Wedgbury soon after and on sixty five minutes Bugiel came on for Keanu, as Noble lined up a free kick on the right side of the area. His kick found Doidge at the back post but the striker mistimed his header and it went wide.

Maidstone were beginning to sense a change in momentum and Pigott hit a shot narrowly wide with Russell diving. Noble replied for Rovers bringing a good save from Worgan stretching to his left. It was a far more open affair now. On seventy five minutes Wishart persisted on the left and made a terrific run into the box and the ball fell for Woolery, whose fierce shot was blocked out to Noble on the edge of the 'D' but his effort grazed the crossbar.

With ten minutes remaining Mullings replaced Doidge. 81mins and it was all square. Substitute Taylor, who had looked lively since coming on, cut inside from the right and tried a speculative shot from twenty five yards that Russell stooped to gather. Calamitous summed up the situation, as the ball bounced off him straight to Pigott, who sent the visiting fans into raptures as he gratefully accepted the gift and smashed the ball into the net from close range. It could have been worse for Rovers three minutes later when Noble gave the ball away and Odubade put Taylor in on Russell, but this time the keeper held on to the ball.

The final chance of the game fell to Woolery whose shot was blocked by Worgan only to see the ball spin back to the striker. He struck his shot against the only defender guarding the open goal.

It was a disappointing end for Forest Green supporters. The clubs third place finish is now under threat from Dagenham & Redbridge. There is already one Shambles in the City of York for all those who travel next week, it is to be hoped Forest Green Rovers do not become another.

## FGR AMBASSADOR REPORT
*Tyler Watson, Eastington Primary School*
My name is Tyler Watson, I am 10 years old and just finishing my second season as the ambassador for Eastington School (close to where our fantastic new stadium will hopefully be built).

I am delighted that I will be doing it again for a 3rd year and looking forward to new challenges in the role.

The best part of being an ambassador is parading out with the FGR players and the pre-season photo shoot. I also enjoy speaking in School Assemblies about the club, writing news and making up competitions in my school newsletter *The Green Devil* and posting the latest updates and match facts on an Instagram page - now with 50 followers.

I have been to most home matches this season, usually with my parents, my older brother and my 5-year-old nephew Alfie who's becoming a real fan. I've also been to Torquay and Macclesfield away. I hope to go to more away matches next season.

Here is my match report: 22nd April 2017. FGR 2-2 Maidstone United.

On a sunny afternoon at the New Lawn with a very noisy visiting crowd, FGR started very brightly with a great goal from Keanu Marsh-Brown on his return to the side, slotting the ball into the far corner

**A**
**P**
**R**
**I**
**L**

after just ten minutes. There were other chances with Kaiyne Woolery and Christian Doidge looking very lively. On 32 minutes 25-goal man Doidge missed narrowly with a super shot on the turn from the edge of the box which the goalkeeper could only push away before gathering safely.

Forest Green dominated the first half and on 43 minutes Dale Bennett couldn't quite finish the job after a sequence of top quality passing. So the score was 1-0 at the break.

Nine minutes into the second half Manny Monthe's cross-field pass found Bennett on the right, who's dangerous low cross was turned into his own net by the unlucky Maidstone defender Kevin Lokko to put the home team 2 up.

Not even 10 minutes later the visitors pulled one back; after some reckless defending Maidstone put in a cross from the right which the usually brilliant Sam Russell spilled directly in front of Maidstone's Harry Phipps who couldn't miss.

A fantastic 70th minute run from inside his own half by Woolery sadly resulted in him skewing the ball wide at the crucial moment. FGR came close multiple times - Dan Wishart did some good work on the left and squared to Woolery whose shot was blocked, then Liam Noble could only manage to hit the bar before it went over.

With Maidstone putting more and more pressure on, Mark Cooper sent on Sam Wedgbury, Omar Bugiel and Shamir Mullings but still FGR could not hold on to their lead. An attack in the 80th minute saw Russell again spill the ball from a long range shot, this time into the path of Joe Piggott who made no mistake with the finish.

Woolery came close to winning it after rounding the keeper but his shot was cleared off the line.

A disappointing result after being 2-0 up, but there was a great atmosphere with 2,030 fans, especially the noisy 280 that made the long trip from Kent.

At least we have made it into the play-offs and can look forward to the possibility of another trip to Wembley.

**Saturday 29.04.17**
**York City 2 FGR 2**
**BUGIEL DOUBLE HELPS ROVERS CLINCH THIRD**
*Richard Joyce*

Omar Bugiel's brace helped Forest Green secure a final finish of third in the National League with a last day draw at York.

Rovers will now prepare to face play-off semi-final opponents Dagenham & Redbridge firstly away before hosting the fourth placed finishers at The New Lawn next Sunday.

In front of the BT Sport cameras, Bugiel's double helped FGR lead twice against a York side who couldn't secure the result needed to stay in the division, after Guiseley's late goal elsewhere in Yorkshire, proved enough to keep them up.

The former Football League side, who have now suffered back-to-back relegations, looked like they were going to hang onto their National League status by a thread, courtesy of two strikes from the outstanding former FGR hero Jon Parkin which didn't prove to be enough.

Bootham Crescent was a cauldron of noise before kick-off. And a dramatic opening few minutes saw the hosts twice hit the bar. Left sider Sam Muggleton's incredible long-distance throw-ins caused chaos as in quick succession he hit the woodwork on two occasions, both after Parkin had tested Sam Russell with a well-taken volley early on.

Bugiel popped up though after just six minutes to open the scoring. He took advantage of a Rovers counter-attack and finished confidently after Dan Wishart's fine run down the left.

York should have levelled on the quarter of an hour mark only to see Vadaine Oliver blast over when he attempted to latch onto Parkin's driven ball across the face of goal.

The hosts finally drew level in a breathless first half, and it was their true leader from the front, Parkin, who like he did so many times in two years at Forest Green, struck the equaliser.

York took advantage of FGR's loss of possession in their own half, and Parkin was on hand to calmly tuck in past the on rushing Russell.

Their joy was short-lived however. Immediately FGR broke down the other end and Fabien Robert fed Bugiel and the German striker did the rest, restoring Rovers lead.

Russell denied Muggleton's curler down the other end before half time, while Bugiel saw a shot saved by Scott Loach as FGR attacked with Shamir Mullings the supplier.

With results not going their way an onslaught came the way of the Forest Green goal early in the second 45 minutes. Russell was in inspired form however and he produced an unbelievable save to push away Asa Hall's drive from the edge of the area.

He was picking the ball out of his own net two minutes later though. That man again, Parkin, got his side back on level terms for a second time as he poked home from close range to give his side hope.

**A**
**P**
**R**
**I**
**L**

The powerful forward then almost sealed his hat-trick with a long range free kick that flew just wide, and another sensational Russell stop denied York, when Hall's header was this time kept out by the stoppers strong trailing leg.

Oliver's sprint clear ended with a wasteful finish, as news elsewhere suggested that with Guiseley behind, a draw would be enough for York to secure safety by goal difference.

The home side pushed on but struggled to create any more major openings. Simon Heslop fired over and a Parkin effort was blocked convincingly.

Teenage striker Olly Mehew came on as a substitute to make his Forest Green debut towards the finish, and as updates came through that Guiseley had bagged a late equaliser in their home tie with Solihull, York began to launch the ball forward in the desperate need for a goal.

Two late corners saw keeper Loach come up from the back in an attempt to be the late hero. But it all proved too much for York, who were to be relegated by just a point, leaving FGR with the security of third place heading into two massive tests up next with the Daggers.

## DESTINATION YORK
*Rambling Man*

Nine gruelling months on from our 'pointless' outing to Boreham Wood, the National League's regular programme was about to draw to a close. Since the Imps deservedly claimed the championship pennant, Rovers seemed to have been playing a 'half-pace' phoney war having accepted that Dagenham & Redbridge will be their foes in the Play-Off legs. Relegated North Ferriby & Southport were the surprised beneficiaries of our end of term generosity.

The clash at Bootham Crescent would be different and memorable. Not least, the home side is in a pickle previously experienced several times by Rovers – win or draw a must, and hope other results go your way. If not, the relegation trap door consigns you to National League North. So, we knew the hosts would be scrapping like Honey Badgers, led by old New Lawn Favourite, 'The Beast' John Parkin, and with Yan Klukowski and Clovis Kamdjo sidelined but looking on.

But that was way down the line on a full and memorable day. Woodchester based Pathfinder Tours was running a regular trip to Scarborough with its period diesel loco and carriages. Happily, the train was due at York Station about an hour before the early kick off time of the National League programme's swan song. With wonderful generosity,

Pathfinder decided to offer places to FGR supporters on a BOGOF basis and the train bore the FGR scarf. All was laid on by Pathfinder's General Manager and FGR guest of the day, Casey Jones, backed up by the friendly and enthusiastic "Frying Scotsman" caterers and all the lovely volunteer Pathfinder hosting staff.

So it was that Mr & Mrs Foggy, Compo, Sir Tomcat and yours truly gathered at Stonehouse's 'Burdett Central' at a an eye-watering 6.15 am, properly decked out in green and black. Regular rail-buff passengers looked a tad confused, but soon caught on. As the local wildlife foraged for its breakfast and gave their dawn chorus a half-hearted rendition, all boarded in party mood. The engine even had and FGR scarf emblazoned across the front windshield.

Now younger readers may not *get* steam trains, antique diesels and musty, tastefully furnished carriages. But those of us of the Six-Five-Special cum Hornby Double O cum Meccano generation are suckers for British Railways before Beeching sank his teeth into the network. We are lost in an epoch when AA men used to salute, gentlemen criminals would 'fess "it's a fair cop" and football used jumpers for goalposts. Hang it all, my phone number was just 3 digits!

Ok nurse, no need for the strait jacket, I'll get back on the narrative. Suffices to say that Casey Jones and his crew treated us like post war royalty. Pathfinder should be on the bucket list of all who reside in the Five Valleys.

Bootham Crescent was also in party mood pre-match, featuring 4,000 friendly, optimistic hosts. Yet despite a characteristically cavalier performance by The Beast, he was upstaged by Rovers' Omar Bugiel. His brace in a 2-2 draw turned the rave into an eerie wake. In post-match commiserations with home fans, we felt like 'spectres at the feast'.

Whilst Rovers' point meant the second play-off leg v Daggers would be at home on Sunday 7th May – the best outcome – the Minstermen supporters had the despair of National League North to haunt their nightmares. We veterans of the cruel Grays debacle a few years back will know the feeling, shudder and sympathise.

But the day was still young for Casey and the gang of five. There followed a leisurely visit to the fantastic National Railway Museum, a walk around the City Wall and along the Ouse Embankment and pints of Yorkshire Pale Ale at the station pub. And to cap that, the splendidly luxurious homeward journey and sumptuous 4 course meal. Literally, our cups runneth over. So ended a day that will live long in the memory.

Delirious happiness! A tense draw at Dagenham & Redbridge had given way to a superb win in the home leg. The depression of Wembley 2016 was blown away, as an astonishing Rovers performance, featuring spell binding goals by Kaiyne Woolery and Christian Doidge, overran the Wirral's finest. Since Dale Vince's arrival, FGR supporters had wondered how it might feel to win promotion to the EFL, not least in front of noisy green hordes at Wembley. The answer is that the reality outshone the dream. I'm so proud and thrilled to have witnessed that momentous day as Coops and his squad showed their true colours.

*sometimes there are no words to find*
*that can express in prose or rhyme*
*this achievement this promotion*
*this relief and this emotion*
*felt in ev'ry single fan*
*who's longed for this since they began*

(Excerpt from 'Sometimes' by Crispin Thomas "Football Poets" which summed up the feelings of all FGR supporters)

**Thursday 04.05.17**
**Dagenham & Redbridge 1 FGR 1**
**(National League play-off semi-final 1st leg)**
**ROVERS AND DAGGERS LEVEL BEFORE SECOND LEG**
*Richard Joyce*

It's level pegging in the fight for a place in this season's National League promotion final as Forest Green and Dagenham & Redbridge couldn't be separated in a fierce first leg at the Chigwell Construction Stadium.

First half goals from both sides mean they're locked level ahead of Sunday's second leg as FGR go in search of a second consecutive end of season trip to Wembley.

Liam Noble powered home from the penalty spot to give Rovers the advantage midway through the first half of a truthfully untidy encounter.

But Dagenham got the equaliser they needed just before the break, when Jordan Maguire-Drew burst through to smash in to level for John Still's men.

The hosts settled into the game early on and FGR were quickly under pressure. Pinball in the box saw Dagenham almost force the ball in after just three minutes, while Corey Whitely's low turn and shot was well kept out by Sam Russell.

Rovers' number one was busy again to prevent the experienced Paul Benson from poking in after he'd latched onto Maguire-Drew's dinked through ball.

There had been little joy for Forest Green in their attempts to put the Daggers under pressure, although it would be them who would strike first from the penalty spot.

Omar Bugiel was upended in the penalty area, and Noble stepped up from 12 yards, sending Mark Cousins the wrong way to put some daylight between the two teams.

Christian Doidge fired wide shortly after on his return to his former club and Benson headed a difficult chance wide minutes before the home side roared back to level.

Maguire-Drew was alert in the box to get on the end of a ball that the Rovers defence had failed to clear, and the Brighton & Hove Albion loan youngster powered in to draw parity.

The opening to the second half was a scrappy affair. The first chance fell through to Fejiri Okenabirhie for the home side but he couldn't direct his low hit on target after bringing the ball down.

Both sides struggled to create chances in a tense but yet quiet half of football, and the next opportunity didn't fall to the hosts until the final minute of normal time, as Whitely couldn't take advantage when he drilled wide.

Encouraging substitute appearances from Shamir Mullings, Keanu Marsh-Brown and the returning from injury Ethan Pinnock will give Mark Cooper food for thought ahead of Sunday's second leg, which is all set up to be a cup final occasion in front of a bumper crowd at The New Lawn.

## DESTINATION DAGENHAM
*Rambling Man*

For the third season running, Rovers' season entered extra time. The dreaded play-offs, product of the English Football League's unwillingness to agree a fair promotion system to the 4th level. Productivity in our corner of Gloucestershire must take a nose dive in each May as GP Surgeries become stacked with patients with nervous complaints.

Our previous record in the first play-off leg is lost one, won one. Maybe the third possibility was inevitable. At any rate, Rovers destination was East London or West Essex, depending on your upbringing. More particularly, The Chigwell Construction Stadium the turf of

Dagenham & Redbridge FC and spiritual home of the Ford Capri and platinum hair dye. Impossible to find a greater contrast to the valleys and scarps of the South Cotswolds.

Meanwhile, over luncheon in the heart of *Merrie England,* Compo hauled up in his silver coach to convey Foggy and me to the 'smoke'. Earlier, in downtown Stroud, I'd spied Wedge, Marcus Kelly & Sincs supping caffeine in Costas and that set us wondering when the team would be travelling and whether the caffeine rush would be put to good use by the popular trio.

An intermediate destination was agreed upon, Hatfield House, conveniently located just north of the midday/midnight position of the M25 clock face. It proved to be a decent decision. Hatfield House in Hertfordshire is the home of the 7th Marquess and Marchioness of Salisbury and their family. Presumably, the geography of their forbears was not too hot?

The original building was a Royal Palace built in 1497 as the Tudors were getting their legs under the dynastic table. It was erected for the Bishop of Ely, but Henry VIII took a fancy to the place and snaffled it up. Down the years, the first Jacobite monarch, James I didn't take to the place. He passed it to the late Queen Bess' Lord Chancellor Robert Cecil. Without more ado, in 1608 he knocked seven bells out of the palace, producing the brick built Hampton Court look-a-like that Foggy, Compo and I were able to gaze upon.

The hour we'd allocated did not merit the tasty £18.00 concession entry ticket to the mansion. So we rubbed shoulders with yeomen and peasants, touring the stable yard and gardens and taking tiffin in ye olde brand-new tea shoppe. All in all, not too shabby and a darned site more picturesque than The Chigwell Construction Stadium.

On arrival at TOWIE, Compo tethered the horses and we collected our pre-ordered tickets. Next stop, the nearest chippy. Munching outside, who did we see but Wedge, Marcus & Fab Robert, returning from hunting provisions at Tesco. Little did we know that the caffeine they'd consumed earlier would turn out to be more useful in keeping them awake until 9.00 pm, than as an energy supplement.

I will not lie. The Chigwell is not a great stadium. It's a cramped place, kind of stuck between older 'non-league' style with a larger modern stand bolted on to one end. It lacks charm and the playing surface proved to contain many a land mine. 250–300 wonderfully noisy and boisterous Rovers fans were packed into a corner of one older stand with several stanchions strategically placed to block the view.

The game was not a classic. As usual, Rovers started slowly and shredded our nerves further with sleepy early defending. Against the run of play, Omar Bugiel got away and was felled by the hosts' keeper. Liam Noble slammed home the penalty as we went bananas. During the final seconds of the first half, more slack defending saw a Daggers equaliser. The second period was slumber inducing, but notable for the re-appearance of Rovers' Rolls Royce, Ethan Pinnock, happily restored to fitness. Quickly back into his classy form, he might well make the difference in the return leg on Sunday. Over all, Rovers were probably the happier of the 2 teams as play-off leg 1 closed.

## ROVERS WARY OF PEAKING TOO SOON
*Jokerman*

The league season ended on Saturday at York. Forest Green Rovers twice led but a desperate York side battled back to level the scores. It was not enough for them to avoid relegation. For Rovers it ensured their third place finish to gain a second leg home tie in the play-offs against this evenings opponents Dagenham & Redbridge.

With little time to contemplate, Rovers supporters headed east. Three coaches, the Kendo Flyer, KB and The Green Army take on the test of endurance that is the M25. Arriving in time for an ale or two in the Daggers bar, fans mix amicably as they await the team news.

To reach this stage Rovers fans have witnessed many changes amongst the playing staff despite an excellent start to the campaign. Manager Mark Cooper has rung so many changes he makes Quasimodo look like a work experience joker. However there is no denying his team is right in the hunt for promotion. Bugiel's two goals at York make him first choice to partner Doidge in attack. Pinnock makes a welcome return on the bench alongside Tilt, Keanu and Mullings. Wedgbury and Kelly have been given the night off, while Carter has left the club and Sinclair appears to have disappeared altogether of late.

The Green Army are in good voice in the sardine corner of the stadium which helps boost the volume. Two hundred in their number in a two thousand plus crowd. Forest Green kick off facing a chilly breeze on a dry overcast evening.

The first fifteen minutes see Dagenham set the pattern that seldom changes for the entirety. A third minute free kick by M-Drew caused concern in the Rovers defence, as a timely block by Monthe, quickly followed by more bodies into the breach to clear the danger. Raiding down the right M-Drew put Whitely through and his snap shot forced

Russell to save low down diving to his right. Benson then had a good half chance but could only prod the ball straight at Russell from twelve yards.

Rovers did force a couple of corners, the first of the game after twenty minutes with no result. On 29mins Bugiel, Rovers most noticeable attacker, took the ball into the Dagenham area where keeper Cousins and a defender attempted to block him. He went to ground and to the joy of Forest Green fans the referee pointed to the spot. It was at the far end away from the sardines who concluded the wall was of the finest stone. Noble stepped up and smashed the ball into the left side of the net. The Green Army gave it the vocals and triggered a couple of smoke bombs in celebration.

It was a goal against the balance of play and Dagenham, unperturbed, continued on the offensive. Rovers' game was not lifted and they remained looking disjointed in their build up play, with the mid-field players constantly giving the ball away, the forwards redundant.

As the game entered added time at the end of the first half, M-Drew brushed off a weak challenge from Wishart inside the area, took a stride and leathered the ball into the roof of the net. The Daggers fans behind the goal were up and on balance it was no more than they deserved at the half time break.

Rovers' fans were left to ponder where the improvement might come from. It didn't take many minutes from the re-start to realise it was going to be more of the same. Good Dagenham build up play on the right saw the ball crossed to Okenabirhie in space on the edge of the area but his shot went narrowly wide. The Forest Green subs were warming up in front of their fans who were keeping up the vocals. On sixty eight minutes Mullings replaced Bugiel. A wheel fell off Keanu's pram. Soon after Pinnock replaced Traore.

Dagenham kept pressing and Okenabirhie in space inside the box again hit the ball wide of the post when he should have done better. Pinnock was making a difference at the back for Rovers, but they were finding no forward momentum. And with ten minutes left Noble, who had experienced a difficult evening was replaced by Keanu. It did little to improve things up front, Mullings spent most of the time defending and when they did get forward there was no threat. The defence at least was holding, but in the ninetieth minute Dagenham's Whitely had a chance which he put wide, to the dismay of one set of fans and relief to another.

Five added minutes was still not enough for Dagenham to capitalise on their superiority against opponents who managed only a single shot on target in the match. At the final whistle the big negative was to see Keanu walk straight down the tunnel and possibly out the door, for all the fans knew, as his team mates stayed to applaud the travelling supporters.

On the positive side Pinnock is back. The defence defied the pressure to get the job done away from home. On Sunday both sides have all to play for. Manager Mark Cooper has two days to persuade Bugs Bunny out of his hat and keep this seasons opportunity to become a legend at FGR alive.

## Sunday 07.05.17
## FGR 2 Dagenham & Redbridge 0
## (National League play-off semi-final 2nd leg)
## DOIDGE AND MARSH-BROWN SCORE THE GOALS TO SEND FOREST GREEN ROVERS BACK TO WEMBLEY
*Richard Joyce*

Forest Green Rovers are on their way back to Wembley after victory over Dagenham & Redbridge sealed the club's place in the National League promotion final.

Already level from the first leg at Dagenham on Thursday, first half goals from Christian Doidge and Keanu Marsh-Brown earned Rovers their opportunity on the biggest stage again this season.

Mark Cooper's men will now take on Tranmere Rovers for a one-off shot at earning promotion into the Football League. Doidge and Marsh-Brown's strikes proved enough to overcome the Daggers in front of a crowd of over 3,200 at The New Lawn.

Earlier, it was actually the hosts who looked threatening despite not dominating possession early on, as Fejiri Okenabirhie and Jordan Maguire-Drew both produced decent efforts on goal.

But Forest Green began to develop the controlled side of their game with a number of chances, and Doidge and Mark Ellis were both presented with chances in front of the Dagenham goal.

The goal Rovers needed to take the lead on aggregate finally came ten minutes before half time.

A well picked out long ball down the right from Ellis was brilliantly seized upon by Kaiyne Woolery, and the Wigan Athletic loanee kept his cool to feed Doidge to power in a strong right footed finish at the near post against his former club.

The pursuit for a second goal to create some daylight between the two teams would come at a perfect point at the start of first half stoppage time.

**M**
**A**
**Y**

Yet again for FGR on the biggest stage it was that man Marsh-Brown who came up with the goods, as he curled in with the benefit of a deflection on his right foot from the left after the outstanding Ethan Pinnock had teed him up.

The two goal lead put Forest Green into a fine position at the break and in the tie, and after overcoming a couple of Dagenham scares at the start of the second half, Rovers looked to increase their lead when Liam Noble put Marsh-Brown through on 65 minutes, only for his shot to be turned behind.

Dagenham pushed on in an attempt to try and get a goal back. Luke Guttridge headed over Luke Howell's cross, while last ditch defending kept the Londoners at bay in the last ten minutes.

FGR managed to fend off their attacking approach successfully, and after substitute Oliver Hawkins headed wide for the visitors, it was Rovers who almost snatched a third goal in the depths of stoppage time.

Shamir Mullings fantastic through ball fell into the path of Woolery, and his finish came within inches of finding the net, as it took a deflection on the way through to hitting the post.

The first half goals Forest Green had accumulated were more than enough though to secure a second trip to Wembley in two seasons, and Rovers will now head to the capital next Sunday seeking another memorable milestone in the club's long 128 year history.

### ROVERS STUFF THE APPLES IN DAGENHAM'S CRUMBLE
*Jokerman*

May 7th, hopefully a lucky day for Forest Green Rovers as they bid to overcome Dagenham & Redbridge this afternoon to progress to the play-off final at Wembley, and a meeting with Tranmere Rovers. Thursday's first leg at Dagenham ended with a 1-1 scoreline that flattered Forest Green whose only shot on target was thankfully a converted 'Tom Daley' penalty by Liam Noble.

The park & ride system helped alleviate congestion in the village as over three thousand fans descended on TNL. The bars were suitably rammed for what aspired to be a tense encounter. The team news for Rovers revealed that Bugiel had picked up an injury and was replaced in attack by Keanu, which should have pleased him after Thursday's disappointment. Pinnock also starts and Wishart is back on the bench with Tilt, Mullings and Wedgbury.

Both sets of fans are in good voice as the teams parade underneath a sky of blue and temperature near twenty degrees. Forest Green get the game under way but as on Thursday it is Dagenham who have the lion's share of possession for the first fifteen minutes. The main danger however came from Bennett in the fifteenth minute, when he hit a square pass across his penalty area that Dagenham striker M-Drew latched onto, but could only strike the ball wide of the right hand post to Russell's relief.

The home side's first foray was sparked by Cooper who hit a pass inside the full back for Woolery to latch onto, but Daggers keeper Cousins was quickly off his line to block the ball away for a corner. Noble stepped up and hit the cross low to the edge of the area to Doidge, whose shot was well gathered by Cousins. For all their possession Dagenham were making little impact on a stout Rovers back four well marshalled by Pinnock and Ellis.

After thirty minutes Forest Green began to impress on the offensive and on 34mins they took the lead. Ellis hit a superb defence splitting pass down the right for Woolery to chase and chase he did to the byline. Under pressure he hooked the ball away from his marker, cut inside the box and pulled the ball back to Doidge, who struck the ball first time inside the near right hand post. The crowd were on their feet and the smoke bombs, well they just smoked.

The goal was a big set-back for Dagenham who again had failed to create a clear chance despite their share of the ball. Cooper was enjoying his best performance in an FGR shirt and encouraged by Bennett and Traore began to look the part.

Indeed it was Cooper as the game entered added time in the first period, who hit the ball wide to the left side where Pinnock and Keanu exchanged passes. Keanu turned twice before turning inside onto his right foot on the corner of the area where he did what his talent allows, sending a beautifully struck shot that sent the ball into the top right hand corner of the net, with Cousins flailing. It was majestic and the crowd were still buzzing as the half ended.

It was the cream on the half time cake as fans tried not to get carried away which was not too difficult given Rovers history. Dagenham had little choice at the re-start but to go for broke. This in turn gave Rovers the opportunity to counter attack and they did this very well.

On fifty minutes a free kick by Noble from the left saw some desperate blocks in the visitors defence to thwart both Woolery and Keanu in turn. Rovers were working hard for each other and when Dagenham threatened from corners, Doidge was in the thick of it.

As the game went on Forest Green began to take a firm grip on proceedings. This forced the inevitable substitutions around the hour mark. For Daggers Hawkins replaced Benson and Howell came on for M-Drew, who was no doubt feeling chastened following earlier comments.

Soon after Keanu nearly added to his score when Noble hit a measured pass to put him through, but Cousins and his defence blocked his shot away for a corner. He was replaced by Wishart. This caused some consternation amongst supporters as it appeared that Rovers were going to play five across the back, which in turn led to Dagenham camping on the edge of the Rovers penalty area.

With twenty minutes left Wedgbury replaced Traore. After some pressure from Dagenham things began to settle and the visitors just ran out of ideas against such a defiant rearguard. The nearest they came was in the closing stages when Boucaud forced Russell to tip the ball on to the top netting, shooting from distance. From the corner Hawkins headed goalwards to Whitely but he in turn could only put the ball wide.

Mullings replaced Doidge for the final ten minutes and like Keanu and Traore before him Doidge was given a standing ovation. The home fans were on their feet for the closing minutes, and into added time it was Mullings who put Woolery through on Cousins, but the keeper made a brave block and the referee sounded the final whistle.

Forest Green Rovers were through to a Wembley play-off final and the fans celebrated with a pitch invasion. The team will take confidence and belief from this performance and will respect Tranmere Rovers next Sunday, but certainly not fear them. One game away from The Football League. Don't you dare miss it. Let's make it happen.

### Sunday 14.05.17
### FGR 3 Tranmere Rovers 1 (National League play-off final)
### FGR PROMOTED TO THE FOOTBALL LEAGUE
*Richard Joyce*

Forest Green Rovers will compete in the Football League for the first time in the club's history next season after promotion final victory over Tranmere Rovers at Wembley.

The club's record breaking 19 year consecutive stay in the National League is over, and FGR will now look forward to hosting the likes of Coventry City, Swindon Town and Port Vale in the fourth tier of English football next season.

A double from Kaiyne Woolery and another strike from leading goal scorer Christian Doidge made history for Rovers, and despite a fine first half goal from Connor Jennings, FGR produced a confident performance to seal their promotion dreams.

Beaten finalists a year ago on the Wembley turf against Grimsby Town, Forest Green started their fourth ever visit to the home of football positively, and Keanu Marsh-Brown had a sniff of a chance early on.

Captain Liam Noble then lifted a free kick over the bar just a couple of minutes before Woolery claimed his crucial first of the afternoon.

Drissa Traore's short forward ball saw Woolery run into the gap in front of him and hammer a tremendous left footed finish out of the reach of Scott Davies.

It was the start FGR deserved, and after Doidge had headed a Mark Ellis long throw over, Tranmere came into the tie a bit more and were rewarded as they snatched a stunning equaliser midway through the half.

Jennings, brother of former Forest Green left back James who had graced Wembley himself for the club a year before, unleashed a fantastic shot from 25 yards which flew into the back of the net.

And they almost took the lead just past the half hour mark only for Sam Russell to pull off a fine stop to deny FGR's all time leading National League goal scorer, James Norwood, who had charged through for Tranmere.

Noble's fabulous ball put Marsh-Brown in the clear shortly afterwards. His excellent touch was followed by a finely executed lob, but Davies produced a fabulous save to prevent the ball from going over the line.

Within a minute another former FGR face in the Tranmere line up almost scored. Andy Mangan couldn't quite finish Jennings' low cross off at the back post when at full stretch.

In the final five minutes of the first half came the two vital goals that would ultimately send Forest Green into the Football League.

Doidge capped his fine first season at The New Lawn by helping his side retake the lead. He controlled Noble's diagonal ball perfectly and cut inside onto his right foot where he smashed home with an unstoppable effort.

And Woolery wrapped up a dream end to the first half when he extended his team's lead, taking full advantage of a Liam Ridehalgh error, and executing a low finish past Davies.

The advantage at the break was firmly with Forest Green, but immediately after half time Russell had to be at his best to deny Cole Stockton's glancing header, while an error from Russell when in possession gifted the Tranmere forward a golden opportunity he couldn't take.

Liverpool loanee Jack Dunn saw his long range effort deflected wide as Tranmere searched desperately for a route back into the game.

**M
A
Y**

Instead though Noble scooped a shot wide after a fine run from Dan Wishart and Northern Ireland international Jeff Hughes' shot for Tranmere was driven off target.

Time was slowly fading away as Forest Green looked to hang on and seal victory. Another Dunn effort went over the target and Ridehalgh's ambitious volley in stoppage time flew over.

The Football League promotion dream so many at FGR had savoured for so long would finally come true at the full time whistle, as after 128 years next season Forest Green will compete in League Two for the first time, after a patient promotion success that will live long in the memory.

## DESTINATION WEMBLEY
*Rambling Man*

Exactly 363 days after the defeat by Grimsby Town, Rovers were back at Wembley playing for promotion to English League Division 2. The promised land, never previously gained by a hamlet club nor town so small as Nailsworth's 5,700 souls.

Our opponents were the second placed team, Tranmere Rovers, proper Northern giants. Their 95 points would be enough to promote sides in any other league (with fair rules for advancement) and they had swatted aside in-form Aldershot in their play-off semis. Old Boys James Norwood – in good scoring form – and Andy Mangan would be lining up for Tranny, both prolific goal hunters in their FGR days.

Ambassador Tsar Compo had organised a coach for the school Ambassadors and their families, with generous help from the Supporters Club and FGR sponsor Grundon. 59 of the 61 spaces were taken, with Mrs Compo and me completing the line up. The passengers were bubbling with excitement as we departed The New Lawn at 10.00 am on a lovely sunny morning.

Do you trust your instincts? I don't know that I do. Though not the superstitious type, I will never predict football scores – it invites retribution. Before FGR matches I am invariably a bundle of shot nerves. Yet despite Rovers' inconsistent form going into the play-offs, I was calm and absolutely convinced we would beat all comers to win promotion. Maybe my votive offering to the household gods at Chedworth Roman Villa a few weeks ago was that powerful?

Sure enough, the scrappy draw at Daggers in Leg 1 of the play-off semis was followed by a glorious 2-0 thumping at The New Lawn, watched by a record crowd of close to 3,300. The noisy support, beautiful weather and slick display grabbed all our attention. The mood change was as tangible as Q-Pie. Surely we would prevail at the third time of asking in the play-off system?

This would be the 5th meeting between the 2 clubs, all being characterised by good relationships between supporters. I have always looked forward to and enjoyed our fixtures. So far, the record is equal – we have both notched 1 away win and 1 away draw, but neither club has won as hosts. Rovers have the bragging rights courtesy of the sneaked 1-0 at Prenton Park in April but Tranny's recent form is far better. For good or for bad, Tranmere Rovers were 9 points ahead of our Rovers at the regular season's end, exactly the same as FGR's advantage over Grimsby in 2016.

The journey passed quickly. Just a short stop at Beaconsfield M40 Services to refuel the youths whilst we adults and seniors took on caffeine and unfurled cardboard stiff limbs. Several Tranny bus loads were there too, as usual ready with friendly Liverpudlian quips.

On arrival, we were directed to Wembley's East side, Grimsby's from last year, another good omen? Soon we had decanted and strove for The Torch, a nominated FGR pub some 10 minutes walk away. There we met up with Miss and Master Compo and their friends and supped ale. Still I felt ridiculously serene like a football supporting Buddha.

Inside the stadium, Rovers supporters were outnumbered 3 or 4 to one by their confident rivals from the Wirral. But what we lacked in numbers we made up for in colourful favours and sheer, joyful racket. The Compos and I were sat next to friends and family of Manny Monthe, Keanu Marsh-Brown and Ethan Pinnock and boy did they yell their acclamations loud and often. In fact all the FGR support was astonishing and unusually raucous all game long. As the sun beat down, it was tremendous.

FGR came out of the blocks like thoroughbreds, passing and tackling confidently. Tranny were struggling for possession. On 11 minutes, Kaiyne Woolery made space, let fly and the green army erupted. 10 minutes later, Connor Jennings hit a miraculous half volley to level matters as the flow of the game evened out. Undaunted, FGR found its stride and Keanu was inches from scoring the goal of the season – an instant trap of a lofted ball into the penalty area, followed by a deft chip over the advancing keeper. But as Christian Doidge tore goal-wards, the keeper made an amazingly athletic back flip and clawed the ball away as it was an inch from crossing the line. That woke us up alright.

As the Cotswold volume switch turned to ear-bleed, Christian decided this was his time. Liam Noble found him with an unerring cross field ball, controlled with ease. Taunting veteran Steve McNulty with feints, he then let rip into the far top corner. Bedlam again as ear drums exploded. Wembley East was party central.

But as we heaved and bounced in song, the half's drama was not done. Kaiyne picked left back Ridehalgh's pocket and beat the keeper's advance. Unbroken wall of green tinnitus. All from the West Country were believing the impossible as the Tranny fans broke for half time, glum and stunned.

Give or take a bit of Bruce Grobbelaar from Sam Russell and one instinctively brilliant save, Rovers played a clever, containing second half. Then, after a full 7 minutes of time added on, the referee's whistle sent FGR players, coaches and the noisy hordes into uncontainable raptures. Unbelievably, fantastically, impossibly, Forest Green Rovers, for all time the little club on the hill (as we will be even at M5 Junction 13!) were an English League Division 2 side. Hold the front page!

The Compos and I kept asking ourselves if it had really happened. Is this what Division 2 felt like? No more National League and no trips to Hartlepool and Halifax next term. Instead, Cheltenham, Swindon, Newport, Wycombe, Yeovil, Coventry and maybe Exeter too. Our joy was palpably painful and cheekbones ached with smile-fatigue. The scenes were unforgettable but Sham Mullings euphoria beat the lot – an instant folk hero.

What more to say? An hour later, the homeward journey was quite pleasant! As we reached Minchinhampton Common a little after 9 pm, the blood red sun was setting. Compo and I exchanged that all we could see around us was English Football League Country. Half an hour later, at home, Mrs Rambling Man had summoned a Chinese Take Away, brought the fizz out of the cold box, and we settled to watch three and a half hours worth of recorded BT Sports Coverage.

In the words of the great poet Giorgio Moroder, "what a feeling, being's believing, I can have it all ..." I trust you never have to watch me do an Irene Cara. No one should.

Finally a dedication. To Dale Vince, your family, all at FGR and Ecotricity including coaches, players and those behind the scenes, and our wonderful supporters. Oh, lest they be insulted, to the household gods of Chedworth Roman Villa. Thank you for realising my dream.

## SPRING SEASON POWERS FOREST GREEN TO GLORY
*Jokerman*

Just six days have passed since Forest Green Rovers clinched a place in the promotion final with an encouraging win against Dagenham &

Redbridge. The build up to today's final against Tranmere Rovers at Wembley has been overshadowed by issues with tickets and particularly ticket prices.

However there is no planned statement from today's match sponsors 'Velcro'. Several coaches have been booked for FGR fans who find it within their budget. Kendo kicks through the gears to haul us out of the valley. National Highways dictate it will be the scenic route. This provides a glimpse of the oriental Mecca of Bibury, before the tailback that is Oxford prior to striking out for Town.

The weather is fine and warm, the outlook bright. All on board hope it is a good omen. Kendo pulled in to park in good time for a convivial pint or more, and following a photo shoot under the watchful gaze of Bobby Moore, it was time to join eighteen thousand eight hundred fans inside the stadium.

The Green Army behind the goal may have been outnumbered but they were giving a good account of themselves. Forest Green manager Mark Cooper kept faith with the same line-up as a week ago. Tranmere named two ex-FGR stars Andy Mangan and James Norwood in their attack. A blast on the referees whistle and the game was underway. Early nerves were on show as both teams gave the ball away. After clearing a Tranmere corner Rovers countered through Noble, who struck a free kick from a promising position over the bar.

Things changed dramatically on 11mins. Attacking down the right, Woolery took a pass mid-way in the Tranmere half, raced forward unchallenged. From twenty yards he drilled the ball unerringly wide of Tranmere keeper Davies outstretched right hand and inside the left hand post. Scored at the Forest Green end, the fans rose as one to acclaim a superb strike. The Tranmere fans were silenced. The goal came as Rovers were showing signs of setting their possession game in motion.

Tranmere had to step it up and on 22mins found a way back into contention. A throw on the left deep in Rovers territory was worked to the edge of the area and a quick exchange of passes left Jennings in space. He promptly leathered the ball past Russell into the left side of the goal. It was the turn of the massed Tranmere fans to roar out a warning; they were back in business. They pressed and on thirty three minutes a mistake by Cooper allowed Norwood to race through on Russell. The Rovers keeper was quickly out to make a terrific block and deny his ex-team mate.

Soon after Tranmere keeper Davies was the hero. A lofted ball into the box was superbly controlled by Keanu, he lifted it high over Davies who somehow twisted himself backwards and clawed the ball away from under the bar. On thirty nine minutes Jennings broke through on the left and hit an inviting low cross along the six yard box. Mangan sliding in could not turn the ball home and Tranmere fans held their heads in dismay. It was to prove costly.

41mins and a raking diagonal pass by Noble picked out Doidge in acres of space on the left. He raced goalwards and with defenders in retreat, he struck a right foot shot he will remember for the rest of his life. The ball sped like an arrow across Davies and buried itself in the right hand corner of the net. Cue the Green Army who were probably a little more hysterical this time.

Three minutes later, with Tranmere still reeling, Woolery again latched on to a ball headed on by Doidge down the right flank. He held off his marker, broke into the area and slipped the ball past the advancing Davies inside the right hand post. Forest Green fans lost the plot completely at this juncture. They were in dreamland. As the game entered added time Tranmere defender McNulty floored Doidge with a crafty one, a degree of desperation perhaps.

At the half time break Forest Green fans were feeling 'spaced out' and went below to watch endless re-plays of the goals on the concourse screens to ensure this was happening. This was some advert for Non-league football.

From the restart Tranmere pressed and from an early corner Stockton glanced a downward header from six yards that had Russell diving to his right to make a spectacular reflex save. Tranmere replaced Mangan with Dunn on fifty four minutes. It was at this time Russell became the villain of the piece when fooling around with a back-pass he gave away possession to Stockton on the edge of his area. The Tranmere striker struck the ball over the crossbar with the goal unguarded.

After this let-off Forest Green fans began to think this might be their day. On the hour Stockton again headed narrowly wide with Russell a spectator. Wishart replaced Keanu and almost immediately went on a fifty yard run to the edge of the Tranmere area. He squared the ball to Noble who under pressure hurried his shot wide. Tranmere were wilting and McNulty and Buxton were looking hippoponderous while Traore, Pinnock, Monthe and Ellis for Forest Green had become dominant.

Mullings and Wedgbury replaced Doidge and Traore inside the final fifteen minutes. As the game entered the closing stages Tranmere were frustrated as Rovers wasted time. Tempers flared but the referee handled the situations well. A final corner for Tranmere and the referee blew his whistle.

Forest Green Rovers were a Football League Club, having written large a significant chapter in their remarkable one hundred and twenty seven year history. Never in the annals of battles for play-off supremacy have so many been conquered by so few. To the victors on this day of days it is theirs to throw cheers to the heavens. To salute their warriors in the theatre of war. While those at home can only wish that they were here to embrace this spirit of victory.

Over the top? Maybe, but Forest Green have made it so. Owner and Chairman Dale Vince has integrated his business philosophy into the football club and made it unique throughout the world. For all those who came before and built the club, and its supporters who stayed, they will remember absent friends at this time. It's emotional.

The future? That will take care of itself. For now, it's all about the glory.

## FGR AMBASSADOR REPORT 1

*Elsie Heslop, Sir William Romney Secondary School, Tetbury*

Elsie's inside view. After a long long journey Forest Green Rovers have managed to reach the play-offs. They have fought so hard this season and are realising the importance of what could happen if they get through into league two. Last year they managed to get all the way to Wembley but sadly suffered a defeat against Grimsby. All season my family and I have been dreaming to redeem ourselves and make our way back to the National Stadium.

On the 7th of May we faced our first challenge against Dagenham and Redbridge. When we played them at the New Lawn it was already 1-1 on aggregate so you could tell it was going to be a tense game. However I was slightly nervous as FGR have been a bit unpredictable this season but I knew that something good would come our way. Forest Green won that match 2-0 and for every goal scored by FGR a green smoke thing exploded creating an atmosphere which was just unbelievable. At the end everyone was buzzing and ran straight onto the pitch to join the players. I couldn't believe my eyes; the New Lawn swarmed with people: singing, cheering, screaming and even more green smoke filled the air. FGR were going back once more to Wembley.

Sunday 14th May. On the way to London I had butterflies in my stomach, Wembley is a humongous stadium and Forest Green Rovers, from little old Nailsworth, were playing to get promoted into the

**M**
**A**
**Y**

football league. For a small club we were taking in every moment of this fantastic experience. The streets were filled with Tranmere supporters who outnumbered us by thousands. But like they say: good things come in small packages! My dad said, "We're parking in the green car park just for luck" and it looked like other supporters had the same idea. I stepped out of the car and immediately saw a big group of Forest Green fans. Because we were so outnumbered everyone acknowledged each other, got along, it was a great and funny environment to be in. It felt as though we were back at the New Lawn.

After grabbing some food we made our way into the stadium and that's when the excitement started to hit me. When you walk around inside you can see those little glimpses of the ground inside. But when you step out to go into your seats you just stand there mesmerised by the size. Despite the fact that we didn't even fill up one of the tiers you could just picture what it would be like if it was. Every goal that was scored by both teams was amazing and showed off what the National League had to offer. At half time it was 3-1 to us and when a goal was scored everyone went mental! If we scored anymore in the second half I'm pretty sure no one would be able to feel their hands or be able to speak because of the noise we were making. There weren't any more goals in the second half although there were some really close attempts. When it went into extra time I think everybody was so excited but also really tense because it seemed as if the final whistle would never go. After 7 minutes of extra time it finally went and Forest Green Rovers are going to be in League 2. The presentation was even better the stadium went crazy! The players were so excited they were getting the crowd up cheering a couple of them did a synchronised worm and obviously they did a massive slide towards the crowd.

Overall, it was a great day and I can't believe that we are going to be in League 2. When I got home I had to pinch myself to make sure that we had just been to Wembley and witnessed our local team get promoted into the football league. What an exciting time! Can't wait to see you all there next season.

Come on you Rovers!

### FGR AMBASSADOR REPORT 2
*Eddy Turner, Avening Primary School*
On the 14th May 2017 Forest Green Rovers played Tranmere Rovers at Wembley for the last promotion place into League 2. To get to this world famous stadium, FGR beat Dagenham and Redbridge 3-1 on aggregate, while Tranmere played Aldershot Town and won 5-2 over both legs.

To travel to this stadium, I went on a long coach journey with lots of other ambassadors. It was roughly a 3 and a ½ hour trip there with a 25-minute stop, but it was worth it when I saw Wembley's famous arch.

To begin with, the game could go anywhere, with continuous attacks and counter-attacks from both teams until Forest Green's Kaiyne Woolery tucked in a bottom corner goal after 11 minutes of play. Tranmere didn't give up though. 10 minutes later Tranmere equalized through Connor Jennings who smacked the ball too high for Sam Russell's reach. Again, numerous attacks were invalidly taken, one of which involved Scott Davies-Tranmere's 'keeper, diving rapidly to his right to prevent a FGR lead. Finally, all that running paid off for FGR after a 42nd minute goal by Christian Doidge and a 44th minute goal, again from Woolery, following an interception just outside the box.

Like the first half, the ball was up and down the pitch, continuously changing ends. One of the most impressive runs was when Forest Green's Emmanuel Monthe single-handedly ran from before the half-way line to near the Tranmere box, but he was tackled before he could do any harm. The game was so action packed, I missed the odd counter-attack whist I was scribbling notes down. Luckily, Tranmere couldn't catch us up so we won, becoming the first ever village club to be in the football league!

"This was even better than watching Spurs miss out on the Premier League title!" said my dad.

Forest Green Rovers are now an official football league club and the New Lawn is an official football league ground. We will definitely need the new stadium now!

The adventure continues...#WEARELEAGUE2FGR

# Poets' Corner

So, you have followed Rovers' tumultuous season in reports and prose provided by a variety of 'commentators'. Now try the experience in verse.

This chapter displays the amazing poetic thoughts posted on the FGR Fans Forum's Poets' Corner during the 2016/17 season. The poems are set out chronologically with a line or two explaining their context. Poets they may be, but in common with all supporters, their mood swings, joy and angst change game by game. If you want to relive the tortured emotions of a season concentrated into a few pages of verse, this chapter for you!

Preseason musing:

ChrisGump11 04.08.16. What foresight this rhymer possessed. How did he foretell the future?

Now so long, National league, it's time that we began
to laugh and cry and cry and laugh about it all again

The Farmacotian

'And so it begins – Our Club'

Same club, but different faces
Same club, new season dawning
Same club, same league
Same club, travelling to familiar places

Same club, but with Coops at the helm
Same club, with same ambitions
Same club, punching above its weight
Same club, aspiring to move to that higher realm

Our club, promotion hopes renewed
Our club, forum reignited with hopes and fears
Our club, friendlies start and we are filled with hope
Our club, excitement of style, hope in all fans imbued

Our club, this is our time, we will prevail
Our club, management have it right
Our club, this is it,come on Rovers
Our club, let battle commence the heights to scale

OUR CLUB - The English Football League to assail.
Now where did I put my scarf?

The season gets under way ...

Pitchfork post Boreham Wood defeat 06.08.16 per Supertramp

Dreamers, we know we are dreamers
Well can we put your hands in our heads, oh no!
I said dreamers, we're nothing but dreamers
Well can we put our hands in our heads, oh no!
I said "Far out, what a day, a year, a laugh it is!"
You know, well you know we had it comin' to us,
Now there's not a lot I can do!

ChrisGump11 11.08.16 in midlife crisis and in search of golf coaching from a
renowned FGR supporting coach

'Dangers'

Dangers takes you over to his golf shack on Minch Common
You can hear the hacks go by
In their shouty Pringle jumpers
You spend countless lessons with him
And you know that he's half-crazy
But that's why you want to be there
And he gives you teas and golf balls
That come all the way from China
And just when you mean to tell him
That you have no skill to give him
Then he gets you on his wavelength
And he lets the video show you
That that you're such a stilted mover
And you want to travel with him
And be a wrinkly golfing find
And you know that he will guide you
For he's coached your aching body with his mind

Crispin Thomas, Football Poets 14.08.16 After FGR 1 Gateshead 0 13.08.16

'Another Season~Another Way'

We're back for more endeavour
while some still holiday
a handful here from Tyneside
have found Another Way*

we wipe away the memories
those seasons in a row
the cruel Play Off lottery
for where we long to go

the Rovers faithful reconvene
they're sampling Vegan food
the Heeds have come here to defend
as deadlock is ensued

# We Did it Our Way: Forest Green Rovers Triumph at Wembley

the Wembley heartbreak is long gone
at last the crowd ignite
it's early doors at The New Lawn
we're showing will and fight

we start to know the faces
the shape the look the new
the season stretches like the hills
as far as we can view

the trees have grown much taller now
the sheep can barely see
we'd take a goal from anywhere
a win will do for me

we leave it late but in the end
we may not have impressed
and need to gel but what the hell
we grab one at the death

and later with the ground all still
I pinch myself and say
how fabulous our hillside home
upon Another Way

The Farmcotian 20.08.17

Following our Jekyl and Hyde start to the season I thought it timely to compose
a poem which reminds us all why we support our Forest Green.

'My Forest Green'

You're precious to me
Like Owen's poetry
And I wish you well
Our Forest Green

When the fans sang with so much pride
We could stem any storm and riptide
Football, passing exemplified
That's our Forest Green

We'll always be there
Our Forest Green

You're precious to me
Like Blake's poetry
And we wish you success
Bold Forest Green

They will be many lows and highs
But we'll raise our heads to the skies

What a mighty team
Our Forest Green

We are still the little club a'top the hill
But we'll show our naysayers with pride and skill
That's our Forest Green
MY Forest Green

Crispin Thomas "Football Poets" 20.08.16 FGR 2 York City 1

'finding voices'

rain drenching toe curling
deep defending wind swirling
early days time to gel
late pen but all is well

signs of something different days
ditch the moaning yell your praise
suddenly we're spoilt for choices
now the main stand's finding voices

long long season lying waiting
good to see us dominating
patient probing from the back
signs of progress in attack

points are points I'm delighted
nothing's easy we're excited
sparks of progress on the pitch
negativity we ditch

make some noise show you care
let them know that we are here
came so close but we'll achieve
believe believe believe believe..

Voodoobluesman 21.08.16

'Brodie haiku'

Oh Brodie why cheat?
Your tackles are a disgrace
Yet your goal was great.

Crispin Thomas "Football Poets" 22.08.16

Onward and Back To Yesterday

how like the pitch and food we are
enveloped in the Green
the stunning wild location

this place has always been
but sometimes as I stand here
and chat with loyal fans
the thoughts go back to yesterday
to how it all began

this tiny hilltop village side
who's changing hut was found
behind the Jovial Forester
a good walk from the ground
a pitch all lined with turnips then
when crowds would flock to see
a local team of local men
so long before TV

as through the lower leagues they rose
a hundred years rolled by
it's sometimes hard imagining
the where and how and why
but I first found the Rovers
back in seventy nine
and under corrugated iron
I stood on that first time
the little stand the breeze blocks
the ancient iron gate
the days under the radar
when hopes were not that great

Hellenic League and Southern League
I dropped by when I could
but die-hard fans stuck by them
through all the bad and good
the FA Vase at Wembley win
it feels like yesterday
the moment when we made it
as the Conf'rence came our way

And now the revolution
the eco sample set
the journey here to where we are
that old fans won't forget
and evr'y time I come here
whenever that may be
I look around and feel so proud
at what has been achieved
while others gaze in wonder
at standards being made
it feels at last it's drawing near
the time to make the grade

we're patient but we sense it
we've seen their fans belief
the Big Boys who have made it from

the hardest league to leave
the Oxfords and the Newports
the Wombles and the Hatters
the 8 win start but in the end
it's finishing that matters
The Pirates and the Chelt'nams
the Grimsbys with their songs
those play-off magic nights so close
to where this team belongs

but through it all a new belief
for little Forest Green
who now command respect and awe
whatever that may mean
but sometimes as I stand here
and chat with loyal fans
the thoughts go back to yesterday
to how it all began

Crispin Thomas "Football Poets": "Plastic fantastic" @ Maidstone United 1
Forest Green Rovers 4. 27 08 16

'Listening To The Game'

sometimes we lock ourselves away
the pressure is immense
it's different at this level
but always always tense~
sometimes it gets confusing
sometimes the crowd are bored
and sometimes you can't figure out
just who has nearly scored~
sometimes it's hard to handle
a feeling you can't name
and clock-watching can be involved
just listening to the game

sometimes it's just impossible
you're working on the day
or distances are massive
on nights when they're away ..
and sometimes you just wonder
where did the derbies go
it's Aldershot or Eastleigh now
at eighty miles or so
but sometimes if we're losing
it always feels the same
and fear and stress get multiplied
listening to the game

sometimes it's so frustrating
we scream until we're blue
but radios can't hear us

there's nothing you can do
and sometimes commentators try
to calm us on the mike
when "truthfully" gets used a lot
or what the food's been like~
sometimes it feels old fashioned
like way back in the day
before TV before BT
we followed games this way...
but sometimes you must ask yourself
there's no-one you can blame
why do we put ourselves through this
listening to the game?

Chrisgump11 28.08.16

Coops says that he will never see
Plastic to beat something grassy.
That the players sparkled effortlessly
Made me think they disagree

Crispin Thomas "Football Poets" 29.08.16 FGR 5 Southport 1

'Easy Now'

easy now easy now
the only thing to say
is bear in mind it's not the time
to get carried away

we've all been here before my friends
we've watched the passion drain
it's nineteen years and counting
let's not jump guns again

the déja vu is valid
the competition's hot
with Dagenham and Tranmere
and Lincoln in the pot

and one or two surprises
I'll all but guarantee
so easy now yes easy now
let's see what we will see

and if we should be critical
when five goals feels so sweet
remember as the goals go in
we've only two clean sheets

so easy no easy now
the only thing to say

is bear in mind it's not the time
to get carried away

The Farmcotian 30.08.16

Phew – written over a coffee in Waitrose listening to England slaughter the
Pakistani bowling. What a game yesterday – went home with a smile on my face
which surprised the family.

'Dreamscape'

Speed, skills, silky smooth
Goals galore, golden groove
Basking, believing, ball battering
Manouevring, manipulating, mastering

Action, accuracy, astonishment
Cloughie climbing, confident
Passing, perfection, purring
Busy, bombarding, blurring

Moore magnificent, monumental
Exciting, enticing, elemental
Forever FGR, fantasy feeling
Southport, skewered, shattered, squealing

Crowd, crowing, chanting, clapping
Scoring, scorching, searing, snapping
Soaring, sated, smile spreading
Happy, homeward heading

Crispin Thomas "Football Poets" 03.09.16 Chester 1 FGR 2 03.09.16

'Count To Ten & Count The Clichés'

keep your feet upon the ground
the plans of mice and men
outweigh all the clichés here
breathe and count to ten

try to curb emotions
nothing's cast in stone
don't tell me it's over yet
keep your dreams in tow
don't celebrate too early
the die is not yet cast
wiser to remember
lessons in the past ~
don't live in the future
keep your powder dry
many a slip twixt cup and lip
we'll know by and by

just refrain from saying
you feel it in the air
wake me when it's over
pinch me when we're there

don't cross bridges early
see what Winter brings
last word's not been spoken
'til that lady sings
not the time to speculate
one game at a time
keep on doing what we do
it'll work out fine
we're not down to brass tacks
season isn't done
put that ol' champagne on ice
battle's not yet won
keep on digging out results
never change your tune
déja vu will never do
don't let's peak too soon

keep your feet upon the ground
the plans of mice and men
are worse than all the clichés here
just breathe and count to ten

Voodoobluesman 05.09.16

Of Eddie Izzard, of Mice & Men

The plans of men we can understand, but the mice? What're they planning?

Crispin Thomas "Football Poets" 10.09.16 Dover 4 FGR 3

'Only one match of the day'

perhaps it was that mid-day kick off
with a fever all over the land
and aside from Manchester and Glasgow
this was the one for real fans

on a day like today you could feel it
in a match that will stir memories
when two of the big boys faced battle
where you can't see the pitch for the trees

but the media didn't quite notice
and we never quite grab their attention
it might be entitled the National
but we never get much of a mention

If you're outside the North and you're not overseas
if you live near to where your team play
forget all the hype in the papers
there was only one match of the day

you could say that we're just poor relations
if you went in your pub they would jeer
but with only two screens when the big boys are on
then you wouldn't see Forest Green there

you could call up the club and the Green Man
but they're closed and your plans looked all over
and none of your mates had got BT installed
who were showing the Rovers at Dover

and what did they miss at Old Trafford
or at Celtic Park on such a day
they missed out a seven goal thriller
in a game Forest Green threw away

perhaps it was sloppy- complacent
and we ran out the losers 4-3
we're a swashbuckling side and we're learning
we move on..que sera...we will see

Crispin Thomas "Football Poets" 25.09.16

'In Good Time'

this is for those who travel
this is for those who care
this is for those who give up their time
to follow their team evr'ywhere

this is for seeing new places
by car or by coach or by train
this is for being outnumbered
and standing outside in the rain

this is where adverts are local
on big wooden old fashioned signs
where terraces still rise in concrete
with raffles read out at half time

this is for those who are loyal
the faces you spot on the day
and this is for those who are faithful
who turn up at home come what may

and this is for keeping it going
whether in village or town
where new boys and giants who've dropped from the league
compete in their half empty grounds

and this is for those who no longer
are drawn by the Premier's sway
where stadiums rise up like space ships
and TV dictates when the play

and this is for always believing
success is a very fine line
and should it be ours in this season or next
it will happen for sure in good time

Crispin Thomas "Football Poets" 06.10.16 After FGR goes top of National
League with 4-0 win at Aldershot Town 04.10.16

'Top Today'

for all of the times that we've been here
ahead of the pack in the chase
be it fleeting or long we will need to be strong
in this joyous precarious place

it's a mountain to climb when you struggle
if you dare take your eye off the ball
you can be there or thereabout all season long
but right at the death you can fall

you can heed all your manager's cliches
and never get carried away
just av'rage two points and we'll be there
but for now... we are still.... top today

Voodoobluesman 06.10.16

'Football friends'

Every other week or so
We'll watch them kick it to and fro
Every other week, we all
Jane, Tom, Alan, Peter, Maggie, Judith and Paul
Sit, chat
Talk about this and that
Every other week,
we'll share
in how our FGR does fare

Crispin Thomas "Football Poets" 17.10.16. After FGR loses 2-1 at Sutton United
in FA Cup 15.10.16

'Clichés In The Wind'

how many times
must a fan turn his head
and pretend that he cares much at all?

yes and how many times
are you glad when your'e when out
before the First Round draw is called
the answer my friend's
a Cliché in the wind
the answer's a cliché in the wind

yes and how many times
must we all pinch ourselves
and remind us all why we believe
there's only thing that we must focus on
and that's getting out of this League
and Man U or Chelsea at home in the Cup
is not what we're longing to win
the answer my friends is always the same
who cares if it's clichés in the wind

yes and how many times
will the moaners all cry
as we chase for the ultimate prize
and Derby was great but I'd much rather wait
for the one dream that fills up my eyes
and now we can concentrate all of our minds
and the Cup is just clichés in the wind

Crispin Thomas "Football Poets" 29.10.16 after FGR 1 Dagenham & Redbridge 1

'These Are The Ones'

these are the ones that matter
this is the acid test
these are the ones that you don't wanna lose
when you're out there ahead of the rest

it's as tight at the top as it always will be
too many good teams are here
and they're names that you've known since your childhood
but you pray we can do it this year

in this lottery league where consistency counts
and the Tranmeres and Lincolns keep pace
it's a really close call and another long haul
it's a knife edge and nail-biting chase

and the moment your mind starts to wander
remember to keep your head strong
as you lift up your voice and you pump up the noise
who cares how our rivals get on

and I know what you're thinking and saying
there's another three quarters to go

and none of us want to go down to the wire
but its upward and on with the show

when the South Stand are belting their hearts out
and the main stand awake and respond
as the energy shifts and the atmosphere lifts
and we join in to cheer them along

but the feeling is growing and growing
it's clear as an old country mile
and we'd love to be ten points ahead of the rest
and to dazzle our way up in style

but we've so far to go in this battle
for our goal to be fin'lly achieved
so batten the hatch and hang on to your hats
just believe and believe and believe

Voodoobluesman 04.11.16

'If Only'

If only we had Ricky Miller
His goals make him a killer.
If only Tubbs would score
We'd have won a lot more.

If only the linesman had seen
The player's hand in-between.
If only the ref saw this and that
But he's just such a blind "cat"

If only the East Stand would make more noise
To match the South Stand boys.
If only the Carol Embrey Suite
Would serve us more Tout-suite.

What we have is where we are
Where people mock from afar
When we're top of the league
And they're just jealous, indeed
We play some great games
Edge of seat stuff, most times
We have ethics, passion, fire and heart
We're the pride of the Cotswolds, and we all play our part.

It's just...
If only....

Crispin Thomas "Football Poets" 29.10.16
Written alone in the East Stand on a cold evening after Tannoy and sound-check
run through with Richard Joyce 03.11.16 ahead of FGR v Aldershot.

'The only person in the football ground'

I'm the only person in the football ground
silence fills the stadium there's no-one around
a pin could be deafening you can't hear a sound
I'm the only person in the football ground

the only soul in the home of expectation
a reservoir of dreams or an outlet for frustration
seats all empty fans on vacation
stand lies waiting like a train at the station

tree-lined terraces underneath the stars
solar panels sparkle green electric cars
here where kids dream of being superstars
up upon the hill but I could be on Mars

where is the manager and where are the team?
where is the kit man who keeps the boots clean?
you can't quite label it or classify by name
I wonder when I leave will I ever feel the same

standing like a statue with the lights down low
dreaming of promotion but there's so far to go
and where there'd be maybe two thousand or so
there's me and myself and this faint white glow

moments like this you can never ever buy
they just get given like a secret or a sigh
clear green canvas of a waiting football ground
security are absent but they're looking I'll be bound

I shouldn't really be here but it's great to stick around
a pin could be deafening you can't hear a sound
nipped through a side door and suddenly I found
I'm the only person in the football ground

The Farmcotian 05.11.16
I'm back - but only in spirit at the moment. Bored at Schipol waiting for my third
flight of the day - let's hope we have a great win. Hopefully will soon be able to
pen verses to the delight and/or annoyance of all whilst actually having seen a
game in the flesh.

'The Leavers/Believers'

Podgorica for early morning airport tea
Touch down in Vienna for a welcome brunch
Flight now to Schipol for a late Dutch lunch
Onto Bristol, missing the match as mainland Europe I flee

The half starts brightly Drissa in control
Ethan and Cloughie the centre to patrol

## We Did it Our Way: Forest Green Rovers Triumph at Wembley

Liam marshals the flanks as Noble as an eagle
Swooping on its prey, haughty and regal

And now the Shots are outgunned
Rhys, Keanu et al out think and out run
It cannot be long now it seems before our artillery
Burst like a torrent through every capillary

Thoroughly sated on the remains of our foe
Coopers men toy with their prey
It should be more but why heap woe upon woe
Keep some powder dry for further affrays

And then ...

I wake with a start over the English Coast at Dover
The match in my dreamlike head is over
Aldershot four nil defeated – toast
Just the hope of an absent Rovers rover

By the time I really know the score
I will be touching down at Lulsgate airport once more
Another game missed and just hoping for the win
The match in my head has flashed by and bemused passengers
Can see my inane grin!

I hope that the dream came true.

The death of Leonard Cohen was announced 11.11.16. Loved by legions, FGR poets
found his words right for most occasions and parodied them with great affection

The Farmcotian 05.11.16

'RIP Leonard Cohen – First we take the Conference"

Pennock sentenced us to 2 years of tedium
But Coop's changing the system from within
We're motoring now, They're going to reward us
First we take the Conference, then we take the League

We're guided by a visionary
We're guided by an eco warrior pure
We're guided by the beauty of our football
First we take the Conference, then we take the League

I really like our movement it's groovy
I love our sinuous, silky, sensuous style
But you see that hard work has to move everyone
It's not easy, not easy, not easy it's how the season goes

Ah I loved you as a loser, but now we just might win
You know they think they have ways to stop us but they'll don't have the guts

How many seasons we prayed for this, to let our work unfold
First we take the Conference, then we take the League

Thanks Leonard for the memories

The Farmcotian 13.11.16. A reaction to Macclesfield Town 0 FGR 1 12.11.16
and social media hate messages from some MTFC "fans" which he felt to be
horribly inappropriate just a day after Remembrance Day

'Fate or Hate?"

Should there be hate in our beloved game?
What makes us utter a word so profane?
Is it really envy, jealousy or desire?
How can hate help us to understand or inspire?

What motivates us to love and support?
It's not hate makes me turn out, opposition to thwart
But joy, anticipation, expectation, frustration, dream
A test of loyalty, true but surely hatred should not be screamed

On a day like today hate surely has no place in anyone's lexicon
Do we truly "detest", "abhor", "loathe" want the other gone
Surely we should admire, inspire or aspire to want to be the best
It's football for goodness sake, we come for community not to detest

Sport is played on home and foreign fields
People who hate must not hide beneath its shield
Let's tease, "take the Michael" have some fun at the oppo's expense
But hate - get real - let us support with passion and with common sense

We will remember

Fartvs Antiqvvs 18.11.16

'Oldies'. (With apologies to Willie Wordy.)

Up Nympsfield road I lonely ploughed
That rises steep o'er vales and hills
When all at once I saw a crowd,
A host, of oldies taking pills;
Around the ground, beneath the stand,
Gasping for air, not feeling grand.

Continuous as the stars that shine
And twinkle in the milky way,
They crouched in never ending lines,
Of east stand seats but nought to say;
Two thousand saw I at a glance,
Singing songs? Nay, not a chance.

## We Did it Our Way: Forest Green Rovers Triumph at Wembley

The Farmcotian 18.11.16

'Big Ben'

Young Ben Jefford has moved to my former club
My other team I still support from afar
It was no good him being excluded from even being a sub
I am sure at Sutton he will become a star

With Cloughie and Dan coming from the U's
We have to give them something back
Ben will be the first full back or midfielder they chose
And will provide many passes for Sutton to attack

And so farewell to a lovely lad
Who in earlier years would have been first choice
Sutton will stop him from becoming a wandering nomad
So come on the chocolate and amber cheer him with hearty voice

Crispin Thomas "Football Poets" 23.11.16 after FGR 2 Lincoln City 3 on
19.11.16 followed by FGR 2 Tranmere Rovers 2 on 22.11.16

'Make Some Noise for Rovers'

when the winner won't go in
when the main stand will not sing
when the late match nerves kick in
make some noise for Rovers

when you've had your mash and pie
gritted teeth as time flies by
take your gloves off have a try
make some noise for Rovers

is it really just the young
who refuse to be outsung
and implore you with the drum
to make some noise for Rovers?

I've seen people stop and stare
parents shudder turn and glare
at my trusty clapper there
making noise for Rovers

as a child upon the Shed
on those chants and noise was fed
swapped allegiance ... there it's said
to make some noise for Rovers

and I for one care not a fig
any match here small or big
and though it's sometimes like a gig
just make some noise for Rovers

are we embarrassed or just shy?
and sit there as the the game flies by
afraid to raise our voices high
and make some noise for Rovers?

Ray Clegg 24.11.16

The tension the thrill with plenty of skill
The boys in green serve up a cracker on top of the hill
We all watch with joy as we cheer the boys on
but at the end we sure need a pill.

Top of the league we sit there still
We all take a breath and urge with goodwill
For the boys in green on top of the hill
to finish with style with panache and with skill.

The Farmcotian 28.11.16

'Sing – Silence – it's still Support'

"'Forest Green, Forest Green, Forest Green"
They say that the East stand voices are rarely heard
We're little boys and girls who don't want to be heard but seen
Just because we don't always sing - that's absurd

Some like to watch the match - and discuss quietly together
You don't have to shout to support your team
They'll still support the Rovers forever
Others are reserved and it's not in their psyche to shout and scream

We all support our club in different ways
Some bang the drum, chant and cheer
Others watch with passion, but don't sing just gaze
So let's accept the differences, TNL still has atmosphere

The Farmcotian 12.12.16

The Farmcotian sums up 'supporters' angst', an emotion felt by all, mid season.
Euphoria has turned to doubt and despair as results go badly and players come
into and leave the club

'Too many cooks spoil the broth?'

Who is now plays for Forest Green?
Who is on loan or at The New Lawn?
What are the names of those seldom seen?
Who will get us to the Rubicon?

Personally I am fed up with all the changes
So many players are here and then not here
Some are supposedly better but Coops just rearranges!
Continuity is what makes a great team I fear

But Racine – the captain of the club
Is banished to a foreign field
And others have too received the Cooper snub
And yet to our main contenders we yield and yield

Forwards Moore and Murphy who we desperately need
Are banished to other clubs whilst whilst we suffer
And others, reputably better have come to help us succeed
But will they be good and messiahs or yet more in season duffers

These opinions are of course mine and mine alone
But I am fed up seeing squad changes every week
We have players, loyal, fine who the coup have not flown
Others performing great things whilst promotion we seek

Continuity for me is an essential part of a happy team
We have a squad of disproportional size in my view
Players come and sometimes go and then return it seems
It's time to rethink our strategy anew

Players have to get to know each other and form a bond
The best time is at pre-season one should start
So many games in – how does Coops wave a magic wand
The continuity, cohesion (and fitness!) he should impart

You look at teams who perform so well through a season
They usually have a team with a spine so stable
Players are told when dropped or loaned – with positive reasons
It could be seen that loyalty is a betrayal

And so with Christmas tide approaching so fast
It's the time of family, loving and giving
Let's look at reducing a squad so vast
And others find first team footy and make a good living!

Merry Christmas everyone and a new player free New Year!

Meanwhile Voodoobluesman turned to his wife and Dean Friedman for
inspiration ...

Voodoobluesman 17.12.16 after FGR 1 Dover Athlectic 1

'Lucky Stars'

"What are you saying ?
How on earth can you say what you just said?"

"I was saying to myself
"Our title dreams are dead."
By the way I forgot to say
I watched forest green rovers play today"

"Did you see Cooper?'
"Yes I saw Cooper"
"And was he angry?"
"He wasn't angry"
"Maybe a little?"

"Well possibly maybe!
But how am I supposed to feel
With all the games we just can't steal.
And I can't thank my lucky stars
Cause we're not as good as we like to think we are."

"Would you like to talk about it?"
"There's not much to say.
We played Dover this afternoon
And let it slip away.
We just ran around as if
We were stumbling off a cliff."

"Do you still like them ?"
"What are you saying?"
"You still support them?"
"Every time they're playing."
"Really I mean it
Can you forget them?"

"Wait now, just stop it,
You should know better
I know this is hard to seem
There's no one quite like Forest Green
but I can't thank my lucky stars
Cause we're not as good as we like to think we are."

Wait I'm sorry, it's going wrong
And you have no alibis
You're just playing like some tools
You should apologise.
Listen boys I know your glum
But that's OK
We could still get a good run.
Do you still want it?
Cause we all want it.
Not just playing nice
Not just playing nice
Are you still winners?
Yes you're still winners
Then get right back out there
Cause we might not be all that loud
You'll never find a more loyal crowd
And I can thank my lucky stars
That I support the mighty FGR

# We Did it Our Way: Forest Green Rovers Triumph at Wembley

Crispin Thomas "Football Poets" 19.12.16

'The Road To Gel'

feeling felt ...sentiment shared
kind of glad that I couldn't be there
a gig at the Sub Rooms kept me away
followed the drama by phone through the day
old school fog like days of yore
same old problems.. been here before

conspiracy theories why we go wrong
always 'big boys' coming on strong
this times Lincoln ...Barrow... Tranmere
how many times have we been here?
blame the manager.. choices he makes
endless chances... defensive mistakes

there at his fingertips there in his grasp
the endless friendless thankless task
Coops has my back - the team as well
here on the long hard road to gel

feels like an age since we won in the League
let's get going and batter Torquay
ditch all the moaning and groaning somehow
the past will be last year.. focus on now
build ups and play are a pleasure to see
time to click let the goals flow free

bring on next Year make a new start
let's score freely and rip teams apart
away with the nervousness swlrling around
it hangs in the air like a mist coming down
away with the negative bring on the plus
pressure possession and all that stuff

have a good Christmas welcome the New
at least we've created a vegan or two
enough about Rovers who we go to watch ...
think about those who just go for the nosh!

so...altogether now:

Vegan Vegan Vegan Pie
Covered in gravy give it a try
Offer me Turkey and I reply
Vegan Vegan Vegan Pie

one vegan club
there's only one vegan club

one vegan cluuuuuuuuuuuuuuuuuuuu-ub
there's only one vegan club

on our way..we're on our way
for a vegan meal we're on our way
if we win we don't care
if we lose we we still don't care
to a vegan meal ..we're on our way

Forest Green FC..in the Carol Embrey
Forest Green FC..for a nice cup of tea
soya milk or rice .. that'll be so nice
Forest Green FC ..in the Carol Embrey

Crispin Thomas "Football Poets" 01.01.17 hot on the heels on 2 extraordinary
results, Torquay United 4 FGR 3 26.12.16 & FGR 5 Torquay United 5 01.01.17

'Defending the Indefensible'

protection shown against attack ?
invisible ? absent ?. Check
unjustified by argument ?
excuses ?.what the heck
regrettable ? lamentable ?
supporter value? High
defenders indefensible
no matter how we try

but sitting with Farmcotian
our poet hearts were torn
ripped open like our back men
bereft inept and shorn
we're shipping goals like stuff online
we're ebay in disguise
we're Amazon we're Dagenham
at least we've got the pies

so where did this all come from ?
and did it hold the fans ?
it could have been eleven all
our heads were in our hands
defend the Indefensible
and grumble as you will
I'd still prefer to share it all
than watch some drab nil-nil

this topsy turvy National League
that begs consistency
and longs for confidence to breed
from club to fan to team
but still there's not a person here
woman child or man

who cannot question what we saw
nor ever understand
for sheer and mad excitement
no time to hold your breath
at one moment I almost thought
that Parkin was the ref

as ten goals came and went today
what still seems fair to see
is at 2-4... and then 3-5
a point is fine for me

The Farmcotian 01.01.16, in seasonal vein. Just off the top of my head as it is Panto season after all - oh no it isn't!

New FGR Panto for 2017 – Passing Strangers'

Ethan, may I introduce Charlie, he is to be a friend of yours
Charlie, this is Dale and he'll also be your chum
And this is Dan who may occasionally be close by
You will come together and gesticulate after the opposition scores
But don't look blue or feel too glum
It's part of my dastardly plan to make friends and foe as bemused as I

We'll fool our oppo's into thinking it's so easy
To win a game in passing right through strangers is sublime
With bafflement complete we'll then move forward with elan
And discover the Torquay manager has a similar plan
Two defences that haven't a clue makes one quite queasy
But it's January and "oh yes it is" it's time for FGR pantomime!

As our doughty manager's selection will confirm
He is playing this panto season for laughs and japes
Seeing how bad the tactics can be and still not lose
And by how much he could make the fans wince and squirm
Could we be so bad and yet "with one bound" escape?
Or will the plan of passing strangers fail totally to bemuse

It is us the fans that are bemused to the n'th degree
We laughed, we cried, the joke was on us
If they didn't know who was playing with who how could we know?
We weren't in on the manager's plan of a goal scoring frenzy
And that even rudimentary knowledge of defence was surplus
And passing strangers is FGR's plan for 2017 to fool both friend and foe

Ho Ho Ho - it's going to be a fun 2017 - All together "Oh No It Isn't"!

Epilogue

A little plea from this humble fan
For Chrissakes Coops get a defensive plan!

Crispin Thomas "Football Poets" 01.01.17 gave his re-joiner in like vein

look out...they're behind you..
who? What?
five goals in your net?
whose net ....what our net ?
yeah ...but what about their net?
..what five goals?...yeah...oh right
....great to see you today mate..
we go again!

Voodoobluesman 07.01.17 after Bromley 1 FGR 5. Yet another seasonal mood swing

The return of the wingers
Turned us into winners
And silenced us whingers

Andymac26 08.01.17

When the team sheet showed Elliott Frear,
It didn't half fill us with cheer.
The difference he made,
And the way that we played,
The way forward is surely now clear?

Crispin Thomas "Football Poets" 16.01.17

'How Many?'

So many questions always on the go
rumours and grumbles that never seem to stop
but only one question in the heart of ev'ry fan
how many coats has Mark Cooper got?

negative comments about the boss
transfers and new loans bubbling in the pot
but far more important than all of that stuff..
how many coats has Mark Cooper got?

heard it mentioned on the last comment'ry
and suddenly the penny just finally dropped
Elliott and Keifer must wonder as they leave
how many coats has Mark Cooper got?

takes some stick on the ol' touchline
Facebook rants that have lost the plot
promotion is there but we still wanna know...
how many coats has Mark Cooper got?

are they chosen for each new formation
diff'rent at the back..diff'rent up top
Motherwell Ipswich I don't care....
but how many coats has Mark Cooper got?

wrapped in a scarf like a snowman on the line
zip- ups... fur-lined ..he's got the lot
forget about Lincoln...all we wanna know
is how many coats has Mark Cooper got?

The Farmcotian 16.01.17. The comings and goings had all got too much for
FGR's poet laureate as he departed for a lie down, or in his words:

"That's it – I will now resort to coming each week, reading the increasingly
insane and hysterical comment and leave it to others to make sense of what is
occurring. Goodbye gentle reader"

'Get me off this insane roundabout'

I'll be at each home match as usual
But I am signing off from the forum except for perusal
I once went to matches to see the same 18-20 players
Who turned out for the club, not on loan or here for favours

Now all I read and see is he's left/arrived on loan
Aren't there any now that a club can call their own
But now I am sick of it all to the nth degree
Players are a commodity, to be bought and sold with no loyalty

We live in a disposable and throwaway society it's true
The same for our players, don't like one get one anew
I go to a match and I now know more from the other side
"weren't they once ours", no tossed carelessly aside

I feel doesn't really matter who we support anymore
FGR - a name for a club with players in/out an ever revolving door
"Who's in the team today - are there 11 I will know
Or have another 9 or 10 arrived and then on loan the others go?

I may be in a minority of one but I am sick of all the upheaval
I never realised that the diaspora had hit FGR - frankly primeval
So I will turn up each week in hope that I'll recognise at least 8-9 of our side
'Cause if I don't what's the point - is it now the season our team died?

Frear, Moore, Murphy, Racine et al were our players who I got to know
Mostly in the team, loyal and help the team and club to grow
But - no let's get loanees in and loan others out
Cooper shows no loyalty or stepping off the temporary contract roundabout

So I'll be there on Saturday to support my FGR team
Regardless of who Cooper feels is the latest pawns in his ridiculous scheme
But if I can hope for one last request on matchday
Can I please see those who for FGR really want to play and stay

Fartvs Antiqvvs 17.11.17. Similarly troubled, he turned to Peter Sarstedt

You talk like Jose Morinho
And you dance like Fred Astaire
Your clothes are all made by Burton
And there's dye and gel in your hair, yes there is

You live in a fancy apartment
By the curtesy of D. Vince
Where you keep players' records
And a friend of that big star Paul Ince, yes you are

You go to Carol's embassy gatherings
Where you talk Russian and Greek
And the young men that play in your line-up
They hang on every word that you speak, yes they do

But where do you go to my leader
When you're alone in your bed?
Tell me the thoughts that surround you
I want to look inside your head, yes I do

I've seen all your qualifications
You got from Ess-WIn-don
And the knowledge you stole from MacDonald
The enigma goes on and on, yes it does

When you go on your summer vacation
Do you to Robin Hood Bay go back?
With your carefully designed Budgie swimsuit
You get an even suntan on your back, and on you legs

And when the snow falls you're found in Nailsworth
With others of the same set
And you sip your hot Vegan coffee
But you never get your lips wet, no you don't.

But where do you go to my leader
When you're alone in your bed?
Won't you tell me the thoughts that surround you
I want to look inside your head, yes I do

You're in between forty and fifty
That's a very desirable age
Your body is firm and still fighting
But you live on a Manager's wage, yes you do, yes you do

Your name is heard in high places
You know well the Chair-man
He sent you a contract for Christmas
And you keep it just for fun, for a laugh. Ha-ha-ha

They say that when you are fired
You will be a millionaire

We Did it Our Way: Forest Green Rovers Triumph at Wembley

But they don't realise where you came from
And I wonder if they really care, or give a damn

But where do you go to my leader
When you're alone in your bed?
Tell me the thoughts that surround you
I want to look inside your head, yes I do

I remember the back streets of Wakefield
Two children begging in rags
Both touched with a burning ambition
To shake off their lowly-born tags, they tried

So look in my face, Nicholas Cooper
And remember just who you are
Then go and forget us forever
But I know you will still bear the scar, deep inside

I know where you go to my leader
When you're alone in your bed
I know the thoughts that surround you
Cause I can look inside your head

All in the best possible taste Mark. All in the best possible taste.

Crispin Thomas "Football Poets" 22.01.17 after FGR 1 Braintree 1 21.01.17

'Too Bright for Comfort'

we weren't too great again out there
it's hard to watch for sure
perhaps they were too bright for us
i thought we'd never score
it feels bizarre..familiar
before a restless crowd
who barely raise the noise at all
as though they're not allowed..

the glaring garb the visitors
arrived in ..took us back
to when the future looked so bright
as we began to crack
to be outsung by 42
all standing in the shade
at least we haven't lost this year
when will we make the grade?

you listen in on moans and groans
from those who've watched for years
the pessimism swirls around
increasing long-felt fears
the panic button's being pressed

we beg consistency
we only sing when we're winning
which is not constantly

they chop and change so often
they come and go like mist
our two new subs looked fine indeed
it's time to stick not twist
we have no right to win this league
we flatter to deceive
from the sublime to poor sometimes
whatever we believe

ok we were hard done by
but there we were again
with 7 added minutes
it's deja-vu my friends
as though we've never known a team
put ten behind the ball
or watched dismayed as they waste time
is no surprise at all

so how to lift the feeling
for confidence to soar ?
except to keep on keeping on
it's square one time once more...
and what to say to stand out more
when pressure is incessant
it's time for even bolder shirts
we must..

.be more..

.fluorescent

Crispin Thomas "Football Poets" 28.01.17 after Barrow 2 FGR 3

we may not have a Miller
a Hawkins or a Conte
but we have Nobes and Doidgey
and a late late late full Monthe

The Farmcotian 31.01.17. (Welcome back Farmcotian!) Perked up by the Barrow win, our poets saw fit to deal with a persistent, abusive Barrow supporter who made frequent intemperate posts on the Forum.

There was a coarse youth from Barrow
Who hadn't heard of Eton or Harrow
The toffs from the south
Failed to speak trench mouth
Which bamboozled the coarse youth from Barrow

We Did it Our Way: Forest Green Rovers Triumph at Wembley

Crispin Thomas "Football Poets" immediately added a second verse:

you managed to keep that one narrow
your verses get right to the marrow
it remains to be seen
if our fine village team
can shoot our way there like an arrow

Thus reinvigorated, 10.02.17 The Farmcotian turned to the Bard ahead of the home match with Boreham Wood

'MacCoops - a modern translation'

MacCoops: Bring me no more reports let's get the game underway
Till Boreham Wood remove to dunces again
We cannot quake with fear. Who's on loan this week, the boy Gosling?
Was he born of women? Only the spirits that know where he and the others called "loaners" come
from
All mortal consequences have been allowed for I hope

'Fear not, MacCoops; no man that's born of Boreham
Shall e'er have power upon the Forest of Green
Then fly, false thanes of the forum
And mingle with the English epicures at our vegan feast:
The team I pick (I know not all their names)
But they shall never sag with doubt nor shake with fear.

(enter Dale of the Vince)

MacCoops: The devil damn thee black, thou new age loon!
Where got'st thou that disheveled look?

Dale of the Vince: There is two –

MacCoops: million pounds villain ?

Dale of the Vince: No two pounds sire

MacCoops: Go prick thy face, and conquer your fear with more cash,
Thou lily-liver'd boy. I need more dodgy players!
Death of thy soul! We can top those Lincoln upstarts
Are Boreham Wood to be feared. What's the score going to be, whey-face?

Dale of the Vince: The English compromise 1-1, so please you my Lord.

MacCoops: Bugger off!

(exit Dale of the Vince)

The Farmcotian 13.02.17. Right on cue, new lad Omar Bugiel bought from Worthing made a very good impression

'A Clarion Call'

Oh me Oh my Omar
Methinks this lad will go far
Attacking from the very start
Raising spirits, playing with skill and heart

Before Omar arrived to take centre stage
Utilitarian and uninspiring was our play
Graft and grit did not the crowd assuage
It needed a spark the fans to gainsay
Eviscerating the opposition, carnage he waged
Legend from day one this was truly Omar's Valentine's Day

The Farmcotian 24.02.17. Defeat at Gateshead on 18th February induced further consternation in a topsy turvy new year for FGR supporters

'Delusion and Derision?'

The loss of Traore
Has caused such a furore
He must be reinstated now
I really don't care how

We had a formidable midfield then
Traore and Kelly (and Carter) made us play like men
Who knew what they were doing
Since then midfield's gone to wrack and ruin

Sinclair, Kelly, Traore perhaps Carter
Makes me feel more confident for starters
So why have they been excluded
Or I am crazy, dreaming or deluded

Direct questions need to be put to Cooper, Ash
Why no Drissa, Robert, Marcus, Darren - a backlash?
Fans have a right to know what is the situation
Because speculation becomes form of frustration

Surely it is easy to tell us why they are not picked
Because it is this equivocation the fans it doth afflict
An explanation to friend and foes will go some way
As to why these players are not picked on matchdays

Crispin Thomas "Football Poets" 05.03.17 after swashbuckling wins over Woking & Macclesfield Town

'Swapping Roles with Shakespeare'

When William claimed our world is just a stage
And we are merely players one and all

We Did it Our Way: Forest Green Rovers Triumph at Wembley

Was he inspired with quill upon the page
Or horrified and shocked by this football?

Did our great Bard endure and watch them play
That rough and tumble long 'ere rules began,
From his window on any given day
In muddy streets with bladder spheres to hand.

Did his namesake see how oft seasons arch
Or expect that he'd be coach instead?
Did Claudio beware the Ideas of March
Did some backstage cry out 'Off with his head'?

Can Craig dismiss this dark and barren spell
So we can all say all's well that ends well ?

Crispin Thomas "Football Poets" 21.03.17 inspired by green smoke bombs at
The New Lawn

'Smoke Flares Limerick'

a smoker who came from round here
loved width in the trousers he'd wear
he would press them and coax them
he'd iron them and smoke them
he just loved how the bottoms would flare

The Farmcotian 22.03.17

As my son said at the end of the match: "If you can keep your head when all
about you are losing theirs - you have clearly misread the situation"

'Diamonds in the Rough'

Ever seen a diamond pattern disintegrate from afar
Backwards and forwards with a lump in the throat
Russell to Wedge, Ellis, Dale, Wish, tactics totally bizarre
Chances of winning the game and championship remote

There are times when one has to wonder what tactics work
Never getting out of our half, two attacking forwards start the game
Nothing to their feet, made the fans go berserk
Were these tactics for the insane?

No Kells, Carter, Sincs, which was Drissapointing
But Fabian was fabulous and Noble his usual aggressive presence
But the shadows of the past with our team superior but lacking was haunting
And Liam was lucky to survive with an act of footballing misfeasance

The fans Wish to bring on the mighty Marcus to add class and pace
Was answered and suddenly there was an outlet on the left
And with more speed from Kane we were able to be back in the race
It provided the desire for the fans and Christian to not be left bereft

And there it was with the moaners ready to swamp the forum
We Doidged the bullet with a 94th minute winner
Our saviour once again brought peace, euphoria and little decorum
Cooper had moved to tactical saint and was no longer a tactical sinner

With our beloved FGR in impish mood this coming weekend
We could be six points clear of the Lincoln machine
But on picking the heroes of the Wrexham game it could depend
And we could become champions - and the world will truly turn Green!

Voodoobluesman 02.04.17. In common with the Forum as a whole, Voodoobluesman sprang to the defence of a tiny minority of vociferous fans who were targeting the manager's son Charlie with abuse. It put him in mind of a Madness song:

Heard a "fan" just the other day,
Don't seem they wanna know you no more,
They've laid it down when you just couldn't score,
Within the first two lines they bluntly said.

"You're not to come and play us no more,
Keep away from our door,
Don't play 'round here no more"
What on earth did you do that for?

Our true fans, we don't wanna know you,
You are a disgrace to the human race we say,
How can you show your face,
When you're a disgrace to the human race?

No supporting, you're an embarrassment,
Yes, an embarrassment, a living endorsement,
The intention that you have booked,
Was an intention that was overlooked.

We say, stay away,
Don't want you at The New Lawn today,
Keep away from our door,
Don't come 'round here no more.

Our true fans, we don't wanna know, we says,
This is a serious matter,
Too late to reconsider,
No one's gonna wanna know ya!

You're an embarrassment...

Crispin Thomas "Football Poets" 03.05.17 on the impending play-off semi-final legs with Dagenham & Redbridge

'On Our Way'

## We Did it Our Way: Forest Green Rovers Triumph at Wembley

I'm tempting fate to get this down
amid the hopes that swirl around
but has the moment comes around
to get into the league?

It's not about the vegan pies
nor playing under Cotswold skies
our taste is for a greater prize
to get into the league

it's not the eco world that's planned
electric cars beside the stand
we climb the hill with heart in hand
to get into the league

we've been here only twice before
sometimes it's hard to not ignore
the days and nights that we endure
to get into the league

we've dreamt and waited for so long
to rectify where we went wrong
we're on our way we sing this song
to get into the league

the time for superstition's done
but battle lost or battle won
our goal will still remain as one
to get into the league

Crispin Thomas "Football Poets" 09.05.17. With Dagenham & Redbridge
defeated and another Wembley final beckoning, Crispin posted a new poem
written by Stuart Butler (Radical/Local Historical Walk Organiser /Teacher and
Co-founder Football Poets in Stroud in 1996)

Blake, Bunyan, Wordsworth and Forest Green

And lo, it came to pass that when the Forest Green fans sang
'Stand up for the Forest Green',
All fans throughout the ground and stands,
Stood up.
And when the Forest Green fans sang
'Sit down for the Forest Green',
All fans throughout the ground and stands,
Sat down.
Truly, this was a paradisal state of beatitude:
An epiphany where all was a New Lawn of harmony,
Where all division and dissent disappeared
In a blissful unification of opposites,
Where lion stood up with lamb,
And where lamb sat down with lion,
In a self-governing collective of joy;

And when the final whistle blew,
The public address system filled the valleys and hills
With Jerusalem and its effulgent message,
And the football poets and the People's Republic of Stroud
Did walk upon the mountains green,
In Forest Green,
Far above the dark satanic mills of old Stroud-water –

But even in the midst of heaven, there is temptation,
For it is an arduous path of the pilgrim to the football league:
Past the Wicket Gate, the Slough of Despond,
The Hill of Difficulty, the Valley of Humiliation,
The Shining Light, the River of Death,
The Delectable Mountain,
Vanity Fair,
Half Man Half Biscuit
(For verily, these are the constituent parts of Tranmere Rovers),
If we are to reach the Celestial City,

Where there will be happiness in the by and by,
And quorn pie in the sky,
And we will walk with Wordsworth on Westminster Bridge,
And through the lanes and paths of Nailsworth,
Horsley, Forest Green, Shortwood and Newmarket:

For 'Earth' will not have
'Anything to show more fair:
Dull would he be of soul who could pass by
A sight so touching in its majesty.'

Details on a performative, celebratory, historical walk to follow if triumphant at Wembley.


Crispin Thomas "Football Poets" 18.05.17. Glorious victory at Wembley on 14th May seemed to stun the poets into contented, silent revelry. Crispin was the first to break cover and his verses captured the mood.

'Sometimes'

sometimes there are no words to find
that can express in prose or rhyme
this achievement this promotion
this relief and this emotion
felt in ev'ry single fan
who's longed for this since they began
who dreamt of this through thick and thin
the scrappy loss the narrow win
who came up here to sit or stand
so often with their heart in hand
the quiet stands that saw it all
the final rise after the fall

## We Did it Our Way: Forest Green Rovers Triumph at Wembley

but now our hearts beat louder than
some drum and bass or garage band
like shackled prisoners breaking free
we've fin'lly made it to the league
and care not what they say or do
now we've been shown that dreams comes true

it's had to work it's hard to sleep
the sounds and images that keep
repeating over in our brain
they rumble on just like the train
or coach or car that brought us home
from Wembley that we made our own
we hold our breath we count to ten
but then re-live it all again
and just like little children do
we realize that dreams come true

the changes burst like sun through mist
that some at first tried to resist
convinced they could not work or last
content to wallow in the past
those seasons that would end in tears
for some it lasted decades - years
a century in black and white
the darkest depths that begged for light
those seasons that would end in tears
the struggles here that they endured
the endless longing oft ignored
when for so long what kept hopes up
was some big draw here in the Cup
the ship that nearly ran aground
until by chance a hand was found
whose vision beckoned green and new
to prove that sometimes dreams come true

but now with concepts blown aside
the moans and groans replaced with pride
we rub our eyes we cant believe
this thing that we've at last achieved
and though the road looms large ahead
with tougher tests and days ahead
how great that now after so long
we've fin'lly found our voice and song
and sound and look like the real thing
what dramas will next season bring
it just reminds us - me and you
that yes sometimes dreams do come true

Greeners Jnr 25.05.17 submitted his first of the season (in time added on!), with apologies to Sir Rod Stewart

You're an essay in ecology
Don't care bout the geography
Coz your every footie fans dream
Not Celtic or United, Forest Green I've decided
Your the best team we've ever seen.

Your in our heart your in our soul
We hold breath when you score a goal
You are our friend you are our love
You in our souls?

# Afterword

Do not look for logic in a football supporter. However rational we try to be, and may be in everyday life, the emotional commitment to a football club sends common sense and reason into the long grass. Asking a dyed in the wool Forest Green Rovers supporter to be reasonable is like trying to calm a tantrum possessed toddler with "count your blessings". For the 9 months of our over-long season, we live on our nerves and for the other 3 we worry more gently!

At the start of the season, Ashley Loveridge (revered Sports Editor of Stroud News & Journal and long standing friend) asked me to do player ratings after each match. I did, but stopped by Christmas as it was making me fret! I could not be objective because it was my team and each year I get to know and like the players. What right had I to mark their performances like a (deaf, old) school teacher? Anyway, I refused to give anyone less than 6 out of 10 (including the manager) as I knew that their parents were often being sent the appraisals too! The contestants on *Strictly* would have loved me as a judge.

Nonetheless, when Ashley invited me to pen some thoughts for SNJ's celebratory edition after the Wembley triumph, I could not wait:

*"Ash asked me for some thoughts and player ratings.*

*Well lets start at the end. As our coach, chock full with bubbling FGR Ambassadors, headed over Minchinhampton Common into the sun's dying embers, Pitchfork and I exchanged "all around us is EFL country!"*

*Lets be clear on one thing. The following players made yesterday's unforgettable occasion: Aarran Racine, Ben Jefford, Charlie Clough, Charlie Cooper, Christian Doidge, Curtis Tilt, Dale Bennett, Dan Wishart, Darren Carter, Drissa Traore, Elliott Frear, Ethan Pinnock, Fabien Robert, Jake Gosling, Johnny Maxted, Kaiyne Woolery, Keanu Marsh-Brown, Kieffer Moore, Liam Noble, Manny Monthe, Marcus Kelly, Mark Ellis, Matt Tubbs, Mohamed Chemlal, Olly Mehew, Omar Bugiel, Rhys Murphy, Robert Sinclair, Sam Russell, Sam Wedgbury, Sharmir Mullings. On that day of days they all got a 10 from me.*

*More than that, they, Mark Cooper, Scott Lindsay, Scott Bartlett and all the other coaches and backroom staff, have claimed immortality in the 5 valleys. Whatever else they achieve in their lives, it cannot match the unique glory of taking a hamlet into the English Football League.*

*And stuff the knighthoods, Dale Vince is the first President of the Green Republic of Stroud!*

*On the pitch, BT Pundits had wondered whether FGR's youngsters might freeze. Did they heck. Bar a handful of misplaced passes and one occasion when Sam was possessed by the spirit of Bruce Grobbelaar, they performed like energy filled seasoned internationals. All 4 goals were sensational quality and Keanu was inches from topping the lot with an audacious trap and lob. Kaiyne and Christian took the honours but at this level, at the National Stadium and in the most important game of their lives, all shone like the stars they have become. And we love them to bits.*

*The party at The New Lawn tonight will be outrageous"*

The Wembley triumph laid a ghost that had been haunting me and I think the team and management since November 19th 2016. The fateful Saturday when we lost a 2 goal lead in the last 20 minutes to stumble to a 3-2 home defeat against Lincoln City. What would have been a 12 point lead over the Imps was reduced to 6 with a game in hand. It was more than a defeat, as it punctured a very big balloon and shattered everyone's confidence. For months, the taunt of the Imps supporters - "2 nil and you f****d it up" was at the back of my mind at every match we contested. Hardly a verse that The Farmcotian or Football Poets would have been proud of, but devastatingly effective nonetheless. Now we can move on, and look to right that wrong next season.

Forest Green Rovers FC is unlike any other club in my humble opinion. Sure it's small, but for decades size has only been part of the story. Long before Dale Vince came on the scene, FGR punched well above its weight and dreamed big. Ridiculously so for a small Cotswold community in a rugby dominated county.

Yet it has always had that special ingredient be it David/Goliath syndrome, quiet yet welcoming supporters or Green by name and nature. As I remarked earlier in this tome, Dale Vince's ambitions for FGR are a strangely good fit for the club and have enhanced its identity not eradicated it.

But the unspoken fear of any Rovers supporter since we reached the old Conference Premier in the nineties has been "what if we get relegated – what then?" It took Dale ages to instil any sort of belief around The New Lawn and I dare say most supporters will still be hoping for survival in EFL 2 whilst he has his eyes fixed on promotion.

I have never experienced anything like the immediate aftermath of victory at Wembley 2017. I say that reflecting on a life that has embraced sport as a participant and player for better than 6 decades. The elation for me, my friends and for the whole club was overwhelmingly fantastic – an electric charge.

In the stadium, I was sat near Ethan Pinnock's dad, who I've got to know and like over the season. A lovely guy who is a dead ringer for his son, simply with more rings around his trunk. Despite my upbringing (i e to address victory and defeat with the same modest demeanour) it was the most natural thing in the world to be dancing around our seats in ecstatic embrace!

Last season, I longed for my first book, *The Rise of Forest Green Rovers: The Road to Wembley*, to end in triumph. I doubted that I would have the will to write a follow up, so much had it told on my nerves and emotional bank.

I was wrong. I've loved writing this book even if no one buys it! As you are reading these words, you must have, so thanks from a very happy FGR supporter. I hope you enjoyed the ride.

# 2016/17 Statistics

## VANARAMA NATIONAL LEAGUE TABLE 2016/17

|   | Club | Played | Home | | | | | Away | | | | | GD | Pts |
|---|------|--------|---|---|---|---|---|---|---|---|---|---|----|-----|
|   |      |        | W | D | L | F | A | W | D | L | F | A |    |     |
| 1 | Lincoln City | 46 | 17 | 4 | 2 | 48 | 17 | 13 | 5 | 5 | 35 | 23 | 43 | 99 |
| 2 | Tranmere Rovers | 46 | 16 | 3 | 4 | 43 | 19 | 13 | 5 | 5 | 36 | 20 | 40 | 95 |
| **3** | **Forest Green Rovers** | **46** | **12** | **9** | **2** | **46** | **25** | **13** | **2** | **8** | **42** | **31** | **32** | **86** |
| 4 | Dagenham & Redbridge | 46 | 12 | 5 | 6 | 37 | 28 | 14 | 1 | 8 | 42 | 25 | 26 | 84 |
| 5 | Aldershot Town | 46 | 15 | 5 | 3 | 38 | 13 | 8 | 8 | 7 | 28 | 24 | 29 | 82 |
| 6 | Dover Athletic | 46 | 13 | 5 | 5 | 48 | 28 | 11 | 2 | 10 | 37 | 40 | 17 | 79 |
| 7 | Barrow | 46 | 12 | 8 | 3 | 40 | 20 | 8 | 7 | 8 | 32 | 33 | 19 | 75 |
| 8 | Gateshead | 46 | 9 | 9 | 5 | 38 | 23 | 10 | 4 | 9 | 34 | 28 | 21 | 70 |
| 9 | Macclesfield Town | 46 | 9 | 3 | 11 | 30 | 29 | 11 | 5 | 7 | 34 | 28 | 7 | 68 |
| 10 | Bromley | 46 | 11 | 3 | 9 | 33 | 37 | 7 | 5 | 11 | 26 | 31 | -9 | 62 |
| 11 | Boreham Wood | 46 | 8 | 7 | 8 | 23 | 21 | 7 | 6 | 10 | 26 | 27 | 1 | 58 |
| 12 | Sutton United | 46 | 13 | 6 | 4 | 41 | 25 | 2 | 7 | 14 | 20 | 38 | -2 | 58 |
| 13 | Wrexham | 46 | 10 | 5 | 8 | 23 | 24 | 5 | 8 | 10 | 24 | 37 | -14 | 58 |
| 14 | Maidstone United | 46 | 8 | 5 | 10 | 29 | 39 | 8 | 5 | 10 | 30 | 36 | -16 | 58 |
| 15 | Eastleigh | 46 | 8 | 7 | 8 | 28 | 26 | 6 | 8 | 9 | 28 | 37 | -7 | 57 |
| 16 | Solihull Moors | 46 | 8 | 3 | 12 | 35 | 38 | 7 | 7 | 9 | 27 | 37 | -13 | 55 |
| 17 | Torquay United | 46 | 9 | 5 | 9 | 34 | 28 | 5 | 6 | 12 | 20 | 33 | -7 | 53 |
| 18 | Woking | 46 | 9 | 7 | 7 | 32 | 30 | 5 | 4 | 14 | 34 | 50 | -14 | 53 |
| 19 | Chester | 46 | 8 | 3 | 12 | 37 | 35 | 6 | 7 | 10 | 26 | 36 | -8 | 52 |
| 20 | Guiseley | 46 | 9 | 6 | 8 | 32 | 31 | 4 | 6 | 13 | 18 | 36 | -17 | 51 |
| 21 | York City | 46 | 7 | 8 | 8 | 33 | 31 | 4 | 9 | 10 | 22 | 39 | -15 | 50 |
| 22 | Braintree Town | 46 | 6 | 4 | 13 | 23 | 36 | 7 | 5 | 11 | 28 | 40 | -25 | 48 |
| 23 | Southport | 46 | 7 | 5 | 11 | 32 | 41 | 3 | 4 | 16 | 20 | 56 | -45 | 39 |
| 24 | North Ferriby | 46 | 6 | 2 | 15 | 17 | 40 | 6 | 1 | 16 | 15 | 42 | -50 | 39 |

## CLUB STATISTICS

| Date | Opponents | Atten | Result | Goals | MoM | Pos |
|------|-----------|-------|--------|-------|-----|-----|
| 06/08/16 | Boreham Wood | 504 | Lost 1-0 | - | Chemlal | - |
| 09/08/16 | Sutton United | 1369 | Drew 1-1 | Tubbs | Chemlal | 16 |
| 13/08/16 | Gateshead | 1143 | Won 1-0 | Bennett | Traore | 13 |
| 16/08/16 | Woking | 864 | Won 1-0 | Marsh-Brown | Noble | 11 |
| 20/08/16 | York City | 1396 | Won 2-1 | Murphy, Tubbs | Jefford | 6 |
| 27/08/16 | Maidstone United | 2274 | Won 4-1 | Carter, Doidge, Murphy (2) | Murphy | 3 |
| 29/08/16 | Southport | 1621 | Won 5-1 | Moore (2), Chemlal, Clough, Murphy | Moore | 2 |
| 03/09/16 | Chester | 1820 | Won 2-1 | Noble, Carter | Pinnock | 1 |
| 10/09/16 | Dover Athletic | 785 | Lost 4-3 | Noble, Murphy, Doidge | Noble | 2 |
| 13/08/16 | Eastleigh | 1442 | Drew 1-1 | Murphy | Frear | 3 |
| 17/09/16 | Bromley | 1371 | Won 1-0 | Marsh-Brown | Marsh-Brown | 2 |
| 24/09/16 | Braintree Town | 621 | Won 1-0 | Marsh-Brown | Russell | 2 |
| 01/10/16 | Barrow | 2236 | Drew 0-0 | - | Bennett | 2 |
| 04/10/16 | Aldershot Town | 2195 | Won 4-0 | Robert (2), Moore (2) | Robert | 1 |
| 08/08/16 | North Ferriby United | 501 | Won 3-0 | Pinnock, Clough, Doidge | Pinnock | 1 |
| 15/10/16 | Sutton United (FAC) | 751 | Lost 2-1 | Noble | Bennett | - |
| 22/10/16 | Guiseley | 1723 | Won 3-0 | Carter, Doidge, og | Doidge | 1 |
| 25/10/16 | Solihull Moors | 919 | Won 1-0 | og | Carter | 1 |
| 29/10/16 | Dagenham & Redbridge | 2268 | Drew 1-1 | Murphy | Traore | 1 |
| 05/11/16 | Aldershot Town | 1638 | Won 2-1 | Doidge (2) | Racine | 1 |
| 12/11/16 | Macclesfield Town | 1749 | Won 1-0 | Marsh-Brown | Sinclair | 1 |
| 19/11/16 | Lincoln City | 2164 | Lost 3-2 | Doidge, Marsh-Brown | Sinclair | 1 |
| 22/11/16 | Tranmere Rovers | 2040 | Drew 2-2 | Doidge, Noble | Traore | 1 |
| 26/11/16 | Wrexham | 3472 | Lost 3-1 | Carter | Pinnock | 2 |
| 10/12/16 | Truro City (FAT 1st round) | 626 | Drew 1-1 | Marsh-Brown | Sinclair | - |

| Date | Opponents | Atten | Result | Goals | MoM | Pos |
|------|-----------|-------|--------|-------|-----|-----|
| 13/12/16 | Truro City (FAT 1st round replay) | 336 | Won 1-1 AET | Carter | Cooper | - |
| 17/12/16 | **Dover Athletic** | **1818** | **Drew 1-1** | **Moore** | **Noble** | **3** |
| 26/12/16 | Torquay United | 2540 | Lost 4-3 | Doidge, Clough, Pinnock | Noble | 3 |
| **01/01/17** | **Torquay United** | **2383** | **Drew 5-5** | **Doidge (2), Marsh Brown (2), og** | **Marsh-Brown** | **3** |
| 07/01/17 | Bromley | 1247 | Won 5-1 | Marsh-Brown, Doidge (2), Frear, Pinnock | Noble | 3 |
| 10/01/17 | Eastleigh | 1917 | Drew 1-1 | Doidge | Doidge | 2 |
| 14/01/17 | Chester (FAT 2nd round) | 1250 | Won 2-0 | Kelly (2) | Kelly | - |
| **21/01/17** | **Braintree Town** | **1735** | **Drew 1-1** | **Clough** | **Noble** | **2** |
| 28/01/17 | Barrow | 1422 | Won 3-2 | Doidge, Noble, Marsh-Brown | Noble | 2 |
| 04/02/17 | Macclesfield Town (FAT 3rd round) | 967 | Lost 1-0 | - | Pinnock | - |
| **11/02/17** | **Boreham Wood** | **1575** | **Won 2-0** | **Doidge, Bugiel** | **Sinclair** | **3** |
| 18/02/17 | Gateshead | 916 | Lost 3-1 | Woolery | Pinnock | 3 |
| **25/02/17** | **Woking** | **1566** | **Won 4-3** | **Marsh-Brown, Doidge, Bugiel (2)** | **Ellis** | **3** |
| **04/03/17** | **Macclesfield Town** | **1569** | **Won 3-0** | **Doidge, Noble, Ellis** | **Ellis** | **2** |
| 11/03/17 | Dagenham & Redbridge | 1459 | Lost 2-1 | Doidge | Pinnock | 3 |
| 14/03/17 | Sutton United | 1446 | Won 2-1 | Ellis, Doidge | Wedgbury | 2 |
| **18/03/17** | **Wrexham** | **2146** | **Won 3-0** | **Bennett, Noble, Doidge** | **Noble** | **2** |
| **21/03/17** | **Solihull Moors** | **1445** | **Won 2-1** | **Robert, Doidge** | **Robert** | **1** |
| 25/03/17 | Lincoln City | 6798 | Lost 3-1 | Doidge | Traore | 2 |
| **01/04/17** | **North Ferriby United** | **1709** | **Lost 1-0** | - | **Bennett** | **3** |
| 08/04/17 | Guiseley | 760 | Won 1-0 | Doidge | Bennett | 3 |
| 11/04/17 | Tranmere Rovers | 6907 | Won 1-0 | Woolery | Russell | 3 |
| **14/04/17** | **Chester** | **1936** | **Won 2-0** | **Doidge, Noble** | **Woolery** | **3** |
| 17/04/17 | Southport | 844 | Lost 2-0 | - | Wedgbury | 3 |

| Date | Opponents | Atten | Result | Goals | MoM | Pos |
|------|-----------|-------|--------|-------|-----|-----|
| **22/04/17** | **Maidstone United** | **2030** | **Drew 2-2** | **Marsh-Brown, og** | **Bennett** | **3** |
| 29/04/17 | York City | 3984 | Drew 2-2 | Bugiel (2) | Russell | 3 |
| 04/05/17 | Dagenham & Redbridge (NL Play Off Semi-final 1st Leg) | 2208 | Drew 1-1 | Noble | Monthe | - |
| **07/05/17** | **Dagenham & Redbridge (NL Play Off Semi-final 1st Leg)** | **3237** | **Won 2-0** | **Doidge, Marsh-Brown** | **Traore** | **-** |
| 14/05/17 | Tranmere Rovers (NL Promotion Final, Wembley) | 18801 | Won 3-1 1-3 | Woolery (2), Doidge | Woolery | - |

# Acknowledgements

Even a publication as inferior as this comes on the back of much hard work and help by a cast of thousands. In no particular order, I owe much to the following:

**Forest Green Rovers FC**, the 'Little Club on the Hill'. My inspiration. With the backing of The Electric Chair, FGR is no longer the tiny David of old. Yet it still has the same values which snare the casual supporter and lock them in an unbreakable embrace. Supporters argue long and hard whether Forest Green is a village or hamlet or whether neighbouring Nailsworth is a village or town! Either way, there is something special that has propelled this community of less than 5,800 souls to The English Football League, easily the lowest population to so aspire.

**Dale Vince** and his directors and team at Ecotricity and FGR. Dale is a game-changer and unlike any other football club Chair you are likely to come across. A genuine football man, Stroud local and possessor of a strong moral compass. At FGR asserts his personal values, including veganism, support to ecological causes and charities, sustainable policies in a number of operational areas and customer-first initiatives. Anyone who spends time with him will know that he 'does not do short term'. Yet he uses sound commercial management practise to allow his management and coaches to do what they are employed for without unwelcome interference. 7 years on, many of his 'shocking' initiatives now seem mainstream for other clubs and organisations. He has my sincere gratitude for policies that I value and for supporting charities dear to my heart, not least Gloucestershire Deaf Association of which I am honoured to be chair. Thanks too for the foreword, Dale. I am delighted for him that his principled support of FGR has brought success and national appreciation.

**Peter Whitbread, Crispin Thomas & David Kerry:** All have kindly volunteered many of their finest works to fill these pages under their pseudonyms The Farmcotian, Football Poets & Jokerman, or is it vice versa? They are the mainstay of a lively Fans Forum and true supporters in the best sense of the words. I highly recommend a visit to Football Poets' website: http://footballpoets.org

**David Drew MP & Phil Butterworth,** Foggy and Compo, not necessarily in that order. Long-time friends and constant travelling companions. David lives and breathes FGR, has been Dale's able club vice-chair and chair of the Advisory Board, until his surprise re-election as Stroud's MP in may 2017 forced his reluctant resignation. Even in his busy resurrected political life, David has spearheaded numerous initiatives to support and promote FGR. Phil is a clubman supreme, known to many as Pitchfork. He has had a huge part to play in FGR's community activities and has promoted the FGR Student Ambassador programme that now includes 53 primary, secondary & tertiary schools and colleges in Gloucestershire. His work has done more than any other in raising average attendances from 800–900 ten years back to 1,800 in 2015/16 and 2016/17.

**Richard Joyce, Tim Barnard & Heather Cook**: 'Young Joycey' has been a constant source of help and was the editor of FGR's *Match Day* magazine, stadium announcer and much else besides. He left his role in July 2017 carrying with him generous tributes from numerous supporters. His match reports are the *straightest* contributions to this volume plus a welter of statistics. Tim Barnard's 'Something to Shout About' has been an invaluable reference when my memory has failed, and club statistician Heather Cook is his and Richard's guru.

**Chef Em Franklin** and her assistants. No club eats as well as FGR nor for such good value. Visitors from EFL2 are in for a surprise – they may come expecting *hippy vegan* food but they will leave drooling over very good food. And thanks for the Q-Pie Recipe Em!

**Our local media moguls**: Bob & Billy Hunt, John Light, Paul Furley, Richard Atkins & Ashley Loveridge. One of them is Deep-Throat. We are lucky indeed to have such fine radio and newspaper journalists following our every move. All have helped me in one way or another.

**FGR Fans Forum**. I may be biased, but a funnier more erudite football forum does not exist. I salute you my friends.

The author gratefully acknowledges those who have allowed him use of their images: in particular his thanks go to The National Trust, Brooklands Museum, Jilly Cooper OBE, Hatfield House (The Marquess of Salisbury), Sir Alex Ferguson, Cressing Barns (Essex County Council) and the parents of the FGR Ambassadors.

The local **schools & colleges** involved in FGR's Student Ambassador programme and the peerless **ambassadors** themselves who have so helped to expand FGR as a family-friendly club.

**& everyone else** named in the book and many who are not. They know who they are even if I forget or overlook them. Sincere thanks to you all. I hope the book does you justice

# About the Author

Back in the day (well, 1953), Chris was born and bred a Bristolian. His father was a 'rugger man' and referee of 25 years, though he was sympathetic to that other football played by hooligans. His three elder brothers followed both creeds but as to *soccer*, the quartet split their loyalties between the Bristol clubs: one for City, Chris and his two eldest brothers for Rovers.

Chris's first attendance at a football match was in the early '60s, an uninspiring 0-0 draw at Ashton Gate between City and Walsall, to which he was taken by his three older siblings. Not the start he wanted. But as Chris entered teenagerdom, regular visits to Eastville began, usually watching a mid-table 'long ball' Gas slogging it out in old Division 3.

In the early 1980s, Chris had his first taste of the Nailsworth-based Rovers. Manager Steve Millard would take his squad to train at Easton Sports Centre off the M32 close in on Bristol's East Side. Chris and his work friends played 5-a-side football regularly on Thursday evenings from 8 to 9 with the Rovers squad next on, having warmed up with a run around the locality. They seemed like decent guys. Then he read about their win in the FA Vase and, from afar, kept an eye on the team from a Gloucestershire hamlet.

In 1985, Chris moved to Stroud having taken a job in Gloucester. Not yet cured of the playing bug, he turned out for Whiteshill United in the Gloucestershire Senior League Division 2, carving out a niche as a non-scoring centre forward.

The weekly *Stroud News & Journal* was always full of the exploits of 'The Little Club on the Hill'. Curious, and recalling the Bristol encounters, Chris took in occasional midweek and Saturday matches at The Lawn. His first fixes for an addiction that has held sway since.

In 2010, severe deafness forced Chris into early retirement from his development surveying career. At the invitation of long-time friend David Drew MP, he joined the club's new Advisory Board which initiates and coordinates Rovers' community activities. When asked, he chips in with media interviews and other appointments for the club and writes for the

*Match Day* magazine as Rambling Man. At *Stroud News & Journal*'s invitation, he also supplies occasional articles and reports about FGR.

As a supporter, Chris prefers to stand, holding a south stand season ticket. At home games he's to be found with his friends on the 'wet' terrace, the closest thing they can find to their favoured spot at the 'Old' Lawn. However, last term, the launch of *The Rise of Forest Green Rovers: The Road to Wembley* and regular voluntary duties for the club meant much time spent warming the seats of the East Stand.

Thirty two years after moving to the county, Chris watches all but a handful of FGR games each season, home and away. He always looks out for the results of Bristol Rovers, but they have long since lost out in his affections to their Nailsworth rivals.

Chris's home is the village of Whiteshill, near Stroud, 600 feet up and with a convenient though distant view of The New Lawn. There, he and his wife Jenni are 'empty nesters', their grown up children having flown the coup to Antibes in France and Cardiff. Cats Ness & Gus keep them company.